Robert Dwyer Joyce, P. X. Keating

Ballads of Irish chivalry

songs and poems

Robert Dwyer Joyce, P. X. Keating

Ballads of Irish chivalry
songs and poems

ISBN/EAN: 9783742829030

Manufactured in Europe, USA, Canada, Australia, Japa

Cover: Foto ©Andreas Hilbeck / pixelio.de

Manufactured and distributed by brebook publishing software (www.brebook.com)

Robert Dwyer Joyce, P. X. Keating

Ballads of Irish chivalry

ROBERT D. JOYCE.

BALLADS OF IRISH CHIVALRY;

Songs and Poems.

BY

ROBERT DWYER JOYCE, M.D., M.R.I.A.

COMPLETE EDITION.

ILLUSTRATIONS BY JOHN O'HEA, DUBLIN.
ENGRAVING BY P. X. KEATING, BOSTON.

BOSTON:
PATRICK DONAHOE.
1872.

Entered, according to Act of Congress, in the year 1871,

BY PATRICK DONAHOE,

In the Office of the Librarian of Congress, at Washington.

Electrotyped at the Boston Stereotype Foundry,
No. 19 Spring Lane.

DEDICATION.

TO MY SON GARRIE.

Digitized by the Internet Archive
in 2016

https://archive.org/details/balladsofirishch00joyc

CONTENTS.

BALLADS.

	PAGE		PAGE
Ballad of Barnakill	160	Romance of the Fairy Wand	105
Ballad of Young Brian; or, the Battle of Athenree	98	Sarsfield's Ride; or, the Ambush of Sliav Bloom	179
Clontarf; or, the King's last Battle	154	Sir Donal	162
Crossing the Blackwater, A. D. 1603	196	The Dying Warrior	186
		The Enchanted War-Horse	173
		The Well of the Omen	169
Dunlevy	92	The Prince of the North Countrie	152
Fair Gwendoline and her Dove	58	The Lady of the Sea	149
		The Burning of Kilcoleman	214
Kilbrannon	75	The Death of O'Donnell, A. D. 1257	209
Lady Marion	83	Tyrrell's Pass, A. D. 1579	203
Little Thomas	72	The Red Rose and the White	206
		The Battle of the Raven's Glen, A. D. 1603	198
Mary Lombard	170	The Spalpeen	191
Maud of Desmond	200	The Sack of Dunbui, A. D. 1602	193
		The Battle of Knockinoss	93
Peter Crowley; or, the Worth of a Dead Man	187	The Siege of Clonmel, A. D. 1650	86
		The Two Galloglasses	88
Romance of Meergal and Garmon	217	The Fairy Mill	90
Romance of the Golden Spurs	212	The Bridge of Glanwillan	76
Romance of the Black Robber	81	The Dying Ballad Singer	79
Romance of the Golden Helmet	55	The Battle of Benburb, A. D. 1646	73
Rossnalee	130	The Green Dove and the Raven	68
Rose Condon	122	The Blacksmith of Limerick	70
Romance of the Stone Coffin	113	The Battle of Manning Ford	60
Romance of the Banner	116	The Pilgrim	132

(5)

CONTENTS.

	PAGE
The Taking of Armagh, A. D. 1596	134
The Baron and the Miller	137
The Sorrowful Ballad of Doirémore	142
The Jew's Daughter	145
The Battle of Thurles, A. D. 1174	128
The Three Sisters	118
The Templar Knight	109
The Battle of Kilteely, A. D. 1599	103
The White Ladye	95

	PAGE
The Watch-fire of Barnalee:— Before the Battle	9
The Minstrel's Tale; or, Earl Gerald and the Fair Eileen	10
Ballad of Sir Hugh le Poer; or, the Death-Feud	19
Ballad of Dark Gilliemore; or, the Mournful Squire	32
Romance of Donal Roe; or, the Lady of Mendora	41
After the Battle	51
Young De Rupe	64

SONGS, POEMS, AND SHORT BALLADS.

Almansa; or, O'Mahony's Dragoons	410
Among the fragrant Hay	408
Adieu, Lovely Mary	398
Asthoreen Machree	376
Annie De Clare	330
A Hymn to England	283
Allisdrum's March at the Battle of Knockinoss, A. D. 1648	269
An Irish Morning	266
Along with my Love I'll go	262
A Reaping we will go	256
Address to an Old Pipe	249
By the Shore	423
Brave Donall	315
Come, all you Maids, where'er you be	370
Donall na Greine	334
Donal O'Keeffe's Lament	300
Diarmid Mor	275
Eileen of the Golden Hair	426
Eileen's Lament for Gerald	362
Fanny	395
Fairest and Rarest	369
Fanny Clair	340
Fainge an Lae	333
Fair Maidens' Beauty will soon fade away	322

Fair Helen of the Dell	301
Fair Kate of Glenanner	293
Fineen the Rover	280
Far away	239
Glenara	375
Glenora	307
Garryowen	272
Gra Gal Machree	261
How Sarsfield died in Glory	298
I'm Fourteen Years Old upon Sunday	399
Ireland our Queen	371
I wish I sat by Grena's Side	357
I loved a Maid	349
Ireland's Freedom; or, the Drop of Blood	326
I built me a Bower	321
I still am a Rover	316
I sit on the Hold of Moyallo	308
I'll stay at Home	267
I sit beneath the Sunset Skies	255
I'll deck his Grave with Flowers	240
Ireland, Our Home	230
In Life's Young Morning. To my Wife	225
Johnny Dunlea	390
Johnny's Return	353
Jessy Brien	351
John's Old Wife of Tullyvoe	345

CONTENTS. 7

	PAGE
Life is Bright. Duet.	420
Lament of Marion Creagh.	386
My Love is at my Side.	412
My Handsome Young Man.	382
Margread Ban.	378
Mary, the Pride of the West.	373
My Love is on the River.	374
Merrily, merrily Playing	365
My True Love.	366
Margaret.	348
Moll Roone	317
Maryanne.	313
My First Love.	309
My Flower of Flowers.	279
Mary Earley.	277
Marjory le Poer.	254
My True Love Bright.	251
My Geraldine.	246
My Steed was weary.	238
Mary's Sweetheart.	235
My Boat.	228
My Anna's Eyes.	290
Old Land.	425
O, Blest be the Bower.	422
Over the Morning Dew.	402
Our Song.	383
Over the Hills and far away.	380
O'Sullivan's Flight, A. D. 1603.	344
O, fair shines the Sun on Glenara.	285
Patrick's Day	416
Paddy's Proposal.	276
Roving Brian O'Connell.	358
Saint Stephen's Night.	419
Song of Galloping O'Hogan.	414
Sweet Glengariff's Water.	405
Song of Sarsfield's Trooper.	367
Shane Gow; or, the Boys in Green, A. D. 1798.	355
Sweet Imokilly.	354
Song.	347
Song of the Forest Fairy.	293
Shawn Dhas of Tullyelmer.	288
Snowing.	281
Song of Tren the Fairy.	226
To Mary.	424
There is a Stream.	418
The Laborer.	415
The saddest Breeze.	409
The Faithful Lovers.	406

	PAGE
The Knight's Lay.	403
The Boys of Wexford.	404
The Linnet.	400
The Summer is come.	401
The Brigade's Hurling Match.	396
The Jolly Companie.	391
The first Night I was married.	393
The Night before Fontenoy; or, the Girls we left behind us.	394
The Green Flag.	388
The Joy-Bells.	389
The Withered Rose.	385
The Green and the Gold.	381
The Undertakers.	377
The Wanderer.	368
The Holly Tree.	363
The Advice.	360
The Flame that burned so brightly.	361
The Forsaken.	352
The Rightful Power.	350
The Stormy Sea shall flow in.	347
The Lasses of Ireland.	342
The Hills of Sweet Tipperary.	336
The Coming Bridal.	338
The Wind that shakes the Barley.	339
The March out of Limerick.	331
The Fair Maid's Lament.	332
The Groves of the Pool; or, the Irish Rover.	328
The Waterfall.	323
The Cailin Rue.	324
The Green Ribbon.	325
The Rights of Man.	318
There is a Tree in Darra's Wood.	320
The Oaks of Gleneigh.	314
The Rapparee's Horse and Sword.	310
The Jovial Christmas Days long ago.	311
The Punch Bowl; or, the Croppy's Finger.	302
The Drinan Dhun.	304
The Siege of Limerick.	305
To a Bird.	294
The Stirrup-Cup.	296
The Blind Girl of Glenore.	291
The Girl I left behind Me.	286
This Maid of mine.	287
The Yellow Hair.	282
To Ireland.	278
The Lesson. To my Son.	273
The Little Bird.	271
The Locks of Amber.	268

CONTENTS.

	PAGE
The Spring of the Year	263
The Outlaw of Kilmore	265
The Red Lusmore	258
The People	259
The Banks of Anner	260
The Petticoat	252
The Merry Christmas Fire	248
The Whig's Lamentation	242
The Mountain Ash	243
The Ensign and his Banner. A Brigade Song	244
The Cock and the Sparrow	245
The Cannon	236

	PAGE
The Flower that ne'er shall fade	233
The Song of Lord Goloptious	233
The Mountains High	229
Where are you going, my pretty Maid?	413
Willy Brand	341
Whatever Wind is Blowing	306
Will of the Gap	232
You're a Dear Land to Me	241

THE FOUR COMRADES. — Page 9.

BALLADS.

THE FOUR COMRADES:
OR, THE WATCH-FIRE OF BARNALEE.

BEFORE THE BATTLE.

I.

There were four comrades, stout and free,
Within the Wood of Barnalee,
Under the spreading oaken tree.

II.

The ragged clouds sailed past the moon;
Loud rose the brawling torrent's croon;
The rising winds howled in the wood
Like hungry wolves at scent of blood.
Yet there they sat, in converse free,
Under the spreading oaken tree,—
Garod the Minstrel, with his lyre,
Sir Hugh le Poer, that heart of fire,
Dark Gilliemore, the mournful squire,
And Donal, from the banks of Nier.

III.

Spectrally shone the watch-fire light
On their sun-browned faces and helmets bright,
Showing beneath the woodland glooms
Their swords, and jacks, and waving plumes;

As there they sat, those comrades free,
Within the Wood of Barnalee,
Under the spreading oaken tree,
And told their tales to you and me.

And first the Minstrel took his harp, that oft
　Rang with War's clangorous music, fierce and free,
And now with gentle touch, and prelude soft,
　Began his strain of simple melody.
Of love he sang — her love whose wavy sea
　Shines round the sunny shores of Desmond's land,
And, as his voice arose, wild rhapsody
　Sparkled within his eyes, and music bland
Flowed from the sounding wires beneath his trembling hand.

THE MINSTREL'S TALE; OR, EARL GERALD AND THE FAIR EILEEN.

I.

When love awakes within the youthful breast,
　Its joys gleam brightest in the solitude
Of bloom-starred vale, or purply mountain crest,
　Or where the blue doves build amid the wood;
There memory is sweetest, thought is best,
　Flowing through heart and brain like the clear flood
That hurries down the green glades all day long,
With many a dulcet strain of murmuring song.

II.

In solitude young Eileen stands by him
　She loves the best, while calm skies o'er them gleam,
And grandly on Cnockfierna's purple rim
　Day's huge orb rests, half sunk, short space to seem,
An arch, where through the fiery cherubim
　Might spread their pinions earthward on the beam,
And light upon the mountain tops, and throw
The glory of their eyes on all below.

III.

Young Eileen of Kilmoodan — pure and red
   Her laughing lips as moss-rose in the sun;
As wing of raven on the mountain head
   Her black locks in their glossy brightness shone;
Her brow was like the snowy lustre shed
   By lilies when the winter's dead and gone;
Her form was like the ash-tree, young and light,
Blooming in beauty 'mid the mountains bright.

IV.

She stands beside her youthful Geraldine, —
   The beautiful, the generous, the brave,
The topmost branch of Desmond's princely line,
   The bearer of the sharp unsullied glaive;
Stately and straight as the young mountain pine
   That towers above Glenara's tumbling wave,
And strong in battle as that rushing flood,
And fleet as wild-deer of the vernal wood.

V.

'Tis at Cnockfierna's foot — the enchanted hill
   Where Donn, the fairy king, hath made his hall,
To men ofttimes invisible, but still
   By wanderer sometimes seen, at twilight fall,
Rearing its crystal battlements, until
   They seem to prop the skies, and glittering all
With gold, and snowy pearls, and diamonds bright,
That mock the pale stars on the brow of night.

VI.

And Eileen looks upon her Gerald now,
   Then points unto the crimson west. "And see
How quick," she says, "upon Cnockfierna's brow
   Yon cloud of blackness loometh!" Presently
A fierce wind shaketh every forest bough
   Save the light branches of the rowan-tree*
That shadows o'er their trysting-place, and there
No light leaf trembles in the troublous air.

---

* The peasantry believe that the rowan-tree, or mountain ash, is endowed with great power against fairy spells.

VII.

With lightnings in its front and thunder knell,
  That black-faced cloud comes rolling down the steep,
And flings its sable darkness on the dell
  Where stand the startled lovers; wild winds sweep
Far through the groaning trees with frantic yell;
  Anon a lightning flash, and from the deep
Green bosom of the circling wood, a fawn,
Small, beautiful and white, treads o'er the lawn.

VIII.

The black cloud fades — 'tis bright and still again;
  The birds once more begin their evening tune,
But fear is in young Eileen's heart — she's fain
  To seek her father's hall, for with the croon
Of the lone rill beside she hears full plain
  Weird fairy voices whispering wild, and soon
They're speeding to Kilmoodan's towers below,
The white fawn close behind them as they go!

IX.

It looks on him, as fast away he hies,
  With melancholy fondness in its gaze;
It looks on her with keen, malignant eyes,
  As though each glance would kill her; through the maze
Of woods Kilmoodan's turrets now arise
  Upon their path, and in a gorgeous haze
Of golden vapor fades the fawn away
Beside the barbacan so old and gray.

X.

The warder from the barbacan shouts down,
  He sees Queen Cleena * walking o'er the glade,
With robe of heaven's own blue, and starry crown,
  But nought the lover sees, nor aught the maid,
Save that light golden vapor: crimson brown
  The twilight steals o'er hill and forest shade,
As Gerald and his Eileen gain the hall
Where feast their smiling friends and clansmen tall.

---

* Cleena, the Fairy Queen of South Munster. **She is believed by the peasantry to reside in Carrig Cleena, near Mallow.**

XI.

Next morning rose in all its summer pride
   Upon Kilmoodan's towers and leafy wood,
And love, that scorned all change of time and tide,
   Swelled high in Gerald's heart, as there he stood
Clasping the white hand of his beauteous bride
   Before the glittering altar; and a flood
Of joy swept o'er them when the rite was done,
When both fond hearts in life and death were one.

XII.

And night came o'er the mountains high, and clear
   The wild harps rang within Kilmoodan's hall,
Where o'er the dancers' heads gleamed sword and spear,
   And targe and helm, and banner from the wall;
And Gerald takes his Eileen's hand. "And here,"
   In accents sweet and low, he says, "though all
Dance now for joy, we too will dance for love!"
And down the floor in circlets light they move.

XIII.

At once, as rose the clansmen's loud acclaim,
   A dazzling light through loop and window shone,
That filled the broad hall like a flood of flame,
   Blinding the dancers' eyes; and, when 'twas gone,
Hearts throbbed and cheeks were blanched of knight and dame,
   And stricken with wild fear, all woful, wan,
Young Eileen stood — her loving bridegroom flown —
Amid th' affrighted dancers, all alone!

XIV.

Short time she stood, then fell and closed her eyes,
   Like a white lily frost-blanched in the vale;
And all that night of woe and wild surprise,
   Wordless, and like the marble cold and pale,
She lay on her sad couch; but when the skies
   Blushed red with morn, she woke, and then a wail
Burst from her as she looked her chamber round
Among her maids, and yet no bridegroom found.

XV.

And many a doctor grave and man of lore
   They brought to cure her mind, for she was mad.

Ah! nought could each one do, but loud deplore,
　　As they looked on the bride, her doom so sad.
At length they brought Black Ronan of Kilmore,
　　For many a spell and wondrous cure he had,
That ancient seer, who drank his first draught full
His birthday morning from the raven's skull.*

XVI.

He looked on her. "Thy Gerald is not dead!"
　　He cried aloud; "but 'neath Queen Cleena's chain,
Where Carrig Cleena rears its mossy head,
　　And Avondhu pours down the woods amain,
He lingers in his grief, with hope still fed
　　Of seeing the green earth and thee again.
Go there and ask for him, and well thou'lt prove
That nought but mighty death can conquer love."

XVII.

They would not let her go; but one still noon
　　Of midnight, when deep slumber brooded o'er
Her father's hall, she donned her silken shoon
　　And garments snowy white, and by the shore
Of the lone forest rill, beneath the moon,
　　She stole away. Ah! many a mountain hoar
Lay between home and her when dewy morn
Glittered like golden fire on tree and thorn.

XVIII.

With weary feet she crossed the forest glen,
　　With many a sigh toiled up the mountain slope,
And sat upon its ridge to weep, and then
　　Went down into the woods with wakening hope;
Away by lone Glengartan's reedy fen,
　　And on, where Conail's mountains to the cope
Of heaven towered upward through the purple air,
She rested in the burning noon, and there—

XIX.

There laughed a sunny lakelet 'mid the trees,
　　Aye mirroring a ruin hoar and lone,

---

* About this personage many legends are told in Munster. They say that should an infant get his first draught from the skull of a raven, he is sure ever afterwards to be endowed with prophetic powers.

Like the blue bosom of those fabled seas
　　Where thunders never growl, nor wild winds moan.
Over its azure breast the wild duck flees,
　　The heron broods upon the shore-side stone,
And from its secret home at evening's gloom
The wary bittern sends its quivering boom.

XX.

A little bay beside her from the lake
　　Oped, by the mountain tempests aye unstirred;
The dun deer to its margent came to slake
　　Their thirst in the hot noon; no sound was heard
The deep and pleasant stillness there to break,
　　Save the sweet warbling of some lonely bird,
Borne with the summer breezes warm and bland,
Murmuring in music o'er the yellow sand.

XXI.

Above her was a rugged, lonely pass,
　　Cleft through the splintered mountains like a gate —
A Titan gate; mass towered on ponderous mass
　　Of savage rock each side; all desolate,
Naked it yawned, save where scant gorse and grass
　　Spotted its torrid ribs, or where elate
With life amid the stillness, one small rill
Shot down in gladness from the giant hill.

XXII.

Now in that pass volcanic there appeared
　　A small, light, spiral cloud slow moving on
Unto young Eileen's path, and when it neared,
　　Beneath its whirling base, that snowy fawn
Again looked on her with a wild and weird
　　Light in its bitter orbs of fiery tawn —
A threatening light, a keen, malignant ray,
That struck the poor bride's heart with strange dismay.

XXIII.

She placed her hand within her snowy vest
　　To still the fear with which that lorn heart strove;
There found suspended on her faithful breast
　　A golden cross, her Gerald's gift of love,

And drew it quickly forth. "At His behest,
  Whose holy sign this is, I charge thee move
From off my onward path!" fair Eileen said,
  And at the word the white fawn shrieked and fled.

XXIV.

She kissed that blesséd symbol; went her way;
  With sinking heart o'er many a mile she wept,
And at the solemn close of that bright day
  Within a woodman's hut she ate and slept —
Slept long and sound, until the yellow ray
  Of morn gilt every hill-top; then she crept
Out from her heather couch, and shaped again
Her southern pathway through the forest glen.

XXV.

At last by Cleena's crag she weeping stood
  Within a fairy nook, whose leafy bound
Left but one vista for day's sinking flood
  To light its dreamy depth; there was a sound
Of a lone brooklet in a playful mood,
  As if ten thousand golden bees had found
Amid the starry flowers their queen, and made
Their murmuring music in the slumbery shade.

XXVI.

Before her towered the crag all lightning split
  With battlemented front so stern and high,
As if the earth in some volcanic fit
  Had burst, and cast it upward towards the sky;
And now, while red its topmost spires were lit
  By sunset, Eileen, with a mad, shrill cry,
Called on the queen her bridegroom to restore;
But echo only answered evermore.

XXVII.

She called and wept, and wept and called again,
  On the hard-hearted queen, till twilight fell
Upon each forest hill and drowsy plain;
  Then sped she to a cave far down the dell
Where dwelt an aged hermit. "Moons may wane,
  And years may vanish," sad he 'gan to tell,
As she sat by his side, "ere thou'lt obtain
Thy bridegroom from Queen Cleena's magic chain."

XXVIII.

Nathless as each day rose she took her place
  Before the crag, and called upon the queen
Her bridegroom to restore, and her sad face
  In the rude blasts soon lost its blooming sheen.
And autumn came; the winds began to chase
  The leaves in the brown woods, and winter keen
Soon followed; still poor Eileen sat her there,
Loud calling for her love in wild despair.

XXIX.

At length of Hallowe'en the blood-red morn
  With surly glare toiled up the eastern sky,
And soon the great wind blew its thundering horn
  From the gray, desolate hill-tops, and on high
The ragged clouds across the heavens were borne
  Over Queen Cleena's crag, and many a cry
Rose to their stormy paths in wailing woe
From the poor bride who still knelt lorn below.

XXX.

Ah! there she knelt before that fairy crag
  With wet eyes, and beseeching arms outthrown;
Yet, answerless, each flinty spire and jag
  Towered to the heavens, by wild winds beat and blown:
Ah! there she knelt, till like a tattered flag
  The noonday sky outspread, and with loud groan
The western blast o'er the dark hills did urge
Mountains of rattling cloud from ocean's surge.

XXXI.

And loud the thunder bellowed, and aloud
  Plashed down the roaring rain; yet love kept warm
Her heart, though like a wind-bent flower she bowed
  In misery to the earth. At length the storm
With gathering twilight fell, and o'er a cloud
  The moon showed, like a silver shield, her form,
And blue the heavens spread o'er with many a gleam
Of starlight on brown hill and thundering stream.

XXXII.

With downcast eyes she knelt; anon she raised
  Their blue orbs, wet with many a tear, and bright

Before her the great crag, a palace, blazed
　　With towers, and domes, and halls of golden light;
Through the tall portal a long train, that dazed
　　Her wondering eyes, out came — bold squire, and knight,
And lady, and before them al! most sheen,
With grace immortal, walked the Fairy Queen.

XXXIII.

And, "Come, thou faithful maid!" Queen Cleena said,
　　"I've proved thy love and deathless constancy —
Thy love, that might the dull dust of the dead
　　From its cold sleep awake. O, come with me!"
She took young Eileen by the hand, and led
　　Into the great hall golden bright. "And see,"
Again she said, "the cause of thy sad moan,
Thy Gerald, high upon yon glittering throne!"

XXXIV.

She looked, — her Gerald looked, — but in his eye
　　She saw no sign of welcome warm and fond;
He knew her not; then rose a mighty cry
　　Of woe from the poor bride. Anon her wand
Queen Cleena took, and with a mournful sigh
　　Of disappointed love and sad despond
She laid it on his brow: from fairy charms
He woke, and clasped his young bride in his arms.

XXXV.

"Now choose thee," said the mournful queen again,
　　"'Tween earth and this immortal palace grand."
"I choose," Earl Gerald said, "my broad domain
　　And faithful bride." Young Eileen took his hand,
With joyous heart, 'mid that resplendent train
　　Of dames and knights, and out from Fairyland
She led him through the golden palace door
Into the world of mortal life once more.

XXXVI.

And many a horseman spurred when morning flashed
　　O'er the hills' ruby cones, by dale and down,
The news to tell, and many a weapon clashed
　　On gladsome shield from wall of tower and town;

EILEEN AND THE FAIRY QUEEN. — Page 18.

From where old Ventry's sands are murmuring lashed
  By the gray waves, to Gaultee's stony crown,
The harps rang in each joyful Desmond hall
For the brave bridegroom freed from fairy thrall.

"Gentles," the Minstrel said, "my harp is still;
  Rake up the brands, and raise the watch-fire's glow;
Hand round the brimming bowl; I'll drink my fill
  To the fair maids we loved long, long ago.
Sir Hugh le Poer, thou never yet wert slow
  To tell the tale, or drain the goblet bright,
However Fortune's changeful winds might blow."
  Glinted his armor in the watch-fire light,
As thus began his tale, that gay and gallant knight.

BALLAD OF SIR HUGH LE POER; OR, THE DEATH-FEUD.

I.

I WOULD not give one good green rood
Of the fair lands by Cloda's wood
For all I took in that fierce raid
  Last April morn, when gallantlie
We stormed the Hold of Garranslade,
  And sacked and burned the west countrie;
I would not give one blooming tree
  That bowers sweet Cloda's sunny plain
For the best ransom paid to me
After the Foray of Bunree,
  When each had six good captives ta'en;
And yet I'd give trees, stream, and land,
Beside my love once more to stand
And hear her laugh of gay surprise,
  Her words of welcome, warm and bland,
And look into her gentle eyes,
  And clasp in mine her lily hand;
For she is dear to me as life,
My beautiful, my promised wife.

II.

I saw a rose-tree by the rill
As I rode down from Ballar Hill;
Its blossoms in the sun spread out,
Shedding a glory all about.
Woe is me! full mournfully
I looked upon the lonely tree,
And thought upon my true-love fair,
Bright as the roses smiling there.

III.

As I came out from Carrick town,
By Dangean's wall I sat me down;
Upon its ruined tower there grew
A lady fern of greenest hue.
Woe is me! full mournfully
Of Mabel's form it minded me —
Graceful and slender, young and light,
As ever blessed a mortal's sight.

IV.

In Coolnamoe the thrush's song
Full oft I listed all day long;
And many a morn, by Darra's moat,
I've heard the wandering cuckoo's note.
Woe is me! full mournfully
The song-thrush, on the blooming tree,
The cuckoo, making earth rejoice,
But mind me of my Mabel's voice.

V.

For she is fair and she is good,
And fresh as flowerets of the wood;
And all things bright by hill or shore,
They make me think of her the more.
Woe is me! full mournfully
That war should ever exile me —
Ever take me from her side,
My beautiful, my promised bride!

VI.

There is a height by Cloda's shore
 With a gray crag upon its crown,

And from that height a castle hoar
  Looks over many a dale and down;
And in that castle is a room
Where spent I many an hour of gloom,
For from my birth some malady
Of power malign had seized on me,
So that I was a weakly child,
Cursed with a soul perverse and wild.

VII.

I had four brothers, tall and brave,
Deft at the bridle and the glaive;
I had four sisters, fair to see;
A mother fond as fond could be;
My father was a comely man
As e'er drew sword in battle's van.
But with their woodland sports, and all
Their merry-makings in the hall,
They left me in that room of mine,
Full often by myself to pine —
To make my unavailing moan,
Forgot, neglected, and alone.

VIII.

Was I alone? No! In that room
Strange shapes arose, as evening's gloom
Lowered from the dusky hills each day,
And kept me company alway.
Wild, shadowy forms would then arise,
And pierce me with their searching eyes —
Vast shades of saffron-kilted chiefs,
With beards like foam on Burren's reefs;
Huge Danes, with looks of fire and bale,
Dim glimmering in their shirts of mail;
Stern Norman knights, with hearts as hard
As the blue flints of Blaynamard,
Came in their iron panoply,
Each in his turn, and gazed on me,
With many another phantom train —
The spawn of my distempered brain.

IX.

At morning, too, the playful elves,
Who in the lone raths hide themselves,

Came from each glen and forest glade,
And many a gambol round me played;
They made me laugh, and when it smote
The warders' ears beside the moat,
They crossed themselves, all shuddering,
And said I was no earthly thing,
But a young sprite the Daoine Shee *
Had brought and left in place of me.

X.

Amongst that merry crowd was one,
An imp of mischief and of fun,
From the green rath by Cloda's hill,
Who said his name was Snodnadil; †
I'd but to call, and presently
Up at my elbow started he,
To prompt me to such antics wild
As ne'er were played by mortal child:
Alas! one prank he made me play,
I'll rue until my dying day.

XI.

One morn, my father, freres, and all,
At matin meal sat in the hall;
The steeds outside, all saddled stood,
To hunt the stag in Brona's wood;
When at my elbow Snod appeared,
With many an antic strange and weird
Led down the stair with demon speed,
And bade me mount my father's steed.
A moment — and I sat in selle; ‡
A moment — with a devilish yell
Of savage and exulting glee,
I shook the bossy bridle free,
And pricked the great steed with a knife
I'd stolen from Gil, the falconer's wife.
The steed he danced the court-yard round,
Then crossed the deep moat at a bound,

---

* The Good People — the Fairies.
† Norman — Irish for Snohud-ua-Dhial: the Devil's Needle; the Dragon-fly.
‡ Selle — a saddle.

And, with a short and angry neigh
Of terror, dashed away — away
Like lightning down the forest track,
As if the de'il was on his back!

XII.

At first I was of sense bereft,
The breath my little body left,
So fast and furious was the speed,
The pace of that strong sable steed.
But soon I woke, full fast to find
My father and my freres behind,
Scouring along, with six good men,
To stop my course through Brona's glen —
That fatal gorge of crags and pits,
Where Bron the Banshee moaning sits.
They called, but at their call the more
I yelled, and pricked the good steed sore,
Until I clattered through the pass,
Like the resounding rocky mass
That, loosened from the mountain's cope,
Thunders down Cnoc-an-Affrin's slope.

XIII.

What heard I, in that valley dread,
But vengeful laughter overhead?
What saw I, as I thundered on,
But flash of sword and glint of gun,
And many a mail-clad man crouched down
By leafy brake and boulder brown?
I knew it was some mortal foe
That waited in that gorge of woe,
Perchance to take my father's life,
And shook at them my flashing knife,
And yelled defiance, fierce and high,
Back in their teeth as I swept by;
For though so small and slight my frame,
Good faith! I was a bird of game,
And would have made the charger stand,
And rushed on them with knife in hand, —
But swifter, swifter sped he on,
O'er bank, and brake, and clattering stone,
With mighty and resistless force,
Showering the blossoms from the gorse,

Tearing the greensward's fretted woof
In thunder with his iron hoof,
Scattering the fire-sparks from each jag,
Away from rattling crag to crag, —
Till out we dashed by Cnoc-na-Ree,
Where dwelt my father's enemie.

XIV.

What saw I by that hostile hold,
Within a green glade of the wold?
A little maiden, fair and bright,
Mounted upon a palfrey white;
Her face by golden sunbeams kissed,
A goss-hawk on her slender wrist;
A small page at her bridle-rein,
With long bright plume of yellow stain;
Beside them two young wolf-hounds gray,
Upon the cool green grass at play.
One glimpse I had, and only one,
As doubly mad I thundered on,
To mark the look of wild surprise
And pity in her large gray eyes,
When verged I on that fairy spot,
And passed her like a falcon * shot.

XV.

Away with lightning speed once more
Towards the great moor of Ballandore,
That dreary waste of trembling reeds
And marshes, where the wild duck feeds;
Where o'er the deep pools, black and dim,
The grassy eskers seem to swim, —
Away, till dell and dingle passed,
Like th' arrow from the arbalast,
We tore through splashing mire and scrog,
And plunged, half swallowed, in the bog.

XVI.

Ha! was it thunder from the pass
  That smote mine ear,
Loud rolling o'er the brown morass,
  With sound of fear,

* A small cannon.

When turned the sweltering steed around,
  With dripping breast and mane,
And stamped once more the solid ground,
  And clanged his bridle rein?
No; 'twas the vengeful battle-cry
  That came in that fierce peal,
With the gun's loud volley rolling by,
  And the ringing clash of steel.
Like the autumnal thunder knell
  That shakes the mountains hoar,
From lowland base to highland fell,
  It rose in one wild roar;
Then the gloomy marsh, and the forest dell,
  And the heavens were still once more.

XVII.

My heart swelled in my troubled breast,
Loud throbbing with a wild unrest;
Bitterly did the tear-drops rise,
And burn within mine aching eyes;
For well I knew that slogan yell —
It was my gallant father's knell.
Once more I shook the bridle free,
And bounded off towards Cnoc-na-Ree,
O'er bank, and brake, and quagmire, back
Upon that great steed's torn track —
Past the sweet spot where I had seen
The maiden in that glade of green,
Till up, with arrowy speed again,
I clattered into Brona's Glen.

XVIII.

Ah! well might Bron the Banshee tear
Her shadowy robe and streaming hair,
And raise her unavailing cries,
All mournful to the windy skies;
For there, most foully murdered, lay
My father, freres, and men that day!
And there, above my father's corse, —
Low bending from his foam-flecked horse,
As if he'd ridden far and fast, —
I found Sir John de Prendergast;
My sire's firm friend long, long ago,
But now, for many a year his foe;

The father of the sylvan maid
I saw within the forest glade
That woful morn. Alas! that she
Was daughter of mine enemie!

XIX.

With rage and grief I scarce had breath
To tax him with my father's death,
To brandish high that glittering knife,
And challenge him to mortal strife.
Sadly he looked down on his foe
Upon the bloody turf laid low,
Sadly he smiled at my wild wrath,
And turned him down the forest path
With laboring breast and hollow groan,
And left me with the dead, alone.

XX.

I looked upon my murdered sire,
Low lying in the gore and mire;
I looked upon my brothers brave,
Each grasping still his broken glaive,
And with a ringing shriek of dread
Up the wild valley's womb I fled,
Till, with commingled fear and hate,
Mad yelling, shot I through the gate
On that great horse, in dust and foam,
And brought the direful tidings home.

XXI.

Woe! woe! the keeners' cry,
  How mournful it began!
Now dying low, now swelling high,
  On the ears of the gathered clan; —
Woe! woe! my mother's wail,
  And my sisters' moans of fear,
And the look of the dead, so still and pale,
  Each on his sable bier;
Eleven good corpses in the hall,
And my mad freak the cause of all.
I cursed that fairy, so that he
From that fatal morn ne'er came to me;
I cursed those heroes grim and old,
And their shades did I never again behold;

I cursed myself, and that dark ravine,
Where the murderers slew my kith and kin;
But the murderers never a curse I gave, —
I left them all for the lance and glaive.

XXII.

My mother took me by the hand;
I followed quick at her command;
She led me to my father's side,
And looked upon his corse with pride,
For like a man she knew he died.
She placed my right hand on his breast,
   Where gaped the mortal wound,
And the keeners were still at her behest,
   And the bravest of the clan stood round.
She took my left and placed the palm
Upon his brow so cold and calm,
And a direful vow she bade me say,
His murderers root and branch to slay.
With swelling heart that vow I made,
And the death-feud thus was on me laid.

XXIII.

The suns of ten long years had burned
   O'er widow, and son, and clan,
And the light of health to mine eyes returned —
   I'd grown a stalwart man;
Spearing the salmon in the floods,
Hunting the grim wolf through the woods,
The dun deer up the mountain track,
Fighting in many a bold attack —
And, comrades, by the blessèd sun,
For many a mile there was not one
Could manage the battle charger free,
Or handle the bonnie lance with me!

XXIV.

In those long years of blood and strife
Why took I not my foeman's life?
Why fell I not upon his clan,
Nor slew them all, both child and man?
You'll hear. Within the secret wood
I met that maiden fair and good —

The maiden of the goss-hawk gray,
And little page so bright and gay;
The daughter of my father's foe
I'd seen upon that day of woe!
She loved me, earthly things above,
I loved her with an equal love;
And day by day, when winds were bland,
And flowers were blooming o'er the land,
We met within the forest bower
For many a blissful, secret hour, —
Or by the streamlet's vocal shore,
And told our love-vows o'er and o'er.

XXV.

Alas! that love must bow to hate,
That red revenge its ire must sate!
One day my mother summoned all
Our warlike clan round Cloda's hall,
And sneered, and told them, every one,
I was not like my father's son,
Else I had met my foeman stout,
And fought the bloody death-feud out.

XXVI.

With burning heart and brow full black
I threw my harness on my back,
Resolved my foeman's hold to sack,
And give it o'er to fire and wrack;
For then, as now, there was no law
For injuries, but the sword to draw;
And then, as now, the arméd hand
Was the best Brehon * in the land.
I mounted my battle-charger free,
And I placed my lance beside my knee;
High in the sun by Cloda's shore
I raised the banner of Le Poer.
Merrily on that river marge
Glittered the light on helm and targe;
Merrily did the sunbeams strike
On the glancing points of sword and pike;
Merrily did the war-pipes play,
Yet my heart was sad as we marched away.

* Brehon — a judge.

XXVII.

As we marched down through Brona's Glen
I made a vow unheard of men —
Whatever fortune happed that day,
De Prendergast I would not slay;
However went the coming fight,
To save the daughter pure and bright,
And bear her off to realms afar,
Where we might love 'neath another star —
Might love, from hate and death-feud free,
In some happy land beyond the sea.

XXVIII.

Up for the storming of the gate
Rushed the fierce clan with hearts elate,
That vengeance was their own at last
Upon the stout De Prendergast.
And there a welcome warm they got
Of molten pitch and leaden shot,
That laid their bodies many a row
The barbican's bloody gate below.
Then rose my hot blood boiling high,
And the light of battle lit mine eye
To see the sudden sally out,
The swaying onset stern and stout,
To hear the opposing clansmen shout,
And rattling steel and roaring rout;
And — as a charger that from far
Hears the loud clangor of the war,
Neighs fierce and shrill, and in his might
Bursts through the thickest of the fight —
So rushed I up the castle height,
And raised the war-cry of my clan,
And stormed the stubborn barbican!

XXIX.

Bloody were pike and partisan,
When through the gateway rushed the clan;
Bloody were axe, and skene, and sword,
When 'cross the court-yard fast we poured,
Tumultuous as the mountain flood
That devastates some lowland wood.
My blood was hot, my passion high,
As first in that wild rush went I.

I saw my foeman 'mid the dead
Brandish a huge mace o'er his head;
I marked his eye, so cold and stern,
Glitter like those the mountain ern
Casts savagely upon his prey
Down from his rock so steep and gray;
I saw him strike three clansmen down
With his iron mace, through helm and crown.
I thought upon my murdered sire,
And rushed on him with eyes on fire;
For the devil is strong and the flesh is weak,
And we cannot keep the vows we speak.
I smote him with my bloody sperthe,
And dashed him sorely to the earth;
Sore and heavy was the stroke,
His good steel basnet bar it broke,
And laid him on his back before
The archway of his castle door.
I placed my knee upon his breast,
   And raised my skene on high;
Unshriven all, and unconfessed,
   He was about to die:—
I raised my skene his life to take,
When the solid court-yard seemed to quake,
And I heard a sound like the sounds that break
From the wings of birds o'er the wild sea lake
   When storms are in the sky.
I looked — and by the Holy Rood,
Amid that scene of wrath and blood,
My father's shade before me stood!

XXX.

He raised his shadowy hand
   Slowly and silently —
A strange, weird look of stern command
   In his fixed eye as he gazed on me.
He spoke; his words were like the tone
Of runnels heard remote and lone
'Mong mountain woods — now strangely clear,
Now dying distant on the ear:—
"Strike not!" he said; "for now I know
De Prendergast was ne'er my foe;
True friends were we, long, long ago,

Ere civil warfare's dire behest
With seeming hate filled either breast.
That day he rode five leagues to aid
And warn me 'gainst the ambuscade
Of him, my murderer — Macray,
The robber chief of wild Coumfay!"

XXXI.

Down upon the gory sand
I dropped my dagger from my hand —
Thank Heaven! it did not find a sheath
Within his heart who lay beneath.
I raised mine eyes to look upon
That awful shade again — 'twas gone! —
The form that from my troubled sight
Hid the wild chances of the fight;
The voice that from my spell-bound ear
Shut out the battle's sounds of fear!

XXXII.

I sprang unto my feet, and back
Turned my clan from the attack;
Stopped the battle's thundering din,
Raised the chief and bore him in, —
In to where my long-loved maid
For the souls departing prayed;
There I sat De Prendergast —
He and I were friends at last.
Night came. When morning rose again,
Together through the mountain glen
Up we marched, with sword and fire,
Fought the murderers of my sire
With our clansmen, bold and stanch,
And slew them all, both root and branch!
And scarce one happy week was o'er,
When the clans by Cloda's shore
Stood beneath the sun to see
The plighting of my love and me!

He ceased, and looked upon Dark Gilliemore, —
Dark Gilliemore, the Squire of Dallan Green.
"Sir Squire," he said, "since first a lance I bore
With thee in battle's van, I've ever seen,
With saddened mind, thy dark and mournful mien.
What makes thee such a gloomsome, lonely man?
Hast thou some tale to tell of sorrow keen?" —
The squire sat silent for a little span,
Then heaved a rueful sigh, and thus his tale began: —

BALLAD OF DARK GILLIEMORE; OR, THE MOURNFUL SQUIRE.*

I.

I PLEDGE ye, comrades, in this cup
Of usquebaugh, bright, brimming up;
And now, while howls the tempest rude
Around our camp-fire in the wood,
I'll tell my tale, yet sooth to say,
It will be but a mournful lay.

II.

Glenanner is a lovely sight,
Oun-Tarra's dells are fair and bright,
Sweet are the flowers of Lisnemar,
And gay the glynns 'neath huge Ben Gar;
But still, where'er our banner leads,
'Mid tall green hills or lowland meads,
By storied dale, or mossy down,
My heart goes back to Carrick town.

III.

By Carrick town a castle brave
Towers high above its river wave,
Well belted round by wall and fosse
That foot of foe ne'er strode across.

---

* "They shot her," said the Gillie Grumach, i. e., the *Mournful Page* or *Squire*, "and I bore her to the peaked mountain in the east, and made her a grave." — *Story of the Gillie Grumach.*

Look on me now — a man am I
  Of mournful thoughts and bearing sad,
Yet once my hopes flowed fair and high,
  And once a merry heart I had,
For I was squire to Ormond then,
  First in his train each jovial morn
He flew his hawks by moor and fen,
Or chased the stag by rock and glen
  With bay of hound and mort of horn.

IV.

Within that castle's mighty hall
I saw full many a festival,
When wild harps rang and gitterns played,
And belted knight and noble maid
Danced merry measures on its floor,
In those lost, pleasant days of yore.
Within its tilt-yard, day by day,
I learnt war's gallant game to play;
And there, though young in years was I,
Soon grew I well my trade to ply;
With the steel sparth * to hew and hack
Through buff-coat strong and iron jack;
To spring on steed in full career,
And wield the sword or couch the spear.
And when our tilt-yard games were done,
Or chase was o'er each set of sun,
Gayly we ruffled through the town,
And spent full many a jovial crown.

V.

Young Ormond was a goodly lord
As ever sat at head of board.
If Europe's kings, some festal day,
Sat round the board in revel gay,
And he were there, and I in hall,
The seneschal to place them all,
I'd place him, without pause or fault,
Among their best above the salt.
You need not sneer, Sir Hugh le Poer,
  Nor you, young Donal of Killare;

---

    * Sparth, or sperthe; a battle-axe.

I'd prove my words, ay, o'er and o'er,
　With skian in hand and bosom bare,
Or sword to sword, and jack to jack,
For sake of Thomas Oge the Black! *
But he is dead, mo brón for him,
His heart is cold, his eyes are dim, —
The heart that all dishonor spurned,
Those eyes that oft in battle burned
Like the twin beacon fires that shed
Their lurid glare from Cummeragh's head,
Through the black midnight seen afar,
The harbingers of border war.

VI.

And border wars and hostings free
Full often then, God wot, had we;
For 'twas the time when mortal strife,
Steel axe to axe and knife to knife,
Was waged between the Butler line
And the strong race of Geraldine.
And Desmond was a foeman stout
In battle, siege, or foray rout;
With spur on heel and sword in hand,
Upon the borders of our land,
With his fierce hobbelers he kept
And often on our hamlets swept,
As swoops the eagle from the mountain
On the gray wolf-cubs by the fountain,
And in his talons bears away,
　Before the howling she-wolf's eyes,
To crags remote his bleeding prey
To feast his fledglings day by day
　Where Crotta Clee's † wild summits rise.

And many a goodly tower and town
Before his hot assaults went down;
For blood, and flame, and woful sack
Forever marked his vengeful track.
Yet oft we met him sword to sword,
By mountain pass and lowland ford,

---

* Thomas, surnamed, from his complexion, the Black, or Swarthy, Earl of Ormond.
† *Crotta Clee*, the Gaulty Mountains.

And turned the tide of war again
Far through each Desmond vale and glen,
And venged our wrongs as best we could
In torrents of the foeman's blood.

VII.

The March winds sang through bower and tree,
   And shook the young reeds by the ferry,
And light cloud shades, o'er mount and lea,
Ran like the billows of the sea,
One day that in the tilt-yard we
   Were making merry;
When swift as those light clouds that fled
   Over each vale and moorland brown,
A courier from the mountain head,
With loosened rein his charger led,
   Wild spurring down!
The rushy bog and treacherous moss
Like the light plover did he cross,
And headlong downward to the shore
As the strong mountain stag he bore,
And swam the Suir, where, deep and wide,
It tumbled in an angry tide;
Then rode unto the castle straight,
And blew his bugle at the gate.
The Desie's badge full well we knew,
On the light cap and folluin blue,
   The hasty clansman bore;
And, faith, but small delay had he,
So eager for his news were we,
For back the ponderous bolts we drew,
   And led him straight our chief before.
He told how Desmond and his men
Had crossed Sliav Gua's mountain glen,
   A small but hardy band,
And burned his chieftain's hamlets free,
And levied coign and liverie
   Within the Desie's land.
Then begged the doughty Butler's aid
To stem the Desmond's bloody raid.

VIII.

In sooth, his prayer was not in vain,
For ere one hour o'er hill and plain

Many an eager gillie trode,
And many a rushing easlach * rode,
Till, when the early twilight fell,
From Fallad glen to Graffon's dell,
On turret top and craggy mount
A thousand war-fires you might count.
Old Carrick town rang loud next morn
With flam of drum and roar of horn,
For from each forest, plain, and glynn,
The clansmen all had gathered in.
To me it was a goodly sight
  To see the Butler's strength arrayed,
The spear-points glittering in the light,
The banners waving on the height,
The footmen eager for the fight,
And horsemen all in mail bedight
  Far spread o'er glen and glade.

Then Butler issued from his hall
Among his gallant clansmen all,
And straightway took the southern track,
While we rode gayly at his back,
And never his charger rested he
  By cross of road, or fount, or plain,
Until he reached, where, broad and strong,
Blackwater rushes by crag and tree,
With murmuring roar or plaintive song,
  'Mid the bonnie woods of wild Affane.†
And 'mid those woods we camped that night,
And waited but the morning light
To fall upon proud Desmond's path,
And on his raiders vent our wrath.

IX.

When morn's first beams began to quiver
On crest of rock and wave of river,
A clump of spears we saw far south
Emerging from a valley's mouth,
And knew 'twas Desmond and his men
  By the great flag that waved so proud
Before them in that hollow glen, —
  By sheets of flame and many a cloud
Of murky smoke from rifled pen

---

* Easlach; a mounted messenger.
† Affane; scene of the battle of that name, on the Blackwater.

And burning cot their track behind,
And the great herds that, like the wind,
Rushed towards the river bank before,
Swept on by kern and creachadore.
He saw us by the ford arrayed,
The Desmond bold, and when they prayed,
His bearded knights, that he would flee
Our onset — stoutly answered he,
  With knitted brow and flashing eye —
"Though we are only one to three,
  Beside yon ford I'd rather lie,
Bloody and stiff within my jack,
Than on a Butler turn my back."

And, faith, he made his vaunting good,
For in our teeth he crossed the flood;
But when he gained the other shore,
Right on his front and flanks we tore.
Then hoarsely rose the battle yell,
And fast the Desmond clansmen fell; —
Yet stoutly still our charge they met,
Though gallantly to work we set,
Until Sir Walter's petronel
  Brought Desmond down, and he was ta'en
A prisoner in that gory dell,
  'Mid the bonnie woods of wild Affane.
'Twas then, as five tall Butlers bore
The wounded Desmond by the shore,
" O, where's the mighty Desmond now?"
  They asked, amid that battle's wreck;
He raised himself, all red with gore,
And answered, with exultant brow, —
  " O, where, but on the Butler's neck!"

X.

The fight was fought, the noonday sun
Shone down on banner, glaive, and gun
Of the proud victors, as they sped
  Back to their homes the hills across,
And on the vanquished as they fled
Through tangled woods and paths that led
  O'er dreary plain and desert moss;
And up the lonely tracks that lie
Along the huge-ribbed hills so high, —
And with them, prisoner bound, was I.

XI.

They placed me in a dungeon strong,
Where distant Mulla winds among
The leafy woods of Houra's hills,
Fed by a hundred dancing rills;
And there pined I for many a day,
Till five long seasons passed away; —
Then, when they thought my spirit broke,
They freed me from their cursed yoke,
And bade me wander as I might —
Yet warned me 'gainst escape or flight.
I well remember, ay, and will
Till some brave foe my blood shall spill,
The day I crossed my dungeon door,
   And sought the wild woods free
The summer sky was laughing o'er;
And from green glen, and height, and shore
The jocund birds their songs did pour
   So merrilie;
And to mine eyes all nature wore
   A look of wondrous brilliancy.
An infant's strength was more than mine
   As I went forth that morn;
I thought each stream a draught divine,
   I rested 'neath each blossomed thorn,
Or slowly strayed o'er height and hollow,
Long draughts of balmy air to swallow.

XII.

My strength returned. One golden eve
   As up the hills I clomb,
Sweet dreams within my heart to weave,
   And think upon my far-off home,
I gained a valley lone and deep,
Where Ounanar's bright waters leap
And fill the thick green woods with song,
Wild bounding through the dells along.
I sat me by the sounding stream, —
I sat me in a pleasant dream;
For who could pass that valley fair
And stop not for a moment there?
The green ash o'er the torrent grew,
The oak his strong arms wildly threw

To the blue heavens, as if to clasp
Some wandering cloudlet in his grasp;
And all around my seat was still,
From far Knockea to Corrin hill.
The leafy branches thick and green
On all sides made a shadowy screen,
  Save where a little vista showed
Beneath me where the torrent sheen,
  A mimic lake all smoothly flowed,
With many a sparkling ripple stealing
  Over its breast of radiancy, —
Wild beauties on its banks revealing;
  And, O, what it revealed to me!

XIII.

There, on a green and mossy stone,
A young, bright maiden stood alone
Gazing upon the foam-wreaths white
  That sparkled on their pathway rude,
Filling the leafy nooks with light,
And, O, it was so fair a sight!
  Methought that maiden, as she stood,
Some phantom of a vision bright,
  Or lovely spirit of the wood.
A moment — I was standing there
Beside that maid so young and fair;
A moment — and my heart was gone
  With her bright face and sunny hair, —
And, ah! so sweet her blue eyes shone,
  'Twas lost ere I was half aware;
A moment — for time went so fleet,
  Long seasons had been hours to me —
And in that lone and wild retreat,
  O, we were talking pleasantly!
I told her in that wild-wood bower
  How I was prisoner ta'en,
And how I longed for that glad hour
  When I might 'scape their chain;
And found she was a captive, too,
  For three long years, —
A captive from that sweet land where,
Above the blooming woods of Caher,
Wild Gaulty to the skies so blue
  Its tall crest rears.

XIV.

It boots not, comrades, now to tell
How oft we met in that wild dell,
And how we loved, and how we planned
To 'scape, and reach the Butler's land.
One morn a brave black steed I caught, —
   My captor's own fleet steed. —
And rode away to that wild spot
   With headlong speed.
And towards far Ormond, glad and free,
I bore my love away with me.

XV.

But sorrow came too soon — alas!
As we sped down Glendarra's pass,
The foe came thundering on our track
With matchlocks pointed at my back.
Away across Turlaggan's rill,
And by the foot of Gurma's hill,
With gory spur and loosened rein,
For life before them did I strain, —
Away up Gurma's side; and there
A bullet whistled through my hair;
But when I gained its summit high,
Between my foemen and the sky,
Another hurtled through the air
And grazed my side with sudden smart,
And lodged within my true-love's heart.

XVI.

Ah, woe is me! the look she gave,
   It haunts me yet;
Its bitter-anguish but the grave
   Can make my heart forget.
One sudden look of woful pain —
   And she was dead;
And I — far down into the plain,
   O'er rocks and glens I fled,
And left my foemen far behind;
Thundering onward like the wind,
Away, away on that swift horse,
Clasping close my true-love's corse!

XVII.

I bore her to yon peakéd hill,
   And scooped her narrow bed,

And laid the earth, so damp and chill,
  Above my darling's head.
And, comrades, since that woful day
  I've never known
One hour of gladness; and I crave,
When I shall fall amid the fray,
  You'll bear me to yon mountain lone,
And lay me in my true-love's grave!

"Now, Donal Roe, begin thee," quoth the Squire,
"I've spun my thread of melancholy lore;
Hast thou no legend of the sounding Nier?
No tale of fairy wrath? of castle hoar?
Of ford, of moated dun, or haunted shore?"—
Red Donal laughed. "I have a tale," quoth he,
"I cannot help remembering evermore,
Of war and love that happed long syne to me
Far on the pagan strand of burning Barbarie."

ROMANCE OF DONAL ROE; OR, THE LADY OF MENDORA.

I.

In every nook and earthly spot
Lurks grief, though oft we know it not;
The freshest blossoms of the May
Blow side by side with foul decay.
The hectic rose-spots on the cheek
A warning sad will often speak,
Gay tinting o'er the peach-like skin,
With rottenness and death within.

II.

But will the sunshine gild the place
Less bright where human woe we trace?
Will the fresh flower false odor shed
When festering weeds lie on its bed?
And will young beauty smile the less
For life's gay signals of distress?

They will not. If they should, then why
Not pass them with averted eye,
Walking through life the pleasant way
Of sunshine and of blossoms gay,
Ne'er seeking on our path to find
Each woful bane for heart and mind?
You loved, and deep of sorrow quaffed;
I loved as well, but loved and laughed,
For, somehow, though enough I had
Of sorrow, still I ne'er was sad,
But climbed up Life's tempestuous height
As jovial as I seem to-night.

III.

Fill me a cup: I'll drink to one
Whose head now bleaches in the sun
On the grim gate whose 'battled crown
Lowers o'er Kilmallock's ancient town, —
The best of soldier-knights was he,
Sir James Fitz Thomas of Tralee.
Cursed be the heart his fall that planned, —
Cursed be the base and murderous hand
Of him who dealt the traitor blow
That laid my peerless captain low.

IV.

Comrades! 'twere long to tell why we
Fled from the Castle of Tralee, —
'Twere long to tell why from our home
We sailed across the sea to Rome.
Enough, we wanted men and gold
From foreign wolves to guard our fold —
To fight the foreign enemy
For Ireland and for liberty; —
Enough, that, far beyond our hope,
We got them from the royal Pope, —
Money, and ships, and arms, and men,
To fight the battle o'er again.

V.

A proud and gladsome heart was mine
  The morn I saw our homeward sails
Spread from each tower-like mast of pine,
  And bellying o'er the sparkling brine
  Before the Mediterranean gales.

Little that joyous morn I recked
How Italy's gay shores were decked
With cedar groves and orange bowers,
With villas and romantic towers,
And painted cots and princely halls,
And far-off gleaming waterfalls; —
Little, for aye before mine eyes
Glittered an exile's paradise —
The rolling clouds of various hue,
The flashing streams and skies of blue,
The fern-clad slopes and forest brakes,
The foggy moors and glistening lakes,
The hills with heather purpled o'er,
  The rock-bound, wave-resounding strand,
The villaged vales and castles hoar,
  And green fields of my native land.

VI.

Alas! that home-bright vision gay
Was like the sparkling ocean spray
That shines a moment in the ray,
Then melts to nothingness away;
For many a brave man's blood I saw
This faithful sword in battle draw;
And many a long moon waxed and waned,
Before my native land I gained.

VII.

Alas! that he remained in Rome
Should guide our gallant fleet for home,
And left our enterprise to him,
  Stukely, the reckless English knight,
An outlawed soldier, brave and grim
  As ever dashed into a fight;
A man full careless of his trust,
  And fickle as a springtide gale,
Whose promises were dross and dust,
  When self was in the trembling scale.
For when the close Herculean strait
Was passed, we knew our bitter fate.
We steered not for our land away,
  But skirted Portingallo's coast,
And joined in Lisbon's glittering bay
  Sebastian's bannered fleet and host

That with the morning sailed the sea,
To fight the king of Barbarie.

VIII.

The favoring winds soon swept us o'er;
We landed on that pagan shore,
And with high hearts in strength and pride
Marched up the Elmahassen's side,
    Until, upon its windings far,
We reached a sandy region wide —
    The bloody plain of Alcazar.

IX.

'Twas morn: the sun, a disk of blood,
Rose o'er the narrow stripe of wood
    That skirted Elmahassen's water,
Whose wave like crystal ruby shone,
But, ere the setting of the sun,
    Ran redder with the stains of slaughter.
And as before that sultry morn
    Faded the pale moon's silvery shine,
Afar beneath her sinking horn
    Upon the low horizon line
A cloud of dust extended wide,
And nearer rolled its threatening tide,
Like a great storm-wrack on the deep,
From whose grim front the lightnings leap.
And lightnings bright enough, I trow,
Incessant did that dark cloud show;
For, as its course upon the sands
It stayed athwart our halted bands,
Myriads of spears, and banners proud,
Flashed upward through its parting shroud;
And when at last the light winds blew
Its rolling volumes from our view,
Before us, stretching far away,
Glittered the Infidel's array —
A mighty, multitudinous host
As ever Pagandom could boast!

X.

Gallants! good armies have I seen
    In this old fighting land of ours,

The best of England's hostile queen,
  The best of Ormond's, Desmond's powers;
But never since that morn when we
Formed on the sands of Barbarie,
To meet King Muley's chivalrie,
  Heard I such rolls of drum and trump,
Saw I such warlike braverie,
  Barbaric pride and martial pomp.

XI.

And our own host in martial show
Was not one whit behind the foe;
From front to rear, from flank to flank,
Wave after wave, each stately rank,
Shimmered beneath the burning ray
Like sunset on the ocean spray,
Or rain-wet woods 'neath shine and breeze;
Magnificent in blazonries
Of war-steeds' gay caparisons,
Of gilded helms and hacquetons,
Of silver shields and crests of gold,
Of banners glorious to behold;
Pennon, and scroll, and glistening plumes
Bright as the tints May morn assumes
When from his deep cerulean bed
The day-god lifts his flaming head.

XII.

Along our front, from wing to wing,
Like the bright sun all glittering,
Statelily rode the youthful king;
Noble and gallant knight, and squire,
  And page behind him many a one,
With surcoats like the clouds of fire
  Which gleam around the setting sun.
And bright, e'en 'midst that dazzling throng,
I saw two pages sweep along;
So much alike, could scarce be seen
A difference the two between,
Save that the one had eyes of blue,
The other, dark, of darkest hue,
And sturdier frame and mien more free, —
Two brothers fond they seemed to me.

XIII.

You know me passing well, good freres,
I'm not much given to qualms and fears;
But when amid that blaze of light,
With helmet crown all jewel-bright,
And bearing confident and high,
The king swept like a meteor by,
I saw within his eagle glance
A weird that pierced me like a lance;
And a dark thought, — say what you will, —
A black presentiment of ill,
Smote my high heart, now all aflame
Beneath his flag to win a name, —
Smote it as water smites the fire
And turns it into dust and mire.

XIV.

I'll tell you how my rede was read.
I'll tell you how the black weird sped.

XV.

A furlong's length of level sands
Between those myriad hostile bands
Burning for blood, with flashing brands
Ready for battle in their hands;
Unlimbered guns and matches lit,
And good steeds champing at the bit, —
Comrades! you know what soon befell
'Twixt Christian and brown Infidel.

XVI.

The sun had risen high in air,
And smote the sands with torrid glare,
And stilled a moment was the hum
Of voice, of cymbal, and of drum,
Portentous of the storm to come; —
So still, I heard the rustling quiver
Of the green trees beside the river.
 The banners by the hot winds stirred,
Till, breaking through the pause profound,
Like the shrill battle-clarion's sound,
 Sebastian gave the word!

Then, like Atlantic's deafening roar
On stormy Corco-Bascain's shore,
The ready foeman's answering shout
Along his bristling lines burst out.
Many a sharp spur's rowel drank
At the wild charger's reeking flank;
Many a sword-hand high was raised,
And musketoon and matchlock blazed;
Many a cannon, fierce and hot,
Belched through the lines its plunging shot,
As o'er that level space did pass
Each rattling wall of steel and brass,
And midway met with thundering shock
Loud as an iceberg 'gainst a rock.

XVII.

Through the hot noon till eve we fought,
And many a deed of valor wrought,
And thrice that day our battle edge
Pierced through the foemen like a wedge,
Though 'gainst King Muley's myriad men
We counted scarcely one to ten.
Many an Infidel went down
With riven breast or cloven crown;
Many a Christian soldier true,
On the red field his last breath drew;
That knight of knights, bold Christovale,
'Mid heaps of slain lay still and pale;
And Stukely, like a forest boar,
Reeking with Saracenic gore,
Sank in the press to rise no more.

XVIII.

'Twas then, as shot the evening light
Aslant upon the roaring fight,
King Muley Hassan's main array
  Furious and fast around us sped,
As rush the waves some stormy day
Round Arran's precipices gray,
  In bellowing thunder hoarse and dread,
With blinding fogs of hissing spray,
  And the great clouds rolling overhead!

So swept they round us, front and flank,
Scattering each serried square and rank,
Until our broken bands they bore
Down to the Elmahassen's shore.

XIX.

There, as a gallant ship that rides
A long day's space the storm-beat tides,
And still, both wind and wave defying,
Keeps colors at the masthead flying
Till, powerless 'mid night's baleful glooms,
  Sudden it sinks from mortal ken
In that dread gulf whose water booms
  Off the wild shore of Loffoden, —
Sebastian, who, amid the storm,
All day reared high his martial form,
His meteor sword in circles flashing,
His war-horse through the foemen dashing,
Now 'mid the splintering spears and crashing,
With fluttering plumes, with eye of pride,
Sank in the battle's thundering tide;
And guardsmen, bowmen, hackbuteers,
  A moment, when they saw him fall,
  Raised high to heaven their weapons all;
And with fierce eyes and maddening cheers,
  And hearts that wild for vengeance burned,
Amid the universal din
Dashed through the pagan Sarazin,
Many a rood his columns in —
  But never a man returned!

XX.

'Twas then, unhorsed, as 'mid the press
I hacked and stabbed in sore distress,
Fast as the storm-wind in the dell,
To me each incident befell; —
I saw upon the red field nigh
Upon his back Sebastian lie,
With bleeding breast and glazing eye,
The younger page beside him kneel,
  The elder o'er his body bent —
  One sabre stroke and down he went.
I saw him his wild charger wheel,

The pagan dog, the Moorish foe,
Whose weapon dealt the fatal blow,
And raise that weapon once again
To cleave the younger to the brain.
Amid the hubbub and the hum
I felt mine hour of hours was come
To do a brave and gallant deed
Was worthy of my father's breed.
Behind him on the steed I sprang
In one wild bound, with clattering clang
Of corselet 'gainst his Moorish jack,
And plunged this long blade through his back!
Then, with our Irish slogan yell,
I hurled him headlong from the selle,
And turned the horse, careering round
Infuriate on the blood-stained ground,
Up to the spot where Blue-eye knelt,
And seized him by the golden belt;
Drew him unto me tenderly,
And grasped the rein and firmed my knee;
And like the lightning bolts that tear,
Destructive through the forest bare,
Riving and shattering all before,
Out through the Moorish crowd I tore,
And wounded, faint, but unpursued,
Soon left behind that field of blood.

. . . .

XXI.

Dead, 'neath the pale moon's midnight ray,
Our good steed on the greensward lay,
The white foam on his spent flank showing,
The red blood from his nostrils flowing;
And, spattered with the crimson tide,
The rescued page lay low beside,
Motionless, without sigh or groan,
Like a young tree by winds o'erthrown.

XXII.

I looked around: the moonbeams lit
A gorge through crags of granite split,
Whose threatening sides above us towered,
With cedars and wild palms embowered,

And feathery ferns that waved aloft
In the light air their plumage soft,
And wild vines hung from tree to tree
  Down the rude rock sides stark and tall,
Like shreds of ancient tapestry
  Upon some old cathedral wall.
Above us, a long band of light,
The torrent cleared a dizzy height
With a wild bound, and broke below
On the black rocks in feathery snow;
Then gathering in its strength again,
Dashed by us down the echoing glen.
No other sound, save when the fox
Barked shrilly from the upland rocks,
Broke on that ghostly solitude
Of intermingled rock and wood.

XXIII.

With sinking heart, that hope denied,
I knelt me down the page beside;
The helmet bright with gold o'erchased,
And glitering corselet I unbraced,
Parted the silken vest — when, lo!
  Two swelling breasts, like ivory
From wild Siberian wastes of snow,
  The page's sex revealed to me!
As one who on a desert hill,
When all before the storm is still,
Walks musing on, till swift and bright
A keen flash of electric light
Out from the black and sulphurous skies
Flickers before his wildered eyes;
Sudden he stops: his startled ear
The pulses of his heart can hear,
That louder still, and yet more loud,
Throbs at each thunder from the cloud, —
So I, before that beauteous maid,
Stood startled, troubled, half afraid;
So through me, like a flood of flame,
The hot blood bounding went and came.
But as the storm which all night long
Rages the rattling Reeks among,
Calms gently down when morning breaks
Upon Killarney's magic lakes,

So my wild raptures suddenly
Calmed as she oped her eyes on me.

XXIV.

And as she looked, a blush there came
Upon her cheeks, of maiden shame,
And in her eyes a lovely light,
Half confidence and half affright,
That pierced my heart with love's sweet pain,
And made its pulses throb again;
For what blest saint could aught control
The feelings of his burning soul —
What heart of man could keep him wise
'Neath the bright glamour of her eyes?
Comrades! 'twas not in mine to brook
That glance and sweet appealing look;
With love and generous ardor stirred,
Out from its sheath I plucked my sword,
And swore upon its shining cross,
Through weal or woe, through gain or loss,
To shield her with my heart's best blood,
Whate'er befell by field or flood.

XXV.

What answer to my vows I got,
'Tis past and gone, and matters not;
But next bright morning found us twain
Upon the rough shore of the main,
And nigh a red-sailed Moorish boat
Upon the green waves half afloat.
Its master, a stout Moor, when he
Looked on our Christian panoply,
Sprang from the boat with brandished oar
To slay me on his curséd shore;
Deftly I warded off his blow,
And with my good sword laid him low,
And left the pagan dog to lie
And rot beneath his burning sky.
Famished with hunger's pangs, we ate
Of his good scrip of sun-dried date;
And pushed his light boat from the strand,
   And set its red sail to the wind,
And steering for the northern land
   Left Barbary's fatal shore behind.

XXVI.

'Twere vain to tell the misery
  Of hunger, thirst, and sun-wrought pain
We bore upon the lonely sea,
  Until, upon the shore of Spain,
We breathed the blessèd mountain breeze
By the great Rock of Hercules.
And vain the panorama bright
Of lovely Spanish vale and height;
Of forests waving in the breeze,
And castles towering o'er the trees;
Of towns, and plains, and shimmering rills,
Dancing in music down the hills, —
We saw 'neath shade, or sheen of sun,
As northward still we journeyed on.

XXVII.

Enough, that, hand in hand, we stood
Within a Lusitanian wood,
Husband and wife one eve, before
A mighty castle, grim and hoar,
That reared its gray and stately head
To the blue skies all turreted.
She looked into mine eyes a look
That through my soul like lightning strook,
And said, "Brave husband, comrade dear,
Our journey's happy end is here!
For yonder ancient castle-hold,
These hills and vales, this blooming wold,
All once were his, my brother true,
Whom the dark Moor relentless slew,
And I, the last branch of our line,
Take thee for lord, and make them thine!
Of lineage high in wealth and fame,
Of old Mendora's line we came;
Twin children, nurtured at one breast,
We grew in love; at fate's behest
  I followed him across the sea
  Disguised in soldier's panoply,
And saw the pagan cleave his crest
  And leave me none to love — but thee."

XXVIII.

O, sweet and sad our welcome home
To old Mendora's castled dome!
The vassals shouted from the towers,
The maidens garlanded with flowers
The glittering halls, — yet I could trace
Sad recollection on each face,
And, 'mid the gay, sweet garlands, find
Beneath the blossoms intertwined
Some branches of a darker hue, —
The cypress and the mourning yew,
In grief for him whose bones lay far
On the fell field of Alcazar.

XXIX.

Yet ever, as each morning rose,
Died out the memory of our woes,
For as two rose-buds of the Spring,
In some sweet bower where linnets sing,
Beneath the sun in beauty's pride
Open their glowing petals wide,
So our young hearts, 'neath Love's warm ray,
Brightened and bloomed, and passed away
A year in one glad rhapsody
Of bliss I ne'er again shall see.

XXX.

But love, and all the hopes it fed,
Its joys and griefs alike, are dead;
She died, and I knelt by her tomb
Short space in misery and gloom;
For word came o'er that Irishmen
In Ireland's cause were up again.
Then I plucked heart of grace once more,
And sought old Ireland's friendly shore; —
And here I sit, from belt to brand,
From top to toe, from heart to hand,
A soldier of my native land.

AFTER THE BATTLE.

I.

There were two comrades, stout and free,
Within the Wood of Barnalee,
Under the spreading oaken tree.

II.

The sun poured down his ruddy light
On blooming wold and purple height;
The wild birds sang, the streams ran bright.

III.

There they sat at set of sun,
Their battle fought, their victory won:
Sir Hugh le Poer, that heart of fire,
And the dark Minstrel with his lyre,
Thinking, thinking mournfully,
Under the spreading oaken tree,
Of their gallant comrades twain
Lying on the battle plain
Stark and silent with the slain.

IV.

Comrades to their latest breath,
True in life and true in death,
God give them peace, God shield them well,
Those who 'scaped and those who fell.

ROMANCE OF THE GOLDEN HELMET.

I.

ONE glorious Easter even,
  Under the mountain tree,
A young knight sat bereaven,
  A-gazing up and down.
O! wearily and drearily
Along the plains looked he,
  And up the summits brown.

II.

The birds were singing sweetly
  From the wild rowan grove,
The dun deer gambolled fleetly
  Beside the upland rills;
Yet wearily and drearily
He thought upon his love —
  Young Bride of the castled hills.

III.

His wolf-hound, by him lying,
  Looked up into his face,
As though he read the flying
  Thoughts of his master's brain.
O, wearily and drearily,
Through the brain's little space,
  Speeds thought's black train!

IV.

"Around my love's hoar dwelling" —
  'Twas thus Sir Brian said —
"The Norman host is swelling,
  And I a banished man.
O, wearily and drearily
My mournful days have sped
  Under the outlaw's ban!"

V.

Just then a white fawn darted
  Out from the rowan screen,
And up the wolf-hound started,
  And after her away;
And suddenly, O, suddenly,
  Under the copses green
    Soon vanished they!

VI.

Beside a cave's hoar portal
  The wolf-hound lost his chase.
O, was the white fawn mortal,
  His keen eyes thus to blind?
Yet eagerly, O, eagerly,
  He still pursued the trace
    Through the cave like the wind!

VII.

Now came the sunset gleaming
  O'er haunted crag and dell;
The young knight stays his dreaming,
  And looks once more around,
'Till eagerly, O, eagerly,
  Across the silent fell,
    Cometh his brave wolf-hound! —

VIII.

In his mouth a helmet golden
  He'd found in th' ancient cave,
With a scroll decayed and olden
  Fastened beside the crest: —
Who'll bear me, who'll wear me,
  Shall have an army brave
    To do at his behest!

IX.

Sir Brian placed the helmet
  His pluméd cap instead,
And scarce had cried, "O, well met,
  My 'fenceless head and thou!"
When suddenly, O, suddenly,
  He heard an army's tread
    Over the mountain's brow!

X.

And quickly filed before him
  A thousand mounted men.
High in the twilight o'er him
  Their gilded banners sail,
And gallantly, O, gallantly,
  They rode in that wild glen,
    All in their glittering mail!

XI.

One led unto Sir Brian
  A mighty milk-white steed,
And he has mounted high on
  The antique saddle-tree;
And eagerly, O, eagerly
  All cried, "In thy great need,
    O, now we'll follow thee!"

XII.

Away Sir Brian dashes
  With those weird warriors all;
The craggy roadway flashes
  Beneath their horse-hoofs' bound,
'Till rushingly, O, rushingly,
  They speed nigh his true-love's wall,
    By the Norman leaguered round!

XIII.

Behind Sir Brian kept they,
  Their proud plumes dancing high;
With brave Sir Brian swept they
  Upon the Norman crew,
And fearfully, O, fearfully
  Rose their ancient battle-cry,
    'Till every man they slew!

XIV.

His love came forth to meet him
  Beneath the midnight star;
His mountain friends to greet him,
  And those weird warriors all,
Joyfully, O, joyfully,
  All crossed the fortress bar,
    And feasted in the hall!

XV.

'Till morn's white planet lit them,
  These champions could not wait;
The milk-white charger with them
  Towards the lone hills they bore;
Gallantly, O, gallantly
They rode from the castle gate,
  And ne'er were looked on more!

XVI.

Long in that ancient castle,
  'Neath the gray Cummeragh's head,
Bright over feast and wassail
  That golden helmet shone;
And joyfully, O, joyfully
These lovers twain were wed
  Ere the next morn was gone! *

FAIR GWENDOLINE AND HER DOVE.

I.

"Come hither, come hither, thou snowy dove,
  Spread out thy white wings fast and free,
And fly over moorland, and hill, and grove,
  Till thou reach the castle of gay Tralee.
Sir Gerald bides in the northern tower,
  While heather is purple and shamrock green,
Go, bid him come to thy lady's bower
  For the love of his own dear Gwendoline.

II.

"Come hither, come hither, thou lily-white dove,
  Spread out thy white wings fast and free;
When thou'st given Sir Gerald my troth and love,
  In the northern turret of gay Tralee,

---

* The tradition of the enchanted warriors is not confined to one part of Ireland. The peasantry of the Cummeragh valleys say that a troop of those ancient and spell-bound warriors may frequently be seen at night performing their evolutions on the wild mountain tracks, and in the rocky cooms near their dwellings.

Then speed thy flight to Dunkerron gate,
  While heather is purple and shamrock green,
And tell its lord of thy lady's hate,
  That he'll ne'er look more on young Gwendoline."

III.

Away, away went the faithless dove,
  Away over castle, and mount, and tree,
Till he lighted Dunkerron's gate above —
  Not the northern turret of gay Tralee:
"Sir Donal, my lady hath lands and power,
  While heather is purple and shamrock green,
And she bids thee come to her far-off bower
  For the love of thine own dear Gwendoline."

IV.

Away, away went the false, false dove,
  Nor rested by castle, or mount, or tree,
Till he lighted a corbeil-stone above,
  In the northern turret of gay Tralee:
"Sir Gerald, my lady hates thee sore,
  While heather is purple and shamrock green,
While the streams dance down the hills, no more
  Shalt thou look on the face of fair Gwendoline."

V.

"Thou liest, thou liest! O, faithless dove!
  I'll take my good steed speedilie
And hie to the bower of my lady-love,
  And ask at its door if she's false to me:
I'll ne'er believe but her heart is true
  While heather is purple and shamrock green."
And never a bridle-rein he drew
  Till he rode to the bower of his Gwendoline.

VI.

Dunkerron's lord came by the gate, —
  A stout and a deadly foe was he, —
And with lance in rest, and with frown of hate,
  He rode at Sir Gerald of gay Tralee;
Sir Gerald bent o'er his saddle-bow,
  While heather is purple and shamrock green,
Strook his lance through the heart of his bravest foe
  For the love of his own dear Gwendoline.

VII.

"Fair Gwendoline, thou'st a faithless dove,
  Yet I know thou wert ever true to me;
'Twas his words were lies and thy troth to prove
  I rode o'er the mountains from gay Tralee."
He's clasped his arms round that lady gay,
  While heather is purple and shamrock green,
And the summer-tide saw their wedding day—
  That trusting knight and fair Gwendoline.

THE BATTLE OF MANNING FORD.

[This battle was fought in the winter of 1643, by the troops of the Kilkenny Confederation, under Lord Castlehaven, against one of the armies of Murrogh O'Brien, Earl of Inchiquin, commanded by Sir Charles Vavasour. The two armies came in sight of each other in the morning, and marched side by side during the greater part of the day, each looking for an advantageous battle-ground. At length they reached the Ford of Manning, across the Funcheon, near Glanworth. Here Sir Charles Vavasour attempted to cross the river, but was attacked by Lord Castlehaven, and his army cut to pieces, after the manner told in the ballad. Sir Charles Vavasour himself was taken prisoner, and all his principal officers either slain or captured. In this battle all the standards, save one, of the enemy, fell into the hands of the Irish forces, together with the preys of cattle, the baggage, and seven or eight hundred stand of arms.]

I.

I SHARPENED my sword in the morning, and buckled my basnet
  and jack;
I clothed my steed in his harness, and cheerily sprung on his
  back;
I rode over mountain and moorland, and never slacked spur by
  the way,
Till I came to the green Pass of Ballar, and called up young
  Johnnie Dunlea.

II.

Then down through that deep vale we clattered, and on by the
  hoarse-sounding rill,
Till we came to the strong House of Sloragh, and blew up our
  bugle full shrill;

Then Diarmid, the Master of Sloragh, rode gallantly out with his men,
And we shouted, "Hurrah for the battle!" as onward we thundered again.

III.

We swept like the wind through the valley — deep quagmire and trench we defied,
And we knocked at the strong gate of Dangan, where Will of the Wood kept his bride; —
How he pressed her sweet lips at the parting, and kissed off her tears, o'er and o'er!
But, alas! they flowed faster at even, for her bridegroom came back nevermore.

IV.

Through the bog of Glendoran we waded, and up through the sear forest crashed,
Then down o'er the broad-spreading highland, a torrent of bright steel we dashed;
And there how we shouted for gladness, as the glitter of spears we descried
From the army of bold Castlehaven, far off on the green mountain side!

V.

I rode up to the brave Castlehaven, and asked for a place in his rank;
And he said, "Keep ye shoulder to shoulder, and charge ye to-day from our flank!"
And we marched 'neath his banner that morning, till fast by Lis Funcheon we lay,
Just to drink a good *slainthe* to Ireland, and look to our arms for the fray.

VI.

'Twas then, as we gazed down the moorland, a horseman came wild spurring in,
And he stinted his course not for thicket, for deep bog, or crag-strewn ravine,
Till his charger fell dead by our standard, that waved in the bright morning glow;
Then up to our chieftain he tottered, and told him his dark tale of woe!

VII.

"Ho! Baron of broad Castlehaven! last night, in the Tower
of Cloghlea,
The foe battered down our defences — save me, every man did
they slay;
And they brought forth their prisoners this morning, — young
maiden, and matron, and child, —
And led them, for bloodshed still burning, away through the
brown forest wild.

VIII.

"And there, by the Bridge of Glenullin, they murdered these
poor prisoners all,
And the demons they laughed as they slew them — ah! well did
they free them from thrall —
And now look ye sharp to the southward; on Vavasour comes
with his horde;
Then give him the murderer's guerdon, and pay him with bullet
and sword!"

IX.

We looked to the southward, and saw them with many a creast
moving on,
With the spoil of two counties behind them, by murder and
treachery won;
With a waving and flaunting of banners, and bright-flashing
arms did they come,
With the clear, shrilly clamor of trumpets, and the loud rolling
tuck of the drum.

X.

We answered their challenge as proudly, and threw out our
skirmishers bold,
Who pillaged their rear of the cattle, and thinned their broad
van from the wold;
And thus the two armies went onward, each watching its neigh-
bor full keen,
Till we came to the rough slopes of Manning, with the bright
Funcheon rolling between.

XI.

Then out spurred our brave Castlehaven, his sword flashing
bright in his hand,
And he cried, "Now, my children, we've caught them, the foes
of your dear native land!

Brave horsemen, bear down on their rearguard — brave footmen,
    strike hard on their flanks,
Till we give them a bed 'neath the Funcheon, or a grave cold
    and red by its banks."

XII.

O, then came the clanking of harness, and the roar of the onset
    full soon,
And the neighing and champing of chargers, and the crash of
    the loud musquetoon,
And the fierce rolling thunder of cannon, and the rattling of
    lances and swords,
And the gloom and the glitter of battle, as we fell horse and foot
    on their hordes!

XIII.

As the frost-loosened crags thunder downward, through the wild-
    woods of steep Gaultymore,
We rushed on their thick-serried horsemen, and swept them
    adown to the shore;
As the gray wolves rush out from the forest, one flood of white
    fangs on their prey,
Our fierce kerne sprang on their footmen, with blades ready
    pointed to slay.

XIV.

And there 'twas all shouting and swearing, and the clanging of
    hard stroke on stroke,
And the flourish of skeins o'er the vanquished, and the glittering
    of pikes through the smoke, —
Till the ford was half crossed by their footmen, and the river
    all red with their gore, —
Till the horse through their thick ranks retreated, and we at
    their backs striking sore.

XV.

There's a flat on the far side of Manning, with gray cliffs and
    wood every side;
'Tis there, in the blood of the foemen, our pikes and our sabres
    we dyed;
'Tis there you'd have heard the loud clangor, as the steel went
    through corselet and breast,
As we slew them, and slew till the sunset glared red o'er the
    hills of the west.

XVI.

Fierce Vavasour rode by his standard, and stoutly he stood to
    the charge,
But we took him, and all his bold leaders, full soon by that red
    river's marge;
And the pillage he swept from each hamlet, and the gold that he
    robbed from each town,
By the ne'er-failing ordeal of battle, were ours ere the red sun
    went down.

XVII.

And the remnant that 'scaped from the slaughter, we chased
    over valley and wood,
Till each rough path was strewn with their corses, each ford
    running red with their blood;
One flag-bearer 'scaped to Kilmallock, with banner all shattered
    and torn —
Sad news to Black Murrogh, the Burner, the sight of that
    horseman forlorn!

XVIII.

And soon o'er the red Ford of Manning we kindled our camp-
    fires full bright,
And fast by the heaps of the slaughtered, O, wildly we revelled
    that night!
And we drank a good *slainthe* to Ireland, and one to our gen-
    eral brave,
Who led us to triumph and glory that day by the Funcheon's
    wild wave!

YOUNG DE RUPE.

I.

A STRICKEN plain is good to see
  When victory crowns the patriot's sword,
And the gory field seemed fair to me
  Won by our arms at Manning Ford.

II.

'Tis there we smote them hip and thigh,
  Till Funcheon's stream ran red with gore, —
Till its marge was matted far and nigh
  With the slaughtered bands of Vavasour.

III.

As I stooped down my thirst to slake,
   A gallant voice rang in mine ears:—
"Now who this joyful news will take
   Of victory to my goodly peers?"

IV.

I turned me round and right about
   By Funcheon's swift and bloody tide,
And there I saw our leader stout,
   Bold Castlehaven, at my side.

V.

"Now who this joyful news will take
   To far Kilkenny's ancient town,
And win a good knight's spurs, and make
   His name a name of high renown?"

VI.

There fell a silence still as death
   On his bearded captains all around,
And each one cast, with bated breath,
   His stern eyes on the bloody ground.

VII.

For the rivers were deep and the mountains high,
   And the Burner's men held pass and ford,
And the wolves were out, and the night was nigh,
   So each man answered never a word.

VIII.

With that, up spoke a stripling brave
   Where by a captured flag he stood
Wounded, and grimed with dust — his glaive
   Still dripping with the bearer's blood.

IX.

His form was like Bengara's pine,
   His youthful face was fair to see,
And his eyes were like the osprey's eyne
   On the barren crags of Barnalee.

X.

"The foe may lurk in bush and brake,
   The wolves may howl, the night come down,
Yet I — De Rupe — the news will take
   To far Kilkenny's famous town;—

XI.

"And not for blame, nor praise, nor fame,
  Nor smile of lady sweet and bland,
Nor power, nor pomp, nor knighthood's name,—
  But all for love of native land!"

XII.

Cheerily smiled that warlike lord,
  His hand slapped on his mailéd knee, —
"Should thou return, by my knightly word,
  Through many a fray thou'lt ride with me!

XIII.

"But speed thee now, as the wild wind speeds,
  And take this flag thou'st nobly won;
'Twill mind them of thy peerless deeds,
  And tell them best what we have done."

XIV.

He took that rent and gory flag,
  Then vaulted to his saddle-tree;
On his steaming steed, by height and crag,
  Like the lightning bolt away went he.

XV.

He had scarce ridden three leagues or so,
  When the night came down full sullen and black,
And he passed the forest of Rossaroe,
  Its wild wolves howling on his track.

XVI.

They scented his fresh blood on the wind,
  And they whisked their tails in savage glee;
Though they howled and whined, far, far behind
  He left them all full speedilie.

XVII.

O'er many a hill and moorland wide
  On his weary way he toiled full sore,
Till he saw the deep Suir's swollen tide
  Sweep thundering down by Ruscoe's shore.

XVIII.

The foam flakes leapt o'er helmet bright,
  The hungry torrent hissed and roared,
And the lightning's light lit up the night
  One moment as he crossed the ford.

XIX.

"Now, who art thou?" did a horseman say —
 "What news? what news, thou stripling wan?
For the de'il a man shall go this way
 Without Lord Murrogh pass him on."

XX.

"I'm young De Rupe, of Ballar dell;
 Sore is the news I bring to thee;"—
And he dashed right up at that sentinel,
 And pierced him through with the banner-tree!

XXI.

He sprang unto his foeman's selle,
 For his own good steed dropped groaning down;
And away once more o'er moor and fell,
 On his path the young De Rupe is bowne.

XXII.

Before the peers for Ireland's good,
 In far Kilkenny's town next day,
Prelate and priest, in brotherhood,
 Were chanting Mass in the Black Abbaye.

XXIII.

They heard a murmur in the street,
 And anon a cheer that shook the town;
Then the clatter of a charger's feet
 On the stony way came ringing down.

XXIV.

And high again that cheering roar
 Through the bannered aisles like thunder ran,
Till the ancient abbey's sculptured door
 Was darkened by a horse and man.

XXV.

He muttered one prayer his soul to save,—
 That courier good, that wounded wight,—
Then clattered up the echoing nave,
 And stopped before the altar bright.

XXVI.

"Christ shrive thy soul, thou gory youth!"
 Up spake the Primate, old and gray—
"Tidings of joy or tale of ruth
 Bring'st thou to tell us here to-day?"

XXVII.

"I bring ye news from Manning Ford;
  We've smote the foeman gallantlie;
This flag bold Castlehaven's lord
  A token good hath sent by me!"

XXVIII.

Fast at the words his wounded side
  The life-blood spirted o'er hip and selle;
As a tree in its pride, 'neath the wild winds tide,
  With a crash on the stony floor he fell!

XXIX.

They laid his corse by the altar bright,
  They chanted the Mass for the brave youth's weal,
And they prayed to God, in his mercy and might,
  For hearts as that dead heart true and leal.

XXX.

Christ save his soul, that gallant youth, —
  When by the Judgment Seat we stand, —
Who rode that ride of death and ruth,
  And all for love of native land!

THE GREEN DOVE AND THE RAVEN.

I.

There was a dove with wings of green,
  Glistening o'er so radiantly,
With head of blue and golden sheen,
  All sad and wearily
Sitting two red blooms between
  On lovely Barna's wild-wood tree.

II.

There was a letter 'neath its wing,
  Written by a fair ladye,
Safely bound with silken string
  So light and daintily,
And in that letter was a ring,
  On lovely Barna's wild-wood tree.

III.

There was a raven, black and drear,
  Stained with blood all loathsomely,
Perched upon the branches near,
  Croaking mournfully,
And he said, " O, dove, what bring'st thou here
To lovely Barna's wild-wood tree ? "

IV.

" I'm coming from a ladye gay,
  To the young heir of sweet Glenore,
His ring returned, it is to say
  She'll never love him more, —
Alas the hour! alas the day! —
  By murmuring Funcheon's fairy shore."

V.

" O, dove, outspread thy wings of green;
  I'll guide thee many a wild-wood o'er;
I'll bring thee where I last have seen
  The young heir of Glenore,
Beneath the forest's sunless screen,
  By murmuring Funcheon's fairy shore."

VI.

O'er many a long mile did they flee,
  The dove, the raven stained with gore,
And found beneath the Murderer's tree
  The young heir of Glenore, —
A bloody, ghastly corpse was he,
  By murmuring Funcheon's fairy shore.

VII.

" Go back, go back, thou weary dove, —
  To the cruel maid tell o'er and o'er,
He's Death's and mine, her hate or love
  Can never reach him more —
To his ice-cold heart in Molagga's grove,
  By murmuring Funcheon's fairy shore."

THE BLACKSMITH OF LIMERICK.

I.

He grasped his ponderous hammer, he could not stand it more,
To hear the bombshells bursting, and thundering battle's roar;
He said, "The breach they're mounting, the Dutchman's mur-
  dering crew —
I'll try my hammer on their heads, and see what *that* can do!

II.

"Now, swarthy Ned and Moran, make up that iron well,
'Tis Sarsfield's horse that wants the shoes, so mind not shot or
  shell."
"Ah, sure," cried both, "the horse can wait — for Sarsfield's on
  the wall,
And where you go, we'll follow, with you to stand or fall!"

III.

The blacksmith raised his hammer, and rushed into the street,
His 'prentice boys behind him, the ruthless foe to meet —
High on the breach of Limerick, with dauntless hearts they stood,
Where bombshells burst, and shot fell thick, and redly ran the
  blood.

IV.

"Now look you, brown-haired Moran, and mark you, swarthy
  Ned,
This day we'll prove the thickness of many a Dutchman's head!
Hurrah! upon their bloody path they're mounting gallantly;
And now the first that tops the breach, leave him to this and me!"

V.

The first that gained the rampart, he was a captain brave, —
A captain of the grenadiers, with blood-stained dirk and glaive;
He pointed, and he parried, but it was all in vain,
For fast through skull and helmet the hammer found his brain!

VI.

The next that topped the rampart, he was a colonel bold,
Bright, through the dust of battle, his helmet flashed with gold.
"Gold is no match for iron," the doughty blacksmith said,
As with that ponderous hammer he cracked his foeman's head.

VII.

"Hurrah for gallant Limerick!" black Ned and Moran cried,
As on the Dutchmen's leaden heads their hammers well they plied.
A bombshell burst between them — one fell without a groan,
One leaped into the lurid air, and down the breach was thrown.

VIII.

"Brave smith! brave smith!" cried Sarsfield, "beware the
    treacherous mine!
Brave smith! brave smith! fall backward, or surely death is
    thine!"
The smith sprang up the rampart, and leaped the blood-stained
    wall,
As high into the shuddering air went foemen, breach, and all!

IX.

Up, like a red volcano, they thundered wild and high, —
Spear, gun, and shattered standard, and foemen through the sky;
And dark and bloody was the shower that round the blacksmith
    fell; —
He thought upon his 'prentice boys — they were avengéd well.

X.

On foemen and defenders a silence gathered down;
'Twas broken by a triumph-shout that shook the ancient town,
As out its heroes sallied, and bravely charged and slew,
And taught King William and his men what Irish hearts could do!

XI.

Down rushed the swarthy blacksmith unto the river side;
He hammered on the foe's pontoon to sink it in the tide;
The timber it was tough and strong, it took no crack or strain;
"Mavrone! 'twon't break," the blacksmith roared; "I'll try
    their heads again!"

XII.

He rushed upon the flying ranks — his hammer ne'er was slack,
For in through blood and bone it crashed, through helmet and
    through jack; —
He's ta'en a Holland captain, beside the red pontoon,
And "Wait you here," he boldly cries; "I'll send you back full
    soon!

XIII.

" Dost see this gory hammer? It cracked some skulls to-day,
And yours 'twill crack if you don't stand and list to what I say : —
Here! take it to your curséd king, and tell him softly too,
'Twould be acquainted with *his* skull, if he were here, not you!"

XIV.

The blacksmith sought his smithy, and blew his bellows strong;
He shod the steed of Sarsfield, but o'er it sang no song.
" Ochone! my boys are dead," he cried; " their loss I'll long deplore,
But comfort's in my heart — their graves are red with foreign gore!"

LITTLE THOMAS.

I.

'NEATH the towers of old Ardfinnan, by the broad ford's mossy stone,
Down sat the little Thomas, and thus he made his moan : —
" He has perished, he has perished, O, my chieftain young and brave,
And my father, too, sleeps with him underneath the rushing wave!

II.

" Many hearts for John of Desmond,* through the Mumhan valleys pine,
But there beats not one amongst them half so desolate as mine, —
I, the little page, that ever by my dear dead lord would stay, —
I, the orphan lone, whose father hath perished here to-day."

III.

Died the purple of the sunset from the blue and watery sky,
Rose the moon in clear white splendor o'er the peakéd mountains high,
But the little page sat weeping still beside the ford's gray stone,
And to the waters sweeping, thus again he made his moan : —

---

* John, the young Earl of Desmond, was drowned at the Ford of Ardfinnan, on his return from a foray, in the year 1399.

IV.

"Woe is me! that they have perished; here my home, until I find
A master like the Desmond, a lord so good and kind"—
Looked he on the curling water, with a sudden throb of fear,
For the Desmond stood before him in the moonlight cold and clear!

V.

On his limbs the battle harness, on his head bright helm and plume,
But pale, pale were his features, marked that morn with youth's fair bloom.
"Stay thy lorn and bitter weeping, O, my little page," he said,
"For beneath the waters sweeping it has waked the early dead!

VI.

"The good sword that I gave thee on our last victorious day,
It shall carve thy path to glory, if bright honor light the way.
One little maid there dwelleth by the green shores of the Lee,
Only she shall love thee fonder than my constant love for thee."

VII.

Vanished the phantom warrior in the cold light of the moon,
And the little page now heareth but the Suir's loud-thundering tune;
Swift he rusheth from the water, swift he springeth on his steed,
And through the moon-lit forest is he gone with lightning speed.

VIII.

Ten springs more have decked the mountains, and it is a morn of May;
Knightly spurs the page now weareth, for bright honor lit his way;
Before the bridal altar, with a happy heart stands he,
And his bride is that fair maiden by the green shore of the Lee!

THE BATTLE OF BENBURB.
A. D. 1646.

I.

O'er the hills of Benburb rose the red beam of day,
Gleaming bright from our foemen in battle array;
But as brightly again, 'mid the green-woods below,
Shone it back from the troops of our brave Owen Roe.

II.

Munroe had his thousands arrayed at his back,
With their puritan mantles, steel morion, and jack,
And with him Ardes, Blayney, and Conway had come,
To cut Irish throats at the tuck of the drum!

III.

And who with O'Neill on that morn drew the brand?
Bold hearts as ere beat by the Blackwater strand:
Sir Phelim, brave chief, with the bosom of fire,
O'Donnell, MacSweeny, and gallant Maguire.

IV.

From Derry's wild woodlands, from Main's sounding tide,
From Leitrim and Longford, chiefs came to our side,
And stern in the front, with his sabre in hand,
Stood bold Miles the Slasher, the pride of our band.*

V.

The foemen at morn crossed the Blackwater's wave,
Where O'Ferral's five hundred a hot welcome gave;
But soon to our lines came his band pouring in,
Just to tell us the news of Kinnard's wild ravine.

VI.

Thus we kept all the noon the lean Scotsmen at play,
Though we thought of their forays and burned for the fray;
For our chief bade us wait till the eve had begun,
Then rush on the foe with our backs to the sun.

VII.

Then down to our front with his chiefs spurred he fast,—
"My brave men! the day of our weakness is past;
We have hearts now as firm as our sires had before,
When Bagnall they slew by the Blackwater shore.

VIII.

"Hark! their cannon the foe for our columns have set;
Strike! and have them to play 'mid their own columns yet;
For God and green Erin sure and stern be your blow,
As ye fight in my path!" said our brave Owen Roe.

---

* Maolmorrha, or Miles O'Reilly, called *Miles the Slasher*, from his great strength and bravery — a colonel under Owen Roe.

IX.

Hurrah for the Red Hand! And on, to a man,
Horse and foot, poured we down like a storm on their van,
Where they listed a sermon to strengthen their zeal,
And a sermon we gave them — the point of our steel!

X.

The Slasher looked round as we closed in the fight, —
"Ho! Sir Phelim," he called, "reap your harvest ere night!"
Then he dashed at the foe with his long heavy blade,
And, *mavrone*, what a lane through their columns he made!

XI.

There was panic before us and panic beside,
As their horsemen fled back in a wild broken tide;
And we swept them along by the Blackwater shore
Till we reddened its deep tide with Sassenach gore.

XII.

Few foemen escaped on that well-stricken day;
O'er hillock and moorland by thousands they lay;
Fierce Blaney had fallen where he charged by the fen —
'Twas a comfort he slept by the side of his men!

XIII.

A kern by the river held something on high; —
"Saint Columb! is it thus that the Sassenachs fly?
Perchance 'tis my coolun which they clipped long ago, —
Mille Gloria! the rough wig of flying Munroe!"

XIV.

And we took from the foe, ere that calm twilight fall,
Their horses and baggage, and banners and all;
Then we sat by our watch-fires, and drank in the glow
Merry health to our leaders and brave Owen Roe!

KILBRANNON.

I.

"My love, braid up thy golden locks,
    And don thy silken shoon,
We'll sit upon Kilbrannon's rocks,
    Where shines the silvery moon;

And bring thy little babe with thee,
  For his dear father's sake,
The lands where he'll be lord to see,
  By lone Kilbrannon lake."

II.

She's braided up her golden locks,
  She's donned her silken shoon,
And they're away to Kilbrannon's rocks
  By the cold light of the moon:
Sir Hubert he took both wife and child
  Upon that night of woe,
And hurled them over the rocks so wild,
  To the lake's blue depths below.

III.

And he has married another May,
  With the locks of ebonie,
And her looks are sweet, and her heart is gay,
  Yet a woful wight is he;
He wakes the woods with his bugle horn,
  But his heart is heavy and sore;
And he ever shuns those crags forlorn
  By lone Kilbrannon shore.

IV.

For down in the lake the dead won't rest,
  That vengeful murdered one;
With her little babe at her pulseless breast,
  She walks the waters lone;
And she calls at night her murderer's name,
  And will call forevermore,
Till the huge rocks melt in doomsday flame
  By wild Kilbrannon shore.

THE BRIDGE OF GLANWILLAN.

I.

THOUGH the linnets sing sweet from the wildwood,
  Young Kathleen no blithe warbling hears,
And the warm wind that plays o'er the moorland
  Can ne'er dry her fast-falling tears;

And though gay shine the sunlight around her,
  Still her fond heart is sad and forlorn
As she sits by the ford of Glenara
  Awaiting her Dermot's return;
For he's gone to the fray with his kindred,
  The hard-riding clansmen of Mourne.

II.

"There are blood spots full thick on thy charger,
  There are blood gouts full red on thy mail, —
Have ye news, have ye news from the battle,
  Tired horseman, so gory and pale? —
O, were you at the bridge of Glanwillan,
  And saw you my love in the fray?"
"A curse on that bridge!" cried the foeman,
  "There the Irish have conquered to-day!"
Then he dashed through the bright gleaming river,
  And away o'er the moorland, away!

III.

"There's a smile on thy face, gallant horseman,
  That sweeps like the wind to the ford,
On thy steed steams the fresh foam of battle,
  And the blood stains are wet on thy sword;
O, were you at the bridge of Glanwillan?"
  With a wild cry of anguish she prayed;
Reining up with a splash by the water,
  His hot, steaming charger he stayed, —
"Yes, I've news from the bridge of Glanwillan,
  Brave news for old Ireland, fair maid."

IV.

"O, stay thee, brave horseman, O, stay thee,
  And tell how the foeman came down;
Did he drive the good preys from the valleys,
  And burn every hamlet and town?
On the blood-streaming bridge of Glanwillan
  Rode my Dermot in front with the best?"
On his brow shone a bright smile of triumph,
  Like the sunlight on Houra's wild crest,
As the tale of that morning's fierce battle
  He told at the fair maid's behest.

V.

But first he glared over the moorland,
  Where the heathbells laugh bright in the sun,

And shook his red sword at the foeman,
  That wounded and weary toiled on;
'Twas down from the green sloping mountains
  We first saw the Saxons' array,
Riding forth with high hearts to the foray,
  On the broad, smoking plain far away.
Dhar Dhia! like the corn sheaves of autumn,
  By the bridge lie their corses to-day.

VI.

With a jangling of scabbards and bridles
  Dashed we down to the broad Avonmore,
Where the long, narrow bridge of Glanwillan
  Spanned the brown tide from steep shore to shore;
And there in the green, blooming forest
  We halted our ranks on the glade,
And each rider looked close to his pistols,
  And loosened his long, gleaming blade;
Like a bright wall of steel in the sunlight
  We stood for the foeman arrayed.

VII.

You could hear the shrill whine of the otter
  As he quested his prey by the shore;
You could hear the brown trout in the shallow
  Splash up from the wave evermore;
So still we awaited their coming,
  Though each heart for the fight throbbed full fain,
Till we saw through the greenwoods advancing
  Their line like a long serpent train,
Till the psalm-singing troopers of Cromwell
  Poured down o'er the causeway amain.

VIII.

'Twas then like the storm-cloud of autumn
  That rolls over Barna's wild crest,
When its thunder clangs hoarse through the gorges,
  And the lightnings leap out from its breast,
With our loud ringing slogan of battle
  On their thick-serried squadrons we bore,
With a flashing of helmets and sabres,
  And a rattling of matchlocks galore,
Till the fresh green was strewn with their corses,
  And the causeway was slippery with gore.

IX.

'Twas then you would see what the clansmen
  In the cause of old Ireland could do;
Long, long the black troopers of Cromwell
  That brave Irish onset will rue.
'Twas then you'd be scared with the clashing
  Of swords, and the loud cannon booms —
With the rattling of pistols and flashing
  Of fire through the thick, sulphury glooms,
With the shouts, with the fluttering of banners,
  And the tossing and dancing of plumes.

X.

There I rode side by side on the causeway,
  With your true-love so gallant and leal,
As he charged 'mongst the foremost and bravest,
  In his morion and bright jack of steel.
Splashed the blood 'neath his horse-hoofs' loud clanging,
  As he swept o'er the red bridge's crown,
And many a bold Saxon trooper
  'Neath the sweep of his long sword went down.
This day for thy Dermot of Mourne
  Is a bright day of deathless renown.

XI.

Then weep not, fair maid by Glenara;
  In triumph thy love will return,
His plume waved to-day 'midst the foremost
  Of the hard-riding clansmen of Mourne.
His name shall be sacred among us,
  And a watchword in foray and fray!
Then that fierce clansman glared o'er the moorland,
  As the wolf looketh out for his prey,
And dashed through the ford like an arrow
  On the track of his foeman away.

THE DYING BALLAD SINGER.

I.

O, Thady dear, the way is long,
  My heart and feet are sore and weary,

I'll never sing another song
  In tented Fair or Patron cheery;
But since the day I met with you,
  I never envied lord or lady;
No care, nor woe, nor joy I knew
  That was not shared by Rovin' Thady.

II.

It seems that now but days have flown
  Since first you bade to me " Good morrow,"
Though many a year is past and gone, —
  Ah! many a year of want and sorrow.
It was a sunny morn in June,
  The winds and waves were sweetly playing,
And you struck up your favorite tune,
  " The piper in the meadow straying."

III.

Since th' hour I ran from home away,
  O, many a pang my heart has riven!
The worst of all was that Fair day,
  I saw my brother at Knockevan;
"Twas at the dance — now, pause and mind,
  What care, with sorrow, shame, and sin, does, —
The feet were going like the wind,
  For they were dancing " Smash the windows;"

IV.

He saw me, but he took no note, —
  He knew me not, so changed and worn;
The song I sung swelled in my throat —
  'Twas worse than all that I had borne.
I stopped, I gazed upon them there,
  I thought of happy hopes departed,
Then turned and tottered through the Fair,
  And left the place all broken-hearted.

V.

Now wrap me in my old gray cloak,
  And lay me by this path-side fountain;
I think on those whose hearts I broke,
  Far, far away by Barna's mountain;
Long calm they lie where Barna's stream
  Around the church-yard wall is flowing, —

O, on their death-bed did they dream
  Of her that's now so quickly going?

VI.

I fear their bones in earth would stir
  With grief, were their cold earth laid o'er me,
Yet still I long to lie near her,
  The mother dear, that nursed and bore me.
I ask it with my latest breath,
  You won't refuse your Maureen Grady —
O, take me, lay me near in death,
  Near those I kilt, my Rovin' Thady.

ROMANCE OF THE BLACK ROBBER.*

I.

By a Mumhan mountain airy and stern,
A well lies circled by rock and fern,
And fiercely over a precipice near
Rusheth a waterfall, brown and clear.

II.

In a hollow rent by that bright well's foam.
A mighty robber once made his home, —
A man he was full sullen and dark
As ever brooded on murder stark, —

III.

A mighty man of a fearful name,
Who took their treasures from all who came,
Who hated mankind, who murdered for greed,
With an iron heart for each bloody deed.

IV.

As he sat by the torrent ford one day,
A weird-like beldame came down the way:
Red was her mantle, and rich and fine,
But toil and travel had dimmed its shine.

* An incident in an old Fenian romance.

V.

A war-axe in his red hand he took,
And he killed the beldame beside the brook,
And when on the greensward in death she rolled,
In her arms, lo! a babe, clad in pearls and gold.

VI.

He buried the beldame beside the wave,
And he took the child to his mountain cave,
And the first jewel his red hand met,
A Fern and a Hound on its gem were set.

VII.

Yet darkly he raised his hand to kill,
But his fierce heart smote him such blood to spill.
O, the rage for murder was there delayed
By the innocent smile of that infant maid!

VIII.

He made it a bed of the fern leaves green,
And he nursed it well from that evening sheen,
And day by day, as the sweet child grew,
The heart of the Robber grew softer too.

IX.

Ten long years were past and gone,
And the Robber sat by the ford's gray stone,
And there on the eve of a spring-tide day,
A lordly pageant came down the way.

X.

Before them a banner of green and gold,
With a Fern and a Hound on its glittering fold,
Behind it a prince with a sad, pale face, —
A mighty prince of a mighty race.

XI.

The Robber looked on the Fern and Hound,
Then sprang toward the Prince with an eager bound,
And "Why art thou sad, O King?" said he,
In the midst of that lordly companie.

XII.

His kindly purpose they all mistook,
For, though wan and worn, yet fierce his look;

And sudden a noble drew out his glaive,
And cleft his skull on the beldame's grave.

XIII.

"Sad," said the pale Prince, "my fate has been,
Since the dark enchanters have ta'en my queen,
Since they bore my child from the nurse's hand,
And keep her alway in th' enchanted land."

XIV.

The dying Robber half rose by the wave,
"O, enter," he cried, "yon lonely cave."
They entered — the pale Prince found his child,
And all was joy in that mountain wild.

LADY MARION.

"At the first blink of the morning light, they found Lady Marion, lying cold and dead beside the corse of her lover, in the Hollow of Barna." — *Story of the Gillie Crumach.*

I.

In the gold and the purple of sunset,
   The great Hold of Carrick looks down
On its greenwoods and calm, winding river,
   And far-stretching moorlands of brown.
The stout warder leans o'er the turret,
   His helmet afire in the sun,
   And his gay gleaming harness half on;
And out from the draw-bridge rides Marion,
   That bright, blessed Eve of St. John.

II.

Out she rides on her little black palfrey,
   Round the verge of the calm, reedy moat,
And she looks on the deep, glassy water
   Far beneath, where the white lilies float;
But there's not in those depths one white lily
   Can mate with her brow, snowy fair;
   No tall iris bloom flaunting there,
With its golden leaves spread like a banner,
   More bright than her long, yellow hair.

III.

Out she rides through the lone, dreamy woodland,
    Where the rill trickles down crystal clear,
Where the brooding doves coo from the pine trees,
    And the robin sings blithe on the brere;
Where the gorse, with a cincture of yellow,
    Encircles the marge of the fen,
Uncrossed by the pathways of men;
And the foxglove, in crimson and purple,
    Robes the steep, sunny side of the glen.

IV.

There's a mound o'er the verge of the valley,
    Looking out to the far, golden west,
At its green, sloping base a clear streamlet,
    A huge Druid cairn on its crest;
And there 'neath that cairn, by her palfrey,
    With a face like the fresh, smiling dawn,
She rests, as the calm hour steals on,
With the glory of sunset around her,
    That bright, blessèd Eve of St. John.

V.

Ho! knights who are deft in the tourney,
    And victors in foray and fray,
Can ye look on that fair maid unconquered,
    As she rests by the cairn rude and gray?
Ah, many a lance ye have shivered,
    And many a keen, cutting blade,
    Many crests in the mire lowly laid,
In tourney and red tide of battle,
    For the love of that bright Ormond maid..

VI.

But your lances, in vain they are shattered,
    In vain cross your swords in the fight;
For Love is the victor of victors,
    And ye bow to the dust 'neath his might.
And the heart of young Marion is stricken,
    You'll win her sweet smiles never more,
    For her vows they are vowed o'er and o'er
To love but one brave knight forever —
    Despite thee, Sir Bertram le Poer.

VII.

Ah! thou by her stern sire art chosen,
   And thou shouldst be gentle and true;
But a deep vow of vengeance thou'st sworn,
   Be she false, that her falsehood she'll rue.
Yet there, by that lone, ghostly cairn,
   Out-gazing o'er forest and lea,
   She waits on the mound, not for thee,
But for Donat, the lord of her bosom —
   The fearless young Knight of Lisree.

VIII.

Sank the sun in a flood of red glory,
   Afar o'er the broad, bronzéd main,
And at once through the gray, soundless twilight,
   Blazed the Baal-fires o'er mountain and plain.
From Clonmel to the fortress of Graffon,
   And up thy broad breast, Sliavnamon,
   Shooting high to the calm stars they shone,
With a weird glare of far-stretching splendor,
   That sweet, windless Eve of St. John.

IX.

As she looked on the Baal-fires out burning,
   Lighting castle and crag in their glow,
Came a trampling of hoofs from the upland,
   And a tramp from the deep gorge below.
Throbbed her heart with a sweet throb of gladness,
   And anon with a strange fear was still,
   As her little steed turned towards the hill,
Stamped its brazen-shod hoof on the greensward,
   And neighed, with a voice wild and shrill.

X.

Loud, loud sounds the trampling, and louder,
   As nearer and nearer they come,
And she sees, as she looks down the valley,
   Two knights, spurring hard through the gloom;
On they rushed, breast to breast, like the thunder
   On the low, stony verge of the shore, —
   One went down with a crash, in his gore,
Young Donat, the lord of her bosom,
   'Neath the spear of Sir Bertram le Poer.

XI.

There is woe in the great Hold of Carrick,
　There is weeping o'er valley and plain,
There is searching for young Lady Marion,
　But she'll ne'er ope her bright eyes again;
For she lies by the corse of her lover,
　Where the sad little stream hurries on,
And no voice can awake her save One —
The Trumpet that sounds for the Judgment —
　That calm starry Eve of Saint John!

THE SIEGE OF CLONMEL.
A. D. 1650.

I.

I stood beside a gun upon the Western Gate
At the rising of the sun, the battle to await:
In the morning's ruddy glow showed the fire's destroying tracks,
And my comrades all below, with their harness on their backs.

II.

Each with harness on his back, by rampart, street, and tower,
To repel the fierce attack in the sultry noontide hour,
Glittered lance and flashed the glaive, till the work of death begun;
And one cheer my comrades gave as the ruthless foe came on.

III.

As the wild waves dash and vault 'gainst the cliffs of high Dunmore,
Fierce they mounted to th' assault, up the breach, in sweat and gore;
As the billows backward flow at the ebbing of the main,
Back we drove the daring foe to his camp-trench once again.

IV.

Out burst each roaring gun, with its mouth of hissing flame,
From its war-cloud thick and dun, as again the foemen came
For vengeance burning hot; but once more we mowed them down
With spear, and sword, and shot, till we drove them from the town.

V.

Cromwell kept the northern height; — as a spectre pale was he,
When he saw his men of might twice before my comrades flee;

And he pointed with his sword where the red breach smoking lay:
"Go! take it, and the Lord shall be on our side to-day!"

VI.

With psalm and trumpet swell came they on at his behest; —
Then we rammed each cannon well, and we nerved each gallant breast!
And the bloody breach we manned, with fearless hearts and high,
The onset to withstand, or for homes and altars die!

VII.

Tottered mansion, tower, and wall at the thundering fire we gave;
But thro' blood, and smoke, and all, came they on by dint of glaive;
Till with wild and deafening din, fierce, to gorge their hate accurst,
O'er the gory breach, and in, one destroying wave they burst!

VIII.

Breast to breast their charge we met, with the battle's rage and hate,
Hand to hand, unconquered yet, with the foe we tried our fate.
They were many, we were few; they were brave and stalwart men,
But we charged, and charged anew, till we broke their ranks again.

IX.

How we cleared each narrow street when the foemen's flight began! —
How we rushed on their retreat! — how we slew them as they ran! —
How we quaffed the wine so bright, when our bloody task was o'er,
To the men who 'scaped the fight, and the brave who slept in gore!

X

Evening's cloud came o'er the hill — darker clouds on Cromwell's face,
When, with all his force and skill, he could not storm the place.
But our powder all was gone, and our cannon useless lay,
And what man could do was done, so we might no longer stay.

XI.

We buried those who fell, with the silence of the tomb,
And we left thee, brave Clonmel, 'neath the midnight's friendly gloom.
With slow and measured tread, o'er the low Bridge of the Dane,
And that dark breach where we bled, did we ne'er behold again.

THE TWO GALLOGLASSES.

I.

"I look across the moorlands drear,
  To see my Donall coming o'er.
He left me for the wars last year,
And night and day I think and fear
  I'll never, never see him more.
Perchance he's slumbering in his gore!
Killemree! O, Killemree!
  My days are dark, my heart is sore,
To think upon thy lovely lea
  I'll never, never see him more!

II.

"Up towards the black, black north he rode,
  To fight the valiant Norman men;
His light plume in the breezes flowed,
And gallantly his armor glowed,
  As he sped down our native glen;
  I'll never see my love again;
Killemree! O, Killemree!
  My heart is sore with sorrow, when
I think upon thy sunny lea
  I'll never see my love again."

III.

Beneath a tree sat comrades two,—
  Two galloglasses in their mail;
All day they rode the foray through—
Wild Diarmid Keal and Donall Dhue—
  Against the Normans of the Pale.
  Said Donall of the Gilded Mail:
"Killemree! O, Killemree!
  What dost thou fight for, Diarmid Keal?"
"I fight all for my fair countrie,
  Tall Donall of the Gilded Mail."

IV.

"And I fight for my fair countrie,
  But eke for love I draw the brand:
To purchase fame for her and me,
My Mora, of the southern lea,

I've ever worked with heart and hand;
I fight for love and native land;
Killemree! O, Killemree!
If one will fall, sure one will stand,"
Said Donall Dhu all pleasantly,
  As they sat by the Liffey strand.

v.

At blink of morn upon the dell
  The valiant Normans they descried;
Then there was groan and battle-yell;
But ere the noon brave Diarmid fell
  His comrade's rushing steed beside;
  All for his native land he died.
Killemree! O, Killemree!
It was a death of fame and pride,
And his was fame, the bold and free
  Who fell upon the Liffey side.

vi.

And black the oath tall Donall swore, —
"I'll have revenge for him that's slain!"
Then through the Norman ranks he tore,
But in their flight along the shore,
  Deep wounded, he was prisoner ta'en;
  But ere the morn he broke their chain,
Killemree! O, Killemree!
And bore him towards his native plain,
Resolved to die, or to be free,
  And see his true-love once again.

vii.

He climbed the mountain hoar and bare,
  And darted up the highland pass:
Three foemen stood against him there —
His keen sword whirling in the air,
  He stretched the foremost on the grass;
  He clove through shield of hide and brass —
Killemree! O, Killemree!
The next, and from a gray rock's mass
He hurled the last right furiously,
  And 'scaped from death in that wild pass!

VIII.

As by a Norman bridge he came,
   The warder laid his lance full low,
To ask his purport and his name; —
Tall Donall's sword went down like flame,
   And cleft the warder at a blow;
But little food and much of woe,
Killemree! O, Killemree!
   Until he reached her faint and slow,
   And clasped young Mora tenderly,
     Thus 'scaped from bond and brand of foe!

IX.

Each day she nursed him tenderly,
   Her Donall of the Gilded Mail;
'Twas love for her that set him free,
That bore him up in far countrie,
   Else he had died like Diarmid Keal.
'Twas all of joy and none of bale,
Killemree! O, Killemree!
   Within their native southern vale,
   At bridal of that maiden free,
     And Donall of the Gilded Mail.

THE FAIRY MILL.

I.

Away to Ounanar's glancing tide,
   Where the redbreast sings on the hawthorn spray,
O'er craggy hill and moorland wide,
   The wanderer takes his lonely way.
He is a warrior young and bold,
   His path from the revel wild pursuing,
And he sits where down in Glenanar's wold *
   The ring-doves mid the dells are cooing.

II.

It is by the Pool of the Fairy Mill,
   Where the redbreast sings on the hawthorn spray,

---

* Glenanar, a beautiful and romantic valley on the Limerick border, between Doneraile and Kilfinane.

Where heard, but unseen, in the evening still,
  Ceaseless the merry wheel worketh away;
And he lists to its plashing, weird-like sound,
  And he drinks, by all fairy spells undaunted,
Of the crystal wave from his helmet round,
  To the maid who dwells in that mill enchanted.

III.

He looks around in the sunset light,
  Where the redbreast sings on the hawthorn spray,
And he is aware of a maiden bright
  Close at his side by the rock-wall gray;
Darts clear light from her star-bright eyes,
  Sweet is her love-lit smile and tender,
And her shining hair o'er her shoulders lies,
  Yellow and sheen in the sunset splendor.

IV.

"Thou hast drunk," she cries, "to the fairy maid,
  Where the redbreast sings on the hawthorn spray,
Wear in thy plume this small hair braid,
  And think on me at each close of day."
She has placed the braid in his nodding plume,
  She's gone, like sweet Hope from a hall of mourning,
And he hears no sound save the ceaseless hum,
  And the plash of the fairy mill-wheel turning.

V.

He hies away from that haunted glen,
  Where the redbreast sings on the hawthorn spray,
But spell-bound, amid the ways of men,
  He thinks on the maid of the mill alway;
He thinks till his heart is filled with love,
  And that heart ne'er resteth, so fondly laden,
Till he stands once more in Glenanar's grove,
  And eager calls on the fairy maiden.

VI.

He looks around in the sunset light,
  Where the redbreast sings on the hawthorn spray,
And he is aware of that maiden bright
  Close at his side by the rock-wall gray;

"To thee," he cries, "my love, I've come
  By forest green and by mountain hoary;
For thee I leave my own loved home,
  The joys of peace and the battle's glory!

VII.

"Then let me live, fair maid, with thee,
  Where the redbreast sings on the hawthorn spray,
Where the fairy mill sounds merrily,
  And love shall lighten our home alway!"
O, her beaming smile! O, her looks of love!
  As she leads him down by that haunted river,
And there, 'mid Glenanar's flowery grove
  They live in cloudless joy forever!

DUNLEVY.

I.

Dunlevy stands lone in the forest,
  To list to the bells' merry peal,
And their sounds make his young heart the sorest
  That e'er throbbed 'neath corselet and steel;
For they ring the gay bridal of Alice,
  The lady he loved long and pure,
False to him in her sire's feudal palace,
  By the sweet, lovely banks of the Suir.

II.

The Baron, his high Norman neighbor,
  The fond, happy bridegroom is he,
And Dunlevy's right hand's on his sabre,
  To think that such falseness could be;
For the lady had vowed o'er and over,
  That nought could her fondness allure
From Dunlevy, her brave knightly lover,
  By the sweet, lovely banks of the Suir.

III.

The hot noon came burning and shining
  O'er hill-top, and valley, and tower;

Yet still stood Dunlevy repining,
  Dark and lone in that gay wild-wood bower,
Till he saw far away brightly gleaming
  Casque and spear over mountain and moor, —
Till a trumpet blast startled his dreaming,
  By the sweet, lovely banks of the Suir.

IV.

Sudden heard he a trembling and sighing,
  And a-nigh stood his love sorrow-worn,
From her father's gay hall after flying
  Ere the bridal could bind her that morn;
And sudden away they are sweeping
  On his wild steed towards gray Craganure,
Where his bright native torrents are leaping,
  Far away from the banks of the Suir.

V.

From the gray hill that towers o'er the valley
  The bridegroom and father look down,
Where the mailed knights and vassals out sally,
  All searching through green dale and town;
But Dunlevy from stern sire and vassal
  With his bright blooming love's now secure,
Far away in his own native castle
  From the sweet lovely banks of the Suir.

THE BATTLE OF KNOCKINOSS.

SCENE: A camp-fire by the Shannon. — An old Rapparee, who had served in the wars of 1641, relating the battle to his comrades.

I.

ATTEND, ye valiant horsemen, and each bold Rapparee,
And by our blazing camp-fire a tale I'll tell to ye: —
With Murrogh's * savage army, one valley's breadth away,
One noon of bleak November, on Knock'noss hill we lay.

---

* *Murrogh an Theothaun*, or, Murrogh the Burner. He was Baron of Inchiquin, and his name is yet remembered among the peasantry as the most ferocious and bloodthirsty of Cromwell's generals.

II.

Lord Taaffe was our commander, and brave Mac Alisdrum,
And 'cross the lowland meadows we saw the foemen come;
Then up spoke bold Mac Alisdrum, "Now leave their wing to me;"
And soon we crossed our sabres with their artillery.

III.

We swept them down the hill-sides, and took both flag and gun.
And back across the meadows we made them quickly run;
But swift as they retreated, more fast behind we bore,
Until we steeped our sabres from point to hilt in gore.

IV.

Alas, alas! for cowards, and ho! for dauntless men!
Without one cause for flying, Lord Taaffe fled through the glen,
And all our army with him in panic rushed away,
And left us sore surrounded on Knock'noss hill that day.

V.

Then up spoke our commander, the brave Mac Alisdrum, —
" The foe pursues our comrades, this way his horsemen come;
Then out with each good claymore, and strike like brave men still!"
And at his words the foemen came charging o'er the hill!

VI.

Mo brón! Mo brón! the slaughter, when we mixed horse and man!
Loud crashed the roaring battle, like floods the red blood ran;
And few the foemen left us to fight another fray,
And Alisdrum they murdered at Knockinoss that day.

VII.

My curse upon all cowards, and ho! for brave men still! —
Long, long their bones were bleaching upon that blood-stained hill!
Then choose a good commander to lead ye to the fray,
And shun what lost the battle on Knock'noss hill that day!

THE WHITE LADYE.

I.

The Baron of Brugh * took his steel-gray steed,
   And faced the mid-day sun,
And he'd gained Glennavh,† so wild his speed,
   Ere the noontide course was run.

II.

He rode by Glennavh and by many a grave,
   O'er that lone glen's sacred rill,
And he stopped not, nor stayed, till he reached the green glade,
   By the Red Rath of the Hill.

III.

Sitting by the lone Red Rath,
   A charger's tramp heard he,
And riding nigh in the woodland path,
   Soon came the White Ladye.

IV.

She was no fairy of the place,
   Though she shamed the fairies' speed;
Milk-white her dress, pale, pale her face,
   And snow-white was her steed.

V.

The Baron leaped as a knight should leap,
   All in mail, to his saddle-tree,
And away, away through the woods did sweep,
   After the White Ladye.

VI.

Till deep in the lonely Gap of the Blast,
   She turned her steed around,
And charged the Baron all furious and fast,
   As he went with a headlong bound.

---

* Brugh, **in the** old Irish, means a house — a large **dwelling-place.** It is the ancient name of Bruff, in the county Limerick.

† Glennavh — the Holy Glen — lies near the ancient and picturesque churchyard of Ardpatrick, about two miles west of Kilfinane. Raheen Ruadh — the little Red Rath — lies near Cloghanathboy Castle, the beautiful seat of Lord and Lady Ashtown, a few miles south-west of Kilfinane.

VII.

A bright, bright glaive in her hand she bore,
    And she came like a knightly foe,
And the Baron she struck on the helmet so sore,
    That he bent to his saddle bow.

VIII.

There came a rock in his charger's path,
    As that furious course he ran,
And with headlong plunge and with kindled wrath,
    To the ground went horse and man.

IX.

Never he rose from the rocky ground
    Till the sunset o'er him shone,
Then he leapt on his steed, and he looked around,
    But the White Ladye was gone.

X.

Ere waned the next moon's silver light
    He sought that place again,
And there he saw a sad, sad sight,
    All in the hollow glen.

XI.

There lay a dead knight in his path,
    Cloven from crown to crest,
And the White Ladye by the lone Red Rath,
    With an arrow in her breast.

XII.

And over the Ladye the Baron stood,
    As her life began to fail,
And ever as flowed the red, red blood,
    She told her woful tale.

XIII.

"My father lived where yon gray tower
    Frowns o'er the Champion's stream;
There fled my days since childhood's hour,
    All like a pleasant dream.

XIV.

"This bridal dress, with my life-blood red,
    One lovely morn I wore,

For I in gladness was to wed
  The Master of Kilmore.

XV.

"The feast was spread, when in there sped
  The wild young lord of Crom,
And his spearmen tall crowded porch and hall,
  And he said for the bride he'd come.

XVI.

"Up vassal sprang and knightly guest,
  Each answering with a blow,
And soon was changed our bridal feast
  To a scene of blood and woe.

XVII.

"I saw my father falling there,
  And my love lie in his gore,
And in wild despair, I knew not where
  I fled through the wicket door.

XVIII.

"Soon, soon I found my courser white,
  And rushed o'er vale and lea,
But ever still, since that fatal night,
  Crom's false lord follows me.

XIX.

"He chased me all this fatal morn,
  He sent this arrow keen,
But never more to the battle borne
  Shall his proud crest be seen.

XX.

"For ere I fell in this lonely dell,
  My steed leapt forth amain,
And with this good sword of my dead young lord
  I cleft through the false knight's brain."

XXI.

Soon the Ladye died, and the Baron of Brugh
  Was a woful wight that hour,
For the slaughtered man was his brother Hugh,
  The bold knight of Crom's dark tower.

XXII.

And ever since, in the lonely night,
And the twilight, calm and still,
Glides that Ladye's sprite on her palfrey white,
By the Red Rath of the Hill.

BALLAD OF YOUNG BRIAN; OR, THE BATTLE OF ATHENREE.

Fytte the First.

I.

"FULL brightly blooms the heather, like a sun-empurpled sea,
Full merry sing the wild birds on every forest tree,
And the gladsome kine are lowing over hill and lowland lea,
But O, my dark-haired darling, what a day it is to me!"

II.

Thus spake my gallant comrade, young Brian of Lisrone, —
Thus spake he to his sweetheart, fair Roisin Dubh Malone;
He was the boldest rider that e'er grasped steel in hand,
And she — she was the fairest maid in all green Thomond's land.

III.

"Up to the heathery mountain, my darling, come with me,
I'll show you all our lances arrayed by stream and lea, —
Up to the woody hollow where neighs my charger free,
In his bright war harness ready to bear me far from thee!"

IV.

"Up to the hill," she answered, "or far from friends and home,
Through desert, woods, and valleys, with you I'd gladly roam;
This noon of golden summer is to me a woful day,
And my heart will break with sorrow while you are far away."

V.

Into the woody hollow he led his dark-haired maid,
And a shrilly welcome to them his gallant charger neighed;
And there beneath them shining in the sultry summer's sun,
With their flashing spears and banners lay our brave bands every
    one.

VI.

How she wept to see the banners and the glittering pomp of war,
And the ready steed to bear him from her circling arms afar;
How she shuddered at the trumpets ringing upward from the shore,
And vowed to love him truly till the deadly wars were o'er.

VII.

Many a mournful kiss he gave her, as he pressed her to his heart —
"Woe is me," he said, "my true love, that from thee I must depart."
Then he sprang into his saddle, and he gave his steed the rein,
And his words were, "Love me truly till I come to thee again."

VIII.

Then we marched, and we marched over many a glen and glade,
'Neath the banner of Prince Donogh, the Connaught king to aid,
To drive the hostile Norman from our green fields away,
Ere he fastened on his plunder like the wolf upon its prey.

IX.

We marched, and we marched over togher, moor, and ford,
And to every hostile challenge, our answer was the sword;
And in each fierce fray and foray never man so brave was known,
As my true, my gallant comrade, the horseman of Lisrone.

X.

We marched, and we marched over bog and desert way,
Till we came to where King Phelim with his gallant cohorts lay;
Then like thunder up the mountains from their 'campment rolled the din
Of a hundred thousand welcomes, as our bands came pouring in.

Fytte the Second.

I.

When the morn blazed o'er the mountains, then we took our march again,
To the trumpet's shrilly clamor and the war-pipe's martial strain;
And we pierced through many a forest, and we wound by stream and lea,
Till we neared our wily foemen, and we came to Athenrie.

II.

Wirristhru! for the day that we came to Athenrie,
'Twas a mournful day for Ireland, and a woful day for me;

There King Art had fallen in battle in the ages long before,*
And there died our young King Phelim ere that hapless day was
    o'er.

III.

Like a lowering cloud of thunder on the moorland broad we lay,
Like a sunbeam on its ragged skirts, the king rode forth that day,
In his glittering shirt of battle, and his golden helm and plume:
Mo Brón! that such a rider e'er should meet with such a doom!

IV.

O'er our bristling line of battle then he cast his kingly eye,
With a gaze full keen and stern, as his chiefs and he rode by;
Then he turned him round and pointed with his sharp and con-
    quering blade
To the Normans' iron chivalric upon the field arrayed.

V.

" By the blood-red hand that moulders in the cold clay of Knock-
    moy,†
Swear ye now those ranks to shatter, and the Norman power
    destroy —
Then charge ye home, for Ireland's good," was all our brave
    king said,
While from van to rear, from flank to flank, our answering slo-
    gan spread.

VI.

How the hot earth smoked and trembled 'neath the thunder of
    our charge,
As, with hearts for vengeance burning, swept we down the
    streamlet's marge!
How the bloody spray splashed round us, how the battle raged
    and roared,
As we met the mail-clad Normans, breast to breast at that wild
    ford!

VII.

Mo nair! our men had nought to shield their valorous, hardy
    breasts
But their shirts of saffron shining, and their purply satin vests;

---

* Art the Solitary, who, together with the seven sons of Oliol Olum, fell in a battle fought by them near this place against Lughaidh Mac Con. The place where the battle was fought was called Magh Mucruimhe.

† Knockmoy was the burial-place of Cathal **of** the Red Hand, King **of** Connaught.

But with naked breast to steel-clad heart, through the battle's dust and sweat,
Till that woful eve shone o'er us, neither gained the vantage yet.

VIII.

My curse upon the arrow, and the hand that shot it, too,
That struck our young king on the neck, and pierced him through and through;
Down he fell beside his banner on the eve of that sad day,
And amid the roar of battle soon his life-blood ebbed away.

IX.

"Come, follow me, my comrade," said young Brian of Lisrone;
"The king is dead, his foes close round, — he shall not sleep alone;
We'll gather round the gory spot where his fair body lies,
And we'll fight more stern and keenly when we look in his dead eyes."

X.

We fought, and we fought, till the eve closed o'er us dark —
Many a pool of blood was round us, many a body stiff and stark;
For our gory sparths we buried in the brains of many a foe,
To guard King Phelim's body on that hapless field of woe.

XI.

Wirristhru! for the day that we came to Athenrie;
There a fond and gallant comrade, and a king were lost to me —
For the king lay in his gore, in the cause of Ireland slain,
And young Brian by his body was a wounded prisoner ta'en.

Fytte the Third.

I.

On that night of blood and sorrow we fled far away,
With Prince Donogh's torn banner, from the field where Phelim lay;
And we took the southward passes till we reached Bunratty's wall,
Where we swore, before we parted, to avenge our young king's fall.

II.

Then I sought my comrade's sweetheart, and told our tale of grief;
She mourned him for one summer moon, and then she found relief;

For she took another gallant — she that vowed so fond and fain
To love young Brian truly till he'd come to her again.

III.

In the dungeon of Mac Feorais * long my comrade sorely pined,
While the yellow leaves were rustling in the withering autumn wind;
And while the hills were whitening in the frost and wintry snow,
Still he lay a hopeless captive in the dungeon of his foe.

IV.

But Mac Feorais' lovely daughter heard that prisoner's woful state,
And she stole unto his dungeon, and she pitied his sad fate;
And love's rosy footsteps followed on the path where pity trode,
Till her heart for the young captive with a wild affection glowed.

V.

Yet young Brian looked not on her with a lover's gladsome eyes,
He thought of her far, far away, where Cratloe's mountains rise;
He thought of her he loved so true, by his native river shore,
And he told Mac Feorais' daughter that he'd ne'er love woman more.

VI.

The summer birds were singing on every blooming tree,
And brightly shone the heather, like a sun-empurpled sea,
And the gladsome kine were lowing over glen and lowland lea,
As young Brian rode by Cratloe hill, from his weary thrall set free.

VII.

Merry heart had that young horseman, as he rode by rock and dell,
As he looked upon those fairy scenes he knew and loved so well;
Many a gladsome song he carolled as to gay Lisrone he hied,
And found false Roisin Dhuv Malone — a stranger's happy bride!

VIII.

He turned him from his childhood's home, and galloped fast and far;
He joined Prince Donogh's banner, and he rode forth to the war;
He fought for Ireland's honor full faithfully and well,
Till with his prince on Barna's field in Norman blood he fell!

* The Irish name for De Bermingham, who, after the battle, was made baron of Athenrie.

THE BATTLE OF KILTEELY.
A.D. 1599.

I.

The mountains of Limerick frown down on a plain
That laughs all in light to their summits again,
With its towers, and its lakes, and its rivers of song,
And its huge race of peasants so hardy and strong.

II.

O, hardy its peasants, and comely, and tall!
But their spirits are broken, their minds are in thrall:
So, strike we a lilt of the chivalric day,
When their sires swept the foe o'er these mountains away.

III.

To harry rich Coonagh fierce Norris came down
From the towers of Kilmallock, by forest and town,
Swearing castle, and homestead, and temple to sack;
And, O God! what a desert he left in his track!

IV.

The sun of the morning all cheerily smiled
On his ranks by Cnock Rue and by Coola the wild,
And how bright gleamed their spears by the tents white and fair,
As they marshalled, to plunder the green valleys there!

V.

They looked to the east, and they looked to the west,
And they saw where their booty lay fairest and best;
Then they moved like a thick cloud of thunder and gloom
When it rolls o'er the plain from the crags of Sliav Bloom.

VI.

But see! they are halting — what wild music swells
By the founts of Commogue, through the forest's green dells?
'Tis the music of Eire — the fierce fiery strain
Which ne'er called her sons to the combat in vain.

VII.

"By Saint George!" says fierce Norris, and stops in his course,
With his long lance stretched forth o'er the crest of his horse, —

"By Saint George, 'tis the Gael! 'tis his pibroch's wild breath;
But he meets at Kilteely his masters and death!"

VIII.

'Twas the Gael. Slow they wound round the foot of Cnock Rue;
Small, small were their numbers, but steady and true;
And they saw not the foe, where exulting he stood,
Till they reached the green glades from their path in the wood.

IX.

Then changed was their bearing — man closing on man,
With De Burgo, their chieftain so proud, in the van;
With hate in each eye, and defiance in all,
And their deep muttered war-word, "We conquer or fall!"

X.

"By the turrets of Limerick!" De Burgo exclaims,
"Black Norris a meed for his ravaging claims;
Be they countless as hail-drops, we never shall go
Till we measure our pikes with the steel of the foe."

XI.

Have ye seen Avondhu, how he rushes and fills
When the flood-gates of autumn are loosed on the hills?
So the tall men of Limerick sweep down on the spears
Of Norris the proud and his fair cavaliers!

XII.

O Heaven! 'tis a fair sight to see how each file
Of the fierce foe is swept into carnage the while, —
Sweet music to hear over forest and vale
The wild shout of triumph ring up from the Gael.

XIII.

Young Burgo is there in his trappings so bright,
And he follows his chieftain for aye through the fight;
But now he forsakes him, and cleaves his red way
Where the banner of England stands proud in the ray.

XIV.

There Norris receives him with taunt and with sneer,
With his arquebus ball and a lunge of his spear;
But the pike of young Burgo tears fierce through his head,
And he sinks by his banner 'mid piles of the dead.

XV.

On passed the young warrior unscathéd by all,
The rush of his foemen, the spear-thrust and ball;
With haughtiest bearing he treads o'er the slain,
And clears a good road to his chieftain again.

XVI.

And wild cry the Saxons. Their chief — where is he?
Struck down at the foot of his own banner-tree,
And the banner is gone; there is fear on each brow,
And a wild panic spreads through their broken ranks now!

XVII.

And soon they are scattered away through the woods,
Like the gray Connacht sands by the westerly floods;
But they bear their gashed chieftain afar as they fly,
And they lay him in Mallow to rave and to die.

XVIII.

And the dreams of his murders came over him there,
With the shadow of death and the doom of despair;
And the sun had scarce travelled ten times through the blue,
Ere he slept his last sleep by the swift Avondhu.

XIX.

Thus fought the huge men of the plain long ago,
Thus chased they from Limerick the hard-hearted foe; —
May we never meet death till we see them again
Striking up for old Eire as fearless as then!

ROMANCE OF THE FAIRY WAND.

I.

'Mid Gailty's woody highlands, by a torrent's lonely shore,
There dwelt a banished monarch in the dusky days of yore;
Long the pleasant Munster valleys had owned his kingly sway,
Till rose a fierce usurper and reft his throne away.

II.

No vassals filled his chambers, no courtiers thronged his hall;
His bright-eyed little daughter and a gray-haired chief were all, —

Were all the friends that never would forsake him in his woe,
When he fled, a care-worn exile, to that tower in Aherloe.

III.

Around that highland castle, by the shady forest springs.
With a heart forever dreaming of all bright and lovely things,
Roamed that regal little maiden every golden summer e'en,
Watched and loved, where'er she wandered, by the radiant Fairy Queen.

IV.

The sunset light was reddening on the crest of tall Bein Gar,*
As lay that little maiden 'neath the flowery woods afar; —
"Spreads this land," she said, "how lovely 'neath the purple sunset's light,
But Hy Gaura's bard has told me of a world more fair and bright!

V.

"Through that land I'd wish to wander; there I'd ask a warrior train
Of its queen, to set my father on his Munster throne again."
O, the words she scarce had uttered, when there shone a radiance sheen
Up and down the shady valley and the forest depths between!

VI.

On the song-birds fell a silence, was no sound through earth or air,
Till in robes of snowy splendor stood a heaven-browed lady there;
With beaming eyes down-looking on the little maid stood she,
All the glad birds singing round her again from bower and tree.

---

* *Bein Gar* — the sharp summit — the name by which Gailty Mor is principally known among the peasantry. The castle of Dun Grod — the one mentioned in the ballad — lies on the side of a glen to the westward of Bein Gar, and is one of the most ancient buildings of that description in Ireland. *Tir-n-an-Oge*, the Land of Perpetual Youth, was the Heaven of the ancient inhabitants of Ireland. The great Mitchelstown cavern, at the back of the Gailty mountains, is said by the peasantry to be one of the entrances to Tir-n-an-Oge. They say, that should a person cross the stream at the far end of the cavern, he could never, by his own power, return — that he should become an inhabitant of Fairyland forever after.

VII.

Then spoke the Queen of Fairy with a sweet, heart-thrilling tone, —
"Thou hast wished, O, little dreamer, for a sight of our fair zone;
Then a gift of power I bring thee: take this snowy wand, and when
Thou dost long to see our bright land, raise it thrice in this wild glen."

VIII.

Scarce the witching words were spoken when the Fairy Queen was gone,
But a trailing light behind her down the silent valleys shone;
And up stood that beauteous maiden, instant bound in fairy spell,
And thrice she raised the white wand in that flower-starred forest dell.

IX.

Sudden, sudden stood beside her a milk-white palfrey fleet,
And a-nigh a mounted esquire in bright mail from crown to feet;
Spell-bound, mounted that young maiden, and away, wild, wild away,
O'er Gailty's dreamy highlands like a flash of light went they!

X.

Sudden fled the sunset heavens, and a mighty vault instead,
Lit with many-tinted crystals, high o'er their pathway spread;
Cavern spars gleamed all around them with the white stars' silver flame,
Till they crossed th' Enchanted River, and to Tir-n-an-Oge they came!

XI.

O, that land of endless joyance! O, that world of beauty bright,
With its green and heavenly mountains bathed all in silver light, —
With its calm sky ever gleaming all in crystal sheen above,
And its plains of bright wild splendor where the happy spirits rove!

XII.

With its clear streams ever singing pleasant songs by hill and wood,
With its silent, flower-bright valleys, where the soul alone might brood

On the splendors all around it, which gray time can ne'er destroy,
And forever, and forever, on its own immortal joy!

XIII.

Scarce an hour unto the maiden in that land had passed away,
When they found a mighty falchion — beside their path it lay.
"Take this falchion to my father," said the maid, "for some sweet lore,
Some strange power, doth sudden tell me 'twill regain his right once more."

XIV.

Sped the esquire with the falchion to the exiled monarch back,
And alone went forth the maiden on her silent, heavenly track,
Till beside a crystal river towered a diamond palace sheen,
And, with all her court around her, there she found the Fairy Queen.

XV.

"By the magic gift you gave me, — by this wand of strangest power,
Send me back, O, radiant empress, to the world for one short hour, —
Back to Dun Grod's hoary castle, that my father I may see,
And he'll leave dark woe and sorrow, and I'll bring him back with me."

XVI.

"Few are they," said that bright empress, "who would leave this land again;
Yet go! and on thy swift course thou shalt have befitting train."
Away the Munster princess and her fairy train are gone,
Through the green vales, through the cavern, through the darkness, to the sun!

XVII.

When she reached the green Earth's valleys, — O, that wondrous fairy zone! —
'Stead of two short hours of gladness, ten long years away had flown!
In the land were many changes; 'twas the golden summer time,
And they asked a youthful peasant, "Who now reigns in this sweet clime?"

XVIII.

"Duan reigns, our aged monarch; he has slain th' usurping lord,
And regained fair Munster's valleys by the might of his good sword;

But, O, lovely, lovely lady, are you come from Fairyland,
You look so bright and beauteous on this morning fresh and bland?"

XIX.

The lady could not answer, so filled with joy was she;
With her maids and fairy gallants sped she on o'er hill and lea,
Till she reached her father's palace, where it stood by Shannon's wave,
And joyful was the welcome that the gladsome monarch gave!

XX.

Soon he led to his bright daughter a champion young and tall, —
"This be he whose gallant father still was faithful in my fall;
Thou canst ne'er find champion braver, thou canst ne'er find love so fond:
Wilt thou go, then, as thou sayest — wilt thou raise the fairy wand?"

XXI.

She looked on that young champion, and at her fairy train,
Gave the wand, and never turned her unto Tir-n-an-Oge again.
O, merry was the bridal, and as glad the reigning time,
Of that princess and her champion o'er the pleasant Munster clime!

THE TEMPLAR KNIGHT.

I.

'Mid Corrin's haunted wild-woods, where the summer winds are straying,
  Around a glade of brightness, from dells and leafy bowers,
There stands a steed caparisoned, a small steed wildly neighing
  To a boy and fair girl playing by Glendinan's high towers; *
And gayly round them winging, the merry birds are singing,
  And the stream its waves is flinging with a glad voice 'mid the flowers.

---

* Glendinan, an extensive valley at the north side of the Bally-Houra mountains, facing the plain of Limerick. At its upper extremity lies a small, oblong, and dilapidated stone chamber, like a grave, called by the country people *Iscur's Bed*; about a mile below which, on the edge of a glen, are the remains of an old building, which, according to tradition, was an establishment of the Knights Templars.

II.

Moves the steed, with sportful neighings, near and nearer to his master,
  With axe and spear crossed bravely on his gilded saddle-tree,
Where springs the boy with shout of joy, and, than the fleet winds faster,
  His comrade, spurs he past her, with a bearing bold and free;
Then sudden cries, "Ho, yonder! see the magic halls of wonder,
  Where the wizard old doth ponder on his spells to fetter me!"

III.

Like a knight of peerless valor on his wild steed he is sweeping,
  Towards the wizard tower he fancies in the dreamy forest shade, —
With lance in rest for foeman's breast, his magic foe unsleeping,
  In swift course he is keeping across that sunlit glade.
And thus each evening golden, 'mid those mossy wild-woods olden,
  By dark care unbeholden, lived that boy and bright-eyed maid.

IV.

Years have passed — bright years of gladness — and their bridal bells are ringing
  Along the summer mountains from that forest wild and wide;
Ah! thus from early childhood in the heart should love be springing,
  Soul to soul in fondness clinging from its golden morning tide;
Yet, alas! for Gerald's dreaming of a bride in beauty beaming,
  Mora's gone ere morn's first gleaming — falsely fled from Corrin side!

V.

As he waited by the altar, fair and fond the dreams that bound him, —
  Chief of Houra's sunny greenwoods, with a bride as fair as May, —
And his look was calmly joyous to the vassals circled round him,
  Till the tale of sorrow found him that his bride had fled away, —
His love, his anger scorning, a stranger's home adorning,
  To Carrignour that morning with its baron bold and gay.

VI.

The priest hath words of comfort, the mother mournful sighing,
  The vassals' shouts of fury loud as battle trumpets blown,

And, "Bring me," cries young Gerald, "my war-steed, that outflying,
    Ere the purple day be dying, ere her paramour be flown, —
That the traitor lord may learn my vengeance red and stern,
    Ere he treads his native fern by the Funcheon's valleys lone!"

VII.

He has donned his battle harness, and away so wild careering,
    His good steed bears him bravely towards the valleys of Glenroe,
Till in the golden noontide, from a forest hill down peering,
    Little caring, little fearing, so he meet his traitor foe,
Where a stream its tide is sending in many a silver bending,
    He espies the false pair wending through the flowery dells below.

VIII.

By the baron kneels the maid at the evening's calm returning,
    But love is drowned in sorrow, and joy is changed to fear, —
By the baron kneels the maid all alone and wildly mourning,
    And his tales with warm love burning she never more shall hear;
Far away young Gerald straineth from the spot where she remaineth,
    And the baron's life-blood staineth his conquering border spear!

IX.

But revenge ne'er changed the bosom from its dark and dreary madness
    To joy, and thus with Gerald as he rides o'er moor and moss, —
"Ah! the shadow of despair," he cries, "has sunk my hope in sadness,
    Love's gold I sought in gladness, and find it leaden dross;
So away from lovely Mulla, where she sings by height and hollow,
    Another path I'll follow, — a champion of the cross!"

X.

It was a golden morning 'mid summer's reign of splendor,
    Young Gerald took his lance and steed, and sped from Houra's wold;
But the fond farewell, when with sweet spell immortal love doth lend her
    Words mournful, true, and tender, no weeping maiden told,

Yet one true heart weepeth ever since he left his native river,
And no joy the world can give her, his mother sad and old.

XI.

And she cries: " Again, O, never shall I see my Gerald riding
  To the chase in merry greenwood at the blithesome peep of
      morn,
Shall his looks of gladness cheer me, shall his words of love
      come gliding,
  With peace and joy abiding, to my heart so sorrow-torn!"
But with time, despair retreating, hope springeth up unfleeting,
  Else her heart had ceased its beating, — she had died in grief
      forlorn.

XII.

Long she hoped for his returning to his hall with name of glory,
  Till the flowers of ten bright summers lay dead on mead and
      tomb;
Then unseen he stood one morning on Corrin's summit hoary,
  Gazing round that land of story on each well-known scene of
      bloom; —
Dreams of fair maids he was spurning, who might come with
      warm love burning,
  When they heard of his returning, for he wore the Templar
      plume!

XIII.

Many dreams of his sweet childhood there his memory might
      borrow,
  Yet he entered with a sinking heart his native hall once more.
There he found his mother sitting in her lorn and silent sorrow,
  As she sat that golden morrow when he left his home of
      yore; —
Glad and sudden up she started, "O, we'll never more be
      parted!"
  And she died all joyous-hearted in his arms by Mulla's shore!

XIV.

To Glendinan Sir Gerald has brought across the ocean
  Five Templars, he their leader, with all their vassal power,
And thrice each day out ringing with a sad and solemn motion,
  Tolls their bell to meet devotion o'er cot, and hall, and bower:
And long their banner knightly in the sunshine glittered brightly,
  To the breezes fluttered lightly from that ancient Templar
      tower!

ROMANCE OF THE STONE COFFIN.

I.

MOURNFULLY, sing mournfully,
　The hollow cave of green Cnoc-Brōn,*
It faceth to the golden west,
　'Mid the steep mountain's ridge of stone;
Boulder and crag, around it strown,
　Its entrance from the wild wind save, —
Mournfully, sing mournfully
　The maiden of that lonely cave;
The brightest, fairest maid was she
　From dark Sliav Bluim to Cleena's wave.†

II.

Mournfully, sing mournfully,
　In gray Kilmallock stands a tower,
And there her lordly father dwelt,
　Long, long ago, in pride and power;
O, ample was bright Nora's dower,
　And many suitors round her came:
But mournfully, sing mournfully,
　An old, proud chieftain owned his flame;
A false and gloomy man was he,
　Yet high he stood in martial fame.

III.

Mournfully, sing mournfully,
　Some curse was on her father then;
He would not list to her true love
　For young Sir Redmond of the Glen;
They forced her to the shrine, and when

---

* *Cnoc-Brōn*, the Hill of the Millstones. It is situated about two miles north of Kildorrery, on the confines of the County Cork. Between it and Cnoc-Aodh, another steep mountain, there is a narrow and deep pass, called Barna Dearg, — the Red or Bloody Gap, — in consequence of the numerous battles fought there in ancient ages. Cnoc-Brōn is supposed to be the ancient Sliabh Caoin, where Mahon, a Munster prince, was murdered, in the tenth century. In a ridge of rocks, which runs towards the summit of the hill, lies a small cave, called by the peasantry *Shaumer-an-Nora*, or Nora's Chamber. In this cave, according to tradition, a young woman, named Nora, hollowed out her coffin, and died as told in the ballad.

† That part of the ocean round the coast of Cork is called, in Irish poetry, the " Waters of Cleena."

Within its sacred bound they staid,
Mournfully, sing mournfully,
　The withered bridegroom, that fair maid,
You ne'er have seen, and ne'er shall see,
　A bridal match so ill arrayed.

IV.

Mournfully, sing mournfully,
　As died the sunset golden red,
The bridegroom told, to pay her scorn,
　His own dear lady was not dead!
Alas! 'twas truth the old man said;
　Then Nora started from her rest;
And mournfully, sing mournfully,
　She plunged a dagger in his breast,
And fled by glen, and bower, and tree,
　Until she reached Cnoc-Brōn's wild crest!

V.

Mournfully, sing mournfully,
　Her madness, and her guilt, and pain,
As fled that fatal summer night,
　And morn leapt o'er the hills again;
O, tears may gush like autumn rain,
　Yet the heart's sorrow will not go;
And mournfully, sing mournfully,
　Young Nora's guilt, and pain, and woe
From her poor bosom would not flee,
　Howe'er her tears might fall or flow.

VI.

Mournfully, sing mournfully,
　The fruits and wild herbs of the fell
Were her sole food for many a day,
　Her drink a lone and rock-bound well;
At length she prayed, and who can tell
　But God did hear her woful prayer,
That mournfully, O, mournfully!
　She'd die on that wild mountain there,
And leave, for Heaven, her misery,
　Her guilt, her madness, and despair.

VII.

Mournfully, sing mournfully,
　As by the cave one noon she sate,

Far looking towards her father's hall,
  Still as the crags and desolate,
  She saw in burnished harness plate
    Many a fierce charger spurn the grass,
And mournfully, sing mournfully,
    Two armies, each in one bright mass,
Rush into battle thunderingly
    Beneath her in the Bloody Pass!

VIII.

Mournfully, sing mournfully,
  She knew one tall and fatal spear —
'Twas young Sir Redmond of the Glen,
  Forth rushing in his wild career,
  And there the foe's red banner near,
    Where knight and kern lay strewn and killed.
Mournfully, sing mournfully,
    Her brave young lover's blood was spilled,
And there that hapless hour sat she,
    The measure of her sorrows filled!

IX.

Mournfully, sing mournfully,
  She took the huge dirk which had slain
That old, and false, and villain chief,
  Red-crusted with its bloody stain;
  A time-worn crumbling stone had lain
    Beside the cave for many a year,
O, mournfully, sing mournfully,
    "Of this," she cried, "I'll make my bier,
And die where o'er my misery
    No human eye can shed a tear!"

X.

Mournfully, sing mournfully,
  Night, and morn, and sunset red,
The lady plied that dagger strong,
  Till she had scooped her narrow bed.
  Now the sweet summer time was fled,
    And all its flowers decayed and gone;
And mournfully, sing mournfully,
    Weak and worn, and sad and wan,
There on an autumn eve sat she,
    The last that o'er her misery shone.

XI.

Mournfully, sing mournfully,
    She laid her on her bier of stone,
And there and then in that wild cave,
    She died for love, all, all alone;
There 'mid the ridge of stern Cnoc-Brōn,
    The peasants found her lifeless clay,
And mournfully, O mournfully,
    They bare her to the abbey gray,
Where sleeps she lowly, silently,
    Within her coffin stone alway.

ROMANCE OF THE BANNER.

I.

THERE was a banner old, in a tower by th' ocean bound,
Its device a boat of gold, a lady, and a hound;
Then, gentles, sit around, and a tale I'll tell to ye,
All about the old green banner of that tower by Cleena's sea.

II.

"Where away, O, where away?" asked the hoary marinere,
From a rock that towered so gray o'er the waters broad and clear.
"To seek my true love dear, doth he live, or is he dead,"
Cried young Marron with her wolf-hound, as o'er the waves she sped.

III.

Night, with her starry train, o'er the hound and fair ladye —
Rose the shark from out the main, stealing slowly on their lee,
On them dark and wild looked he, — gazed the wolf-hound fierce on him,
While he plunged, and glared, and passed them in the ghostly midnight dim.

IV.

Vanished the starlight pale; came rosy morn once more;
As that boat so small and frail sped the purpling billows o'er,
A tall coast towered before, with great blue hills behind,
And, "Perchance," cried Marron, weeping, "here my true love I may find."

V.

The sharp keel grates the sand; — ah, the sight before her there!
Wrecks on wrecks along the strand, stark bones whitening in the air;
Down she sat in her despair. "Ah, my Turlogh brave!" said she,
"The storm came down upon him, and his bones lie in the sea."

VI.

And floating on the wave, beside the sand below,
The glittering plume she gave her love two moons ago!
O, the madness of her woe, O, her shriek of wild despair.
As she sank, like death had struck her, on the wet sands swooning there!

VII.

A youth with agile bound, of high and princely mien,
Welcomed by Marron's hound, — no foe to her, I ween, —
Has darted from the screen of an old, deserted fane,
And, o'erjoyed, young Marron wakens in her Turlogh's arms again.

VIII.

Sank crew and galley trim, when the wild tempest roared,
And left alive but him, to Marron thus restored;
Nought saved he but his sword from thundering blast and brine,
And he says, "We'll seek green Desmond, and thou never more shalt pine."

IX.

On their course the night came down without one planet bright;
Great clouds of dreary brown quenched all their trembling light.
Up to the lowering height the hound his gaze has thrown,
And a sudden yell breaks from him, and a low, sad, wailing moan.

X.

Sudden the lightning's flash came darting out on high,
And the mighty thunder's crash boomed o'er the boundless sky,
And with a vengeful cry the storm began to rave,
And lowered them in the hollows, and tossed them o'er the wave.

XI.

"O, for the mighty rock where stands my castle gray" —
Amid the tempest's shock, thus the young chief did say: —
"My heart feels no dismay, but all for love and thee,
So soon to sink and perish beneath the roaring sea."

XII.

Out in the rushing wind, upon the greedy wave,
His arm around her twined, — wildly he sprang to save;
The boat whirled stave by stave, on towards the distant shore,
And the wolf-hound plunged and turned, then dashed right on before.

XIII.

The golden morn had broke o'er sea and lovely land,
When calmly they awoke — 'twas on their native strand;
They made a banner grand, and on its gleaming fold
Was the hound and lovely lady, and the boat of ruddy gold.

THE THREE SISTERS.

Part the First.

I.

There stands a crumbling castle by the winding Liffey's shore,
Through its roof the moonbeams glimmer, through its hall the night winds roar;
Fast the fox sleeps on its hearthstone, green the grass grows on its floor,
And through battered wall and window steals the ivy evermore.

II.

In the light of youth and beauty, fair as roses of the May,
Once there dwelt three lovely sisters in that castle old and gray;
One with tresses like the midnight, one with ringlets of the brown,
One with locks all glittering golden on her white neck gleaming down.

III.

'Twas a time of war and trouble, when across our native land
Swept black Cromwell and his crop-ears, with full many a murdering band,
From their new Geneva Bibles twanging forth their creed of sin,
And their long swords for the Irish heads, each text to hammer in! —

IV.

When the holy crag of Cashel wore a ghastly crimson hue
With the blood of all the martyrs that the demon Burner* slew,

---
* Murrogh the Burner, baron of Inchiquin.

When the slain lay thick in Wexford, and like Boyne's autumnal
   wave
Ran the steaming streets of Tredagh * with the best blood of the
   brave.

V.

And from out their turret window could these maidens three
   look down
On many a rifled hamlet, many a blazing tower and town,
On the bands of black marauders, as betimes they crossed the
   flood,
Preaching peace with sword and cannon, every sermon stamped
   in blood.

VI.

But still these bonnie sisters, in their castle old and hoar,
Lived in peace, by none molested — wishing, yearning evermore
For their lovers' quick returning, who the plume and helmet wore
In the hardy ranks of Owen,† far away from Liffey's shore.

VII.

Till a Babe of Grace ‡ one autumn with his riders passed the way,
And he said, " 'Tis writ this castle shall be mine ere close of day."
Quoting texts and ranting Scripture for an hour to show his claim,
Reuben Roast-and-Burn-the-Gentiles was this godly hero's name.

VIII.

He girded well his armor, he raised a holy psalm,
And on his red sword's iron hilt he laid his godly palm;
He cried, " Strike up the timbrel of God's Chosen Babes, and
   come ! "
And at his back they crossed the ford with sound of psalm and
   drum.

IX.

" Ho, Gentiles! yield both sword and gun; ho, traitors! ope the
   gate;
This land it is the Parliament's, and Parliament is fate !
For there ne'er was town or city did not yield to its decree ;
Then doff your flag, and ope your gate, and yield this hold to me."

X.

" Our flag upon the turret top it ever fluttered free,"
Cried Ineen Dhuv, the dark-haired maid, the eldest of the three;
" Our men are few to guard it well, but with that gallant few,
We'll hold our own this day against the Parliament and you ! "

* Tredagh, Drogheda.   † Owen Roe O'Neill.   ‡ A Puritan.

XI.

The outer wall was thick and strong, and strong the iron gate,
And stout the hearts that stood within black Reuben to await;
And though 'twas written, as he preached, that "ere the sun
    should set,
He'd take that gallant tower," these maids they held it stoutly
    yet.

Part the Second.

I.

The night fell down on Liffey's shore, and round that castle gray;
Black Reuben and his Babes of Grace like watchful sleuth-
    hounds lay;
And Ellen Bán, the youngest maid, she called her brother down,
A little boy, with bold, black eyes, and locks of wavy brown —

II.

"My brother Hugh, look yonder, in the forest old and dim;
A foeman's horse stands 'neath a tree — go thou and capture
    him,
And speed thee off to th' Irish camp, and seek my true love dear,
And tell him of our woful plight, and bid him soon be here."

III.

He clambered o'er the outward wall — no fairy's foot more light;
He stole unto the foeman's horse 'neath the friendly shades of
    night;
He crept into the saddle, despite the wary foe,
And dashed away, through bush and brake, for the camp of Owen
    Roe.

IV.

On Liffey shore smiled fair the morn — Black Reuben ranged
    his men,
"And soon," he said, "we'll sap the gate of yon unhallowed
    den;
Think how the Gentiles bowed their necks when the walls of
    Jericho
Fell down before blest Israel's voice, and charge ye on the foe."

V.

They shot the warders on the wall, they rushed unto the gate,
They burst its bars, and bounded in to glut their burning hate;

Round turret, stair, and rampart high, with murderous swords
    they ran,
And dragged the brave defenders forth, and slew them every man.

VI.

And then from out the castle hall they brought those sisters three,
Where Reuben sat, beside a drum, to judge them speedily.
" Ye fought against the Parliament, ye fought 'gainst God's de-
    cree ;
I am his minister, young maid — hast aught to say to me ? "

VII.

" I've nought to say," said Ineen Dhuv, a brave light in her eye —
" No words for thee, thou canting knave ; I am prepared to die.
You'd have another tale to tell, this day you'd deeply rue,
If bold Sir John, my love, were here to measure swords with you."

VIII.

" A curse upon thy pagan tongue ! Ho ! bear her to her fate."
They dragged her 'cross the castle bawn, and shot her by the gate.
Then Reuben looked on Rosaleen, the second of the three —
" Hast aught to say," he grimly said, " to alter our decree ? "

IX.

" I've nought to say," cried Rosaleen ; " but for this deed you've
    done,
You'll sorely pay, perchance this day, ere setting of the sun ;
I hear a horse-tramp on the hill, a plash beside the shore " —
" Ho ! bear her to her sister's doom ; that sound you'll hear no
    more."

X.

With demon frown on Ellen Bán then Reuben cast his eye ;
She met his gaze with steady look. " Art thou prepared to die ? "
" Art *thou* prepared ? " she answered quick ; " for see, with all
    his men,
To pay thee back, comes my true love, Sir Gilbert of the Glen ! "

XI.

Then Reuben sprang unto his feet, and drew his sword — too late !
For young Sir Gilbert and his men came thundering through the
    gate ;
They fell on Reuben's Babes of Grace, and slew them every one,
And 'venged those hapless sisters twain ere the setting of the sun.

XII.

There grew a tree beside the gate, an oak tree, fair and high,
And from its branch black Reuben swung in each wind that
    wandered by
To sing its dirge his victims' graves in the churchyard sadly o'er;
And thus they fared, those sisters three, by the Liffey's winding
    shore.

ROSE CONDON.

I.

Over valley, and rock, and lea,
  Merrily strike the wild harp's strain,
For the fairest maid in the south countrie
  Hath come to our Funcheon's side again;
Far 'mid the mountains of Green Fear-muighe,*
  In lone Crag Thierna † many a day
Dwelt she long with the fairy throng,
  Mourning for her home alway.

II.

An Ardrigh's crown is yellow and bright —
  Fill the glens with the wild harp's tone —
But it may not match those locks of light
  So loosely o'er her fair brows thrown;
And the glance of her eyes, O, mortal wight
  Never such glory saw before;
And her neck, as the wild rose soft and white,
  Lone blooming by the Funcheon's shore.

III.

She is daughter of Condon brave —
  Strike the wild harp's string of pride —

---

* *Fear-Muighe-Feine*, — the plain of the Fenian men, — which anciently included the baronies of Condon and Clongibbon, together with what is at present called the barony of *Fermoy*, is walled in on the south by the Nagles mountains, and on the north by the Gailtees and Bally-Houras, or mountains of Mole. It was called Armoy, and, I believe, Ardmulla, by Spenser. Along its southern side flows the Blackwater, forming a succession of the most beautiful and romantic scenes in the south of Ireland. The whole plain anciently belonged to the O'Keeffes.

† Crag Thierna, or Corrin Thierna, a romantic steep, eastward of Fermoy, and celebrated in the legends of the peasantry as one of the great fairy palaces of Munster.

The fiercest chief where thy waters rave,
  Dark Oun Mór of the rushing tide;
Nine moons have silvered the Funcheon's wave,
  Since by the towers of strong Cloghlee
The fondness of her heart she gave,
  To the banished knight of thy woods, Gailtee!

IV.

O, Love! thy power grows day by day —
  Strike the wild harp high and bold —
Three eves had purpled the mountains gray,
  And young Clongibbon had ta'en his hold,
Reta'en his hold, regained his sway,
  All for the love of Condon's child,
And chased the Saxon far away
  Beyond the pale of his mountains wild!

V.

Three eves more o'er Funcheon's tide —
  Strike the wild harp clear and sweet —
Rose Condon sat by the water side,
  Her brave, triumphant love to meet:
The sunset in his purple pride
  Over the far-off crests of Mole,
And through the glens and forest wide
  A sweet and dreamy silence stole.

VI.

Long she waits her lover's tread —
  Strike the wild harp tenderly —
Till day's bright legions all are fled,
  And the white stars peer through the forest tree;
Ha! now he comes by the river bed,
  With his martial step and bearing high;
But why is the maiden's heart adread,
  As her warrior love draws fondly nigh?

VII.

Does victory paint a warrior's mail —
  Strike the wild harp fearfully —
With swarth gold gems and diamonds pale,
  And his plume with the sunbow's radiancy?
Her lover's armor through the vale
  Sheddeth a wild and elfin gleam,
And strange sounds on the breezes sail,
  Sweet echoing o'er the star-lit stream.

VIII.

The warrior now beside her stands —
  Strike the wild harp sad and low —
And takes in his her trembling hands,
  But her loved knight ne'er gazéd so!
O, 'twas the king of the fairy bands
  That bound her in his spells that night,
And bore her swift to the elfin lands,
  Far, far away in his love-winged flight!

IX.

From Oun Mór's tide to Carrig'nour,* —
  Strike the wild harp rushingly —
From far Mocollop's mighty tower
  To the storied hill of Kil-da-righ,
Many a man ere morning hour
  Through the wildwoods rode amain:
They sought the maid in hall and bower,
  But fruitless was their search, and vain.

X.

Condon sat within his hall, —
  Strike the wild harp mournfully —
Sadness did his heart inthrall,
  Grief for her he might not see;
Searching still, Clongibbon tall
  Roamed the forests lone and drear,
Like maniac man bereft of all
  The joyance of this earthly sphere.

XI.

Joy in lone Crag Thierna's steep! —
  Strike the harp o'er hill and wold —
Glad feasts the Fairy King did keep
  For young Rose with the locks of gold;
But ah! the maid did nought but weep,
  And eight bright moons had lost their flame,
Yet still by Oun Mór swift and deep,
  In sorrow she was still the same.

---

* Carriganour, a very ancient castle, a few miles below Mitchelstown, on the banks of the Funcheon. Mocollop, a huge pile eastward of Cloghleigh, on the shore of the Blackwater. *Kil-da-righ*, — the Church of the two Oaks, — at present Kildorrery, a small town on the Cork border, between Fermoy and Kilmallock.

XII.

Nine sweet nights have robed the dells—
  Strike the wild harp bold and high —
Since out with martial trumpet swells
  The fairy throngs came trooping by;
Round lone Molaga's holy cells,*
  Beneath the midnight moon they played,
While she, the victim of their spells,
  Sat lorn within the ruin's shade.

XIII.

It is beside a fountain fair —
  Strike the wild harp sweet and low —
With sad heart brooding on her care,
  She looks into the wave below;
A shadow glides before her there,
  And looking up, beside her stands
An agéd man with snow-white hair,
  With pitying eyes and claspéd hands!

XIV.

A mitre decked in golden sheen —
  Strike the wild harp wonderingly —
A vestment as the shamrock green,
  And sandals of the mountain tree
He wears: the ancient saint I ween!
  Ah! he hath heard the maiden's moan,
And bids her drink, with brow serene,
  One pure draught from a cup of stone.

XV.

The fays may sport o'er hill and plain —
  Strike the wild harp glad and bold —
But never shall their power again
  In magic gyve that maiden hold;
One cool, bright draught she scarce had ta'en,
  Scarce looked upon the vestment cross,
When fearful died the fairy strain,
  O'er moonlit crag and lonely moss!

* *Teompal Molaga,* — the Temple or Church of Saint Molaga, — an extremely beautiful and picturesque ruin, about a mile north-east of Kildorrery, on a bend of the Funcheon. Beside it is an ancient well, dedicated to the saint, to which the peasantry ascribe many virtues, and of which many strange legends are told.

XVI.

Short time their splendid pageant shone —
  Strike the harp with gladsome thrill —
Then faded in the moonlight wan
  Far o'er Caher Dringa's castled hill; *
Short time the moonbeams glowed upon
  The mitre and the vestment bright,
The maiden turned, the saint was gone,
  Impatient to his home of light!

XVII.

O, joy! she sees the eastern ray —
  Strike the wild harp glad and clear —
The herald of a golden day,
  The fairest in the circling year;
It is the first bright morn of May,
  And stream and plain smile calmly now,
And many a wild bird pours his lay,
  In gladness from the greenwood bough.

XVIII.

O, Freedom leadeth where she list —
  Strike the wild harp's string of pride —
Wild joy the maid can ne'er resist
  Impels towards Oun-na-Geerait's side;
There, while the stream by day is kissed,
  A strange sight meets her wandering eyes, —
It is not golden morning mist
  With glad larks o'er it in the skies:

XIX.

The red fires of a Saxon raid —
  Strike the wild harp fierce and high —
With scattered smoke o'er many a glade,
  Blue curling to the breezeless sky;

---

* Caher Dringa or Fort Prospect, a castle about three miles south-east of Carriganour. *Oun-na-Geerait*, — the River of the Champion, — a tributary of the Funcheon. Glashmona, a stream rising in the Bally-Houri mountains. By the banks of this torrent, the peasantry tell many legends relating to the battles fought there between the ancient tribes. *Aha Phooka* — the Ford of the Spirit — is a steep and dangerous pass leading from the county Limerick into the Clongibbon's country.

Helmet and lance, and well tried blade,
  Gleam brightly from the forest deep,
And many a creacht beneath the shade
  Lie silent in their morning sleep!

XX.

"Ho! wake the tired creachts from their rest!" —
  Strike the harp o'er hill and plain —
On toward Kilfinane's mountain crest
  The raiders take their course again;
Fear gathereth in the maiden's breast,
  As wind away that fierce-browed horde,
Taking their pathway to the west,
  Triumphant through the Spirit's Ford.

XXI.

Is that the thunder of the flood —
  Strike the harp all fiercely now —
She hears wild rising from the wood,
  And echoing up the steep hill's brow?
O, rushing back in panic mood,
  Like leaves before a mountain wind,
The raiders come in dust and blood,
  Her father and his clan behind!

XXII.

And who is he her sire before —
  Strike the wild harp high and grand —
Scattering the raiders evermore
  Before the wide sweep of his brand?
Ah! well within her fond heart's core
  She knows her lover's martial form,
As fiercely on the river's shore
  He sweepeth through the battle storm.

XXIII.

O God! that lance stroke through his side —
  Raise the wild harp's mournful tone —
Stretches her sire where redly glide
  The swift waves o'er their bed of stone!
Down speeds the maid, whate'er betide,
  Swift as Glashmona's startled hare,
And soon — death, danger, all defied —
  She bendeth o'er her father there!

XXIV.

O, joy! it is no mortal wound —
  Strike the glad harp to the skies —
She lifts his faint head from the ground,
  With heaving breast and tearful eyes.
With wondering eyes he looks around,
  As wakening sense asserts its reign —
O, joy of joys! the lost is found
  To cheer his course through life again!

XXV.

The clangor of the fight is o'er —
  Strike the wild harp's proudest lay —
Few raiders from that river shore
  Passed westward through the Spirit's Way;
Glad was the look Clongibbon wore,
  His herds reta'en, his valley free,
As clasped he in his arms once more
  The gold-haired maid of green Fear-muighe!

THE BATTLE OF THURLES.
A. D. 1174.

I.

By the gray walls of Thurles, in O'Fogarty's land,
We came to the trysting with banner and brand,
'Twas no true loves to meet, 'twas no fond vows to say,
But to conquer the foeman, or die in the fray.

II.

Royal Roderick was there with his bravest and best,
The wild fearless clans from the vales of the West;
Royal Donal came up from the green hills of Clare,
With his stately Dalcassians, like lions from their lair.

III.

Where our Ardrigh was resting, the sunburst gleamed wide,
Donal's three bloody lions waved proud at his side,
And *mavrone*, on that morn how we vowed and we swore
To freshen their tints in the black Norman's gore.

IV.

Out rode Earl Strongbow from Waterford gate,
With his bowmen and spearmen in armor of plate,
And they harried rich ploughland, and dangean, and hall,
To O'Fogarty's mountains from fair Carrick's wall.

V.

This news reached Marisco in strong Aha Cliath,*
And he smiled on his warriors a grim smile of glee,
And like wolves scenting carnage, with rapine and flame,
For their share in the booty to Thurles they came.

VI.

In the sun gleamed their armor, waved their flags in the gale;
Few warriors amongst us had helmet or mail;
But the hearts in our bosoms were fearless and strong,
And we clove through their corselets and helmets ere long.

VII.

Out rode the two kings 'mid our gallant array —
Small need then for words: well we knew what they'd say;
But they pointed their spears where they wished us to go,
And we rushed in their path on the iron-clad foe.

VIII.

The foe levelled lances our charge to withstand,
And thick flew their arrows as we closed hand to hand;
And full stoutly they stood, for brave robbers were they,
Who would part with their lives ere they'd part with their prey.

IX.

O, the crash of the onset as steel clanged on steel!
O, the *Ferrah* we gave as our blows made them reel!
O, the joy of our vengeance as onward we poured,
Till we smote them as Brian smote the fierce Danish horde!

X.

Earl Strongbow for life flies towards Waterford Gate;
But few vassals around him his orders await;
By the brave walls of Thurles 'neath our vengeance they died —
Wild we feasted that night by the Suir's reddened tide!

---

* Aha Cliath, Dublin; pronounced *Aha Clee*.

ROSSNALEE.

I.

The fairy woman of the wood,
    Rossnalee! O, Rossnalee!
Hath set the spell in her cave so rude,
And she cries, " Is't for sorrow, or all for good,
That the lovers shall meet in the secret wood,
    By the crystal waters of Rossnalee?"

II.

The fairy woman of the wood,
    Rossnalee! O, Rossnalee!
With her crimson gown and her scarlet hood,
Cries again, " 'Tis for sorrow, and nought for good,
That the lovers shall meet in the secret wood,
    By the crystal waters of Rossnalee!"

III.

Many hearts the wild wars rue,
    Rossnalee! O, Rossnalee!
Mac Donogh's daughter weepeth too,
As she cometh to meet her lover true,
For war's sad chances well she knew,
    By the crystal waters of Rossnalee.

IV.

The first step she took from her father's door,
    Rossnalee! O, Rossnalee!
The ban-dog howled on the barbican floor,
And her little dove cooed in the turret o'er,
With a voice of wailing and sadness sore,
    By the crystal waters of Rossnalee.

V.

The next step she took from her home so dear,
    Rossnalee! O, Rossnalee!
She heard a low voice in her ear,
Though she saw but a white owl floating near —
" Thou'rt the sweetest blossom to grace a bier,
    By the crystal waters of Rossnalee!"

VI.

As she went down where the crags are piled,
    Rossnalee! O, Rossnalee!
She saw a little elfish child,
And it cried with a voice all strange and wild,
"Go back, thou lady fair and mild,
    By the crystal waters of Rossnalee!"

VII.

As she crossed the rath and the war-grave rude,
    Rossnalee! O, Rossnalee!
Cried she of the spells and the scarlet hood,[*]
"If thou goest, thou goest for sorrow, not good,
And the earth shall be dyed with my darling's blood,
    By the crystal waters of Rossnalee!"

VIII.

But 'gainst fair warning and friendly threat,
    Rossnalee! O, Rossnalee!
She answers, "My heart's on the trysting set,
And how can I mourn and how regret,
That I meet with my gallant De Barrette
    By the crystal waters of Rossnalee?"

IX.

Where the mountain ash bends over the wave,
    Rossnalee! O, Rossnalee!
She's clasped in the arms of her lover brave,
Who cries, "Ten kisses for love I crave,
For my new-won knighthood and conquering glaive,
    By the crystal waters of Rossnalee!"

X.

"Mac Donogh, aboo!" From the darksome wood,
    Rossnalee! O, Rossnalee!
Rushed her sire and his vassals in savage mood,—
"Ho! traitor, my vengeance this hour is good,
For thou'st won thy spurs with my best son's blood,
    By the crystal waters of Rossnalee!"

---

[*] Fairies are believed by the peasantry to appear frequently in the form of an old woman clad in red garments, always with some benevolent intention.

XI.

Three vassals were cloven through basnet and brain,
    Rossnalee! O, Rossnalee!
When an arrow shot from the wood amain,
To stretch De Barrette upon the plain,
But the heart of the maiden it cleft in twain,
    By the crystal waters of Rossnalee.

XII.

Down fell the knight by his true-love's side,
    Rossnalee! O, Rossnalee!
With a wound in his breast both deep and wide,—
"O, death in thy arms is sweet!" he cried;
And thus these lovers so faithful died
    By the crystal waters of Rossnalee!

THE PILGRIM.

I.

As I sat at the cross in the village, it was on a bright summer day,
An old man came silently thither, was drooping, and bearded, and gray;
There was dust on his shoon and his garments, the sore dust of many a mile;—
"O, where are you going, gray pilgrim? Come rest 'neath this green tree a while."

II.

"O, God's holy blessing be on you! an hour from my journey I'll steal:
I have wandered from morning till noontide, and foot-sore and weary I feel;
I am going fast, fast to the graveyard, and wish I may reach it full soon,
Till under its green grass, untroubled, I sleep by my Aileen Aroon!

III.

"O, she was an Orangeman's daughter! but wild was her fondness for me;
She dwelt where in glory and splendor broad Barrow sweeps down to the sea:

She was fair as the roses of summer, and mild as a May morning
    bland;
O, a maiden so bright in her beauty was never like her in the
    land!

IV.

"Ah! darkly and sore I remember, it was in the wild Ninety-
    eight,
When peace from our land was uprooted, and sad was the poor
    peasant's fate;
I'd scarce numbered twenty fair summers, the blood ran like fire
    in my veins,
And I rose with the rest for old Ireland, to free her from bondage
    and chains!

V.

"I had a strange power 'mong my neighbors, — my sires had been
    lords in the land, —
And soon on the hills round me gathered a reckless, a wild dar-
    ing band.
Through many a sad scene I led them, by lone cot and strife-
    ruined hall,
Till a dark hour of gloom saw me faithless to God, and my
    country, and all!

VI.

"In the madness of love I had promised, the last time I parted
    my dear,
That I'd ne'er draw the sword 'gainst her father, when met in the
    battle's career;
I kept to that promise too truly, betrayed with old Ireland my
    trust,
And my name was soon named with the traitors, and my idol
    soon crumbled to dust!

VII.

"We'd camped in a gorge of the mountains; the redcoats and
    yeomen were nigh:
'If I wait for the morning's fierce battle, we'll meet 'mid the
    combat,' said I;
'Can I calm the dark foeman, that hates me, with love for his
    child pure and bright?
Can I keep to the promise I made her?' I fled from my com-
    rades that night!

VIII.

"I fled like a deer through the mountains, to the arms of my
    Aileen Aroon; —
O, great God of glory and mercy, the black fate that met me so
    soon!
She lay in her grave-clothes, down-stricken by a sickness full
    sudden and sore,
And my name was the name of traitor, and my bright hopes were
    quenched evermore!

IX.

"From the old pilgrim places around me to gray, holy Derg of
    the lake,
Since that wild time of trouble and vengeance, my slow yearly
    pathway I take;
And I pray that my sins be forgiven, by many a lone ruined
    wall,
And I sleep, — but I'll soon sleep beside her, the sweetest, long
    slumber of all!"

X.

O, mournful stood up the old pilgrim, and mournful took me by
    the hand, —
"May the blessings of love be upon you, and freedom and peace
    in the land!"
Then he drank at the spring in the village, and silently went on
    his way; —
O, God and His mercy go with him, a sure prop by night and by
    day!

THE TAKING OF ARMAGH.
A.D. 1596.

I.

'Twas fast by gray Killoter we made the Saxons run,
We hewed them with the claymore, and smote them with the gun.
"Armagh! Armagh!" cried Norris, as wild he spurred away,
And sore beset and scattered, they reached its walls that day!

II.

Alas! we had no cannon to batter down the gate, —
To level fosse and rampart; so we were forced to wait,

And 'leaguer late and early that place of old renown,
By dint of plague and famine to bring the foeman down.

III.

Then up and spake our general, the great and fearless Hugh, —
"We'll give them fit amusement while we've nought else to do;
Then deftly ply your bullets, and pick the warders down,
And well watch pass and togher, that none may leave the town."

IV.

We camped amid the valleys and bonnie woods about,
But spite of all our watching, one gallant wight got out,
Till far Dundalk he entered by spurring day and night,
And told them of our leaguer, and all their woful plight.

V.

Then Norris raised his gauntlet, and smote his mailéd breast —
"God curse these northern rebels with fire, and plague, and pest.
Ho! captain of the arsenal, send food and succor forth,
For if we lose that stronghold, the Queen must lose the North."

VI.

'Twas on a stormy twilight, when wildly roared the blast,
Up to our prince's standard a scout came spurring fast,
And told him how that convoy — four hundred stalwart men —
Had pitched their camp at sunset by Gartan's woody glen.

VII.

"Then let them take their slumber," said our great prince that
      night;
"God wot, they'll sleep far sounder before the morning's light:
My son, thou'rt ever yearning to win one meed — renown;
Go! if thou slay'st the convoy, then we will take the town."

VIII.

He sprang upon his charger, our prince's gallant son,
And fast his path we followed, till Gartan's glen we won;
And there beside the torrent, with watch-fires burning low,
Deep in their fatal slumber we spied the Saxon foe.

IX.

When booms the autumn thunder, and thickly pours the rain,
From Mourne's great mountain valley the flood sweeps o'er the
      plain —

While up our drums we rattled, and loud our trumpets blew,
Like that wild torrent swept we upon the Saxon crew.

X.

We swept upon their vanguard, we rushed on rear and flank,
Like corn before the sickle, we mowed them rank on rank,
And ere the ghostly midnight we'd slain them every one —
I trow they slept far sounder before the morrow's dawn.

XI.

"Now don the convoy's garments, and take their standard, too."
'Twas thus, at blink of morning, out spake our gallant Hugh;
"And march ye toward the city, with baggage, arms, and all,
With all their promised succor, and see what shall befall."

XII.

We donned their blood-red garments, and shook their banner free,
We marched us towards the city, a gallant sight to see;
Upon their drums we rattled the Saxon point of war,
And soon the foemen heard us, and answered from afar.

XIII.

From dreams of lordly banquets that morn the Saxons woke,
When on their ears our clamor of drums and trumpets broke;
And up they sprang full blithely, and crowded, one and all,
Like lank wolves, gazing greedily from loophole, gate, and wall.

XIV.

There was an ancient abbey, a pile of ruined stone,
Two gun-shots from the ramparts, amid the wild woods lone;
And there he lay in ambush, our tanist brave and young,
And, as we neared the city, upon our flank he sprung!

XV.

With all his rushing troopers, out from the wood he sped,
Their matchlocks filled with powder — they did not want the lead —
And well they feigned the onset, with shot and sabre stroke,
And deftly, too, we met them, with clouds of harmless smoke!

XVI.

Some tossed them from their saddles, to imitate the slain;
Whole ranks fell at each volley, along the bloodless plain;
And groans and hollow murmurs of well-feigned woe and fear,
From that strange fight rang mournfully upon the foeman's ear.

XVII.

Up heaved the huge portcullis, round swang the ponderous gate,
Out rushed the foe to rescue, or share their comrades' fate;
And fiercely waved their banners, and bright their lances shone,
And, "George for merry England!" they cried, as they fell on.

XVIII.

Saint Columb! the storm of laughter that from our ranks arose,
As up the corpses started, and fell upon our foes;
As we, the routed convoy, closed up our thick ranks well,
And met the foe with claymore, red pike, and petronel!*

XIX.

'Twas then from out the forest our mighty chieftain came,
Like a fierce autumn tempest of roaring wind and flame —
So loud his horsemen thundered, and rang their slogan free,
And swept upon th' affrighted foe with all their chivalric!

XX.

Yet stout retired the Saxon, though he was sore distrait,
Till, with his ranks commingled, in burst we through the gate;
Then soon the Red Hand † fluttered upon their highest towers,
And wild we raised our triumph shout, for old Armagh was ours!

THE BARON AND THE MILLER.

I.

There was a steed, a brave, black steed,
    Lithe of body and limb,
And in country or town, for strength or speed,
    There never was one like him.

II.

He had sinews of brass for the chase's flight,
    Eyes of fire as he swept the hill,
He'd a heart of steel for the bloody fight;
    And his master was Hugh of the Mill.

---

* Petronel, a long dag or pistol.
† The Red Hand, the device on the banner of Tyrone.

III.

But Hugh of the Mill had a master, too, —
  The Baron of Darenlawr,*
Whom he served in peace, as a vassal should do,
  And followed in day of war.

IV.

Never were twain, by hill or by plain,
  So matched in passion and ill,
As the baron bold of that castle old,
  And his vassal, wild Hugh of the Mill.

V.

By Cummeragh one morn, with stag-hound and horn,
  They hunted like the wind,
But the black, black steed, with his sinews of speed,
  Left the ireful baron's behind.

VI.

"This brown steed of mine, wild Hugh, shall be thine,
  With fifty crowns so bright;
But I must have thy charger brave,
  For I need his strength in the fight!"

VII.

Then out and told that miller so bold:
  "I care not for favor or pelf;
And this brave steed of mine shall never be thine,
  For I need his strength myself!"

VIII.

Then an ireful man was the dark baron,
  And an angry laugh he gave:
"I will have thy steed, though the demon should feed
  On thy carcass, thou grinding knave!"

---

* Of this ancient castle but one tower, now completely covered with ivy, remains. It stands on the southern bank of the Suir, in the county Waterford, about two Irish miles eastward of Clonmel. The foundations, on arches, can yet be discerned, and from their extent and thickness, it must have been once a fortress of great strength and importance. It was garrisoned for the English, in the days of Queen Elizabeth, by the Butlers, to whom it belonged. The scenery around it is very beautiful and romantic.

IX.

And though Hugh was strong, down, down to the earth
   The vassals they've dragged him amain,
And they've changed each saddle, and rein, and girth,
   And mounted him once again.

X.

On the baron's brown horse now he's mounted perforce,
   And the baron sits on the other;
The baron is glad, but the miller is mad
   With a passion he cannot smother.

XI.

He digs the spurs in the brown steed's sides
   Till it snorts with rage and pain,
Then up with a fiendish frown he rides
   To the baron's bridle rein.

XII.

"May the memory of crime thy bosom freeze,
   The worm that never dies —
Till the flames of Hell on thy dark soul seize,
   And I see it with mine eyes!"

XIII.

Then he plunges and volts, and away he bolts,
   And down the rough mountain he's gone;
While the vassals' laughter rings wildly after,
   And the shout of the fierce baron.

XIV.

There were battles enough, both bloody and tough,
   To employ them both, I wot,
And swift moons ran over master and man,
   Till the curse was all forgot.

XV.

But there came a day when the baron lay
   On his bed of sickness and dole,
And the bells were rung, at the evening gray,
   For his departing soul.

XVI.

There came three knocks to the miller's gate
   In the dead hour of the night,

And the miller he rose at a furious rate,
  And looked in the dim moon's light.

XVII.

And there sat the Baron of Darenlawr
  Upon the swift, black horse,
And his fixed eyes glared 'neath his visor bar,
  And his brow was pale as a corse!

XVIII.

"Come hither, come hither, thou miller brave, —
  Ho! mount and follow me!"
On the dark-brown steed Hugh is mounted with speed
  And away with the baron is he.

XIX.

In their garb of war by old Darenlawr,
  And down by the rushing Suir,
Till they strike on a track, all barren and black,
  O'er a wide and lonely moor.

XX.

Black mountains rise to the pale, dim skies,
  Beyond that desert place,
As side by side away they ride
  In a fierce and furious race.

XXI.

Taller and taller each giant hill,
  And darker their chasms grow,
As away over quagmire and brawling rill
  Like demons of night they go.

XXII.

Redder and redder the baron's eyes glared,
  But 'twas more from rage than fear,
As the bog-fiend's lamp on their pathway flared,
  And they swept that barrier near.

XXIII.

And there at last rose a crag so vast
  That it hid in the clouds its face;
Then the miller reined in, but the baron spurred past
  Till he neared its gloomy base.

XXIV.

Then it rocked and shaked, and it groaned and quaked,
  And its breast burst right before,
And a mighty flame through the broad rent came
  As from Hell's eternal door!

XXV.

Yet on and on spurred the fierce baron
  Till he came to that fiery rent;
Then his teeth he ground, and with one great bound
  Through its flaming throat he went!

XXVI.

One hellish roar through the heavens tore
  As the rent upclosed again,
And the bog-fiend's lamp went out on the swamp,
  And the black cocks crowed by the fen!

XXVII.

The miller he rose at the break of day,
  And looked for the rock and the moor; —
Nought before him lay but that castle gray
  And his own blithe mill by the Suir.

XXVIII.

Then he crossed the mill weir furiously,
  And quick to the stable he sped;
But a humbled and awe-struck man was he
  When he found his steed stark dead!

XXIX.

Then, sore of body and weary of bone,
  To Darenlawr he passed, —
From its gloomy halls rose the vassals' moan,
  For the baron was gone at last.

XXX.

"And now, O, now, my brave black steed,
  I'll have thee!" the miller said,
As he sought the stable with eager speed;
  But the black steed, too, was dead!

THE SORROWFUL BALLAD OF DOIRÉMORE.

TIME — the end of the sixteenth century. SCENE — a hut in the forest of Connilloe. The old woman who had witnessed the murder of the great Earl Garret relating the event to James Fitz Thomas, the new earl, and to Patrick Fitz Maurice, Lord of Lixnaw.

I.

My curse light heavy on thee,
  Ghastly wood of Doirémore!
May the dews of heaven forsake thee,
  Never spring rain on thee pour;
May the clouds hang ever o'er thee,
  A pall of blight and gloom,
And thy best branch never bear a leaf
  Till the mighty Day of Doom!

II.

Within thy traitor fastness
  Flowed the great Earl Garret's blood,
Crying up to Heaven for vengeance
  On his murderers, gloomy wood!
Never green grass grow within thee,
  Never bird above thee soar,
Never flower thy glades enliven,
  Ghastly wood of Doirémore!

III.

Come hither, James of Desmond,
  Thou warrior true and good,
Bring hither, too, yon steel-clad knight
  Who roams with thee the wood:
I see the brave Fitz Maurice
  In his port and eagle eye; —
Fit comrades are ye to avenge
  Earl Garret's death, or die!

IV.

Come nearer, nearer, gallant knights,
  My voice is weak and low;
I, I am she, the agéd wife,
  Who saw the deed of woe, —

Who saw the traitors stain their swords
  In their mighty chieftain's gore,
In that woful spot, that place of shame,
  The wood of Doirémore ; —

v.

'Twas on the blustering even
  Of a bleak November day,
I knelt outside my cabin door
  With my last son to pray
For his brave sire and brothers three
  Who fell by Desmond's side —
For Ireland's cause and Desmond's weal
  With their harness on they died.

vi.

'Twas then, as from our hearts to Heaven
  Uprose our prayer forlorn,
An agéd man came down the way,
  With garments soiled and torn ;
His form like Ballar's blasted oak,
  His steps all faint and slow,
And his matted beard upon his breast
  Like white Benbarna's snow.

vii.

But though so changed by want and grief,
  So worn with woe he came,
I knew the Desmond by his look
  And by his giant frame ; —
The look — the mighty arm that oft
  So well had swayed the sword,
Where the shivered spears gleamed through the dust,
  And the great guns blazed and roared.

viii.

Ah! he was hunted like the wolf
  Of gray Sliav Luchra's scaurs ;
And wild with hunger's pangs was he,
  And worn with ceaseless wars.
We took him in, we nursed him well
  Through that long night of woe,
Till the early dawn began to light
  Benbarna's caps of snow.

IX.

Alas! that ever rose that dawn
  On Munster's stricken land,
That my last son was but a child,
  And mine a woman's hand;
That Desmond's kerne were far away,
  By Dingle's stormy shore,
When the foe with their wild shout of war
  Burst through our cabin door!

X.

In, in black Dhonal Kelly sprang,
  Base Moriarty came;*
A moment quailed they 'neath the glance
  Of the Desmond's eye of flame;
Then up black Dhonal whirled his sword,
  With many a murder dyed,
And the old earl's arm, gashed long and deep,
  Fell nerveless by his side!

XI.

"Back, traitor knave!" then cried the earl —
  "Put back thy caitiff sword;
False Moriarty, sheathe thy skian,
  For I am Desmond's lord!"
But traitor skian and felon sword
  Cleft his brave heart in twain,
And the great earl fell groaning down
  Never to rise again!

XII.

They bore his body up the height,
  Then lopped his head away,
And left me but the bloody trunk
  To *caoine* the livelong day;
I washed it by the mountain stream,
  Then raised the funeral cry,

---

* Dhonal O'Kelly, once a follower of the Earl of Desmond — at the time of the murder a soldier in the pay of the English government. Dhonal Moriarty, son of Dhonal, petty chief of Corkaguinny, and dependant of the Desmond. These two unexampled villains, after the murder, salted the head of their victim, sent it to London, and were well paid by Elizabeth for their treachery.

That lonely swelled from my son and me
  Through the wild November sky.

XIII.

And thus they slew my gallant lord,
  God's curse upon their name,
Be theirs a life of blackest gloom
  And a memory of shame!
They spiked his hoary head above
  The bridge of London town;
But his body sleeps in holy earth
  Full many a good foot down.

XIV.

My curse light heavy on thee,
  Thou gloomy, gory wood,
And on the two base, felon hearts
  That planned that deed of blood; —
Withered, withered, bare and nerveless
  Be their arms and hands of gore,
Like thy lightning-blighted branches,
  Ghastly wood of Doirémore!

THE JEW'S DAUGHTER.

Part the First.

I.

"Ho! get yourselves in readiness, and come along with me!"
Cried Edmond Dhuv of Falad to his jollie companie;
To his hobbelers,* his daltins,† and his foresters full keen,
As they kicked the rolling foot-ball round and round on Falad Green.

II.

Each brown and freckled forester stood listening at the word;
Each hobbeler refixed his belt, laid hand upon his sword;
Each daltin ceased his capers, and to think of war began,
And cocked his baradh o'er his eye, and thought himself a man.

---

* Hobbeler, a horseman.   † Daltin, a horseboy.

III.

"Come! get yourselves in readiness — a hawking we will go;
But bring your harness on your backs — perchance we'll meet a foe;
We'll rouse the merry greenwoods with the sounds of sylvan war,
And we'll end our jovial hawking at the fair of Inis-Corr.*

IV.

"Come here, my brother Edward, you're a horseman keen and bold,
You'll see chargers there with harness all bedecked with steel and gold,
You'll see weapons, costly armor, many another costly thing; —
By the bright shrine of our Lady, 'twill be pillage for a king!

V.

"There the merchants down from Dublin all their treasures will display,
There the foreigners from Waterford their wares will show that day;
But we'll ease them of their merchandise before the sun goes down,
As sure as red Queen Bess's head is stamped upon a crown.

VI.

"Then dress yourselves in motley sheen — go, some like harpers gay,
And some like jolly gamesters, the rattling dice to play,
And some to spae their fortunes, and amuse them all the day,
Till eve falls down on tower and town, and we begin the fray."

VII.

The horseman bold who stood the gap, the applauding shout he gave,
Then took the foot-ball in his hand and stabbed it with his glaive;
His comrades swore, with yells galore, they'd serve each man the same,
Who, at the fair of Inis-Corr, would dare to spoil their game.

---

* Eniscorthy. A great fair was held here every summer-time, at which the goldsmiths, jewellers, and other merchants from Waterford, &c., exhibited their wares, and to which the inhabitants of the county for many miles round came for business, fun, and sight-seeing.

Part the Second.

I.

With hawk on his wrist, and plume on helmet crown,
All glittering in his armor to the fair my lord is bowne;
And merrily we followed as he rode o'er dale and down,
Till the sultry noon gleamed o'er us, and we reached the joyous town.

II.

I went into a tent with "Three Horsemen" for its sign,
I sat down with my comrade and drank a pint o' wine,
Then roved through the fair, and saw the glittering line
Of booths with treasure laden — all the treasures of the mine.

III.

Heaps of gems and costly pearls glittered gorgeously in one,
Gilded armor in another flashed with splendor like the sun;
Rings of gold for dainty fingers, plumes of foreign birds that shone
Like the glory of the heavens when the day-god's course is run.

IV.

I stood beside a booth — 'twas the brightest in the Fair,
All lit with costly silver and with diamonds sparkling rare;
But more bright than blaze of silver, or the diamond's dazzling sheen,
Sat a fair maid 'mid that treasure all — a lovely summer queen!

V.

I looked upon that maiden, deep into her lustrous eyes,
And thought, "When Butler sacks the Fair, she'll be a glorious prize!"
I looked upon her father, and his baleful glance I knew —
Ah! well I ought to know it — 'twas old Mark the Dublin Jew!

VI.

Ah! well I ought to know it, since that day in Dublin street,
An outlawed man, in pillorie, they bound me hands and feet,
When the jeering crowd drew round me, and old Mark glid down the place,
And glanced at me his baleful eyes, and spat upon my face!

VII.

He sat beside his daughter, that young and lovely thing,
With eyes as black as ebonie and locks like raven's wing —
I plucked my dagger from its sheath, 'neath my cloak I held it bare,
And thought how I might slay the sire, and the bonnie daughter spare!

Part the Third.

I.

The golden sun was sinking, still by the booth I stood
With Gambling Dick, my comrade, and Dermot of the Wood,
And they eyed the costly treasure as the eagle eyes his prey,
Before he swoops on arrowy wings from Mora's mountain gray.

II.

And I — from off that maiden bright my glance I never drew
Until my lord rode through the Fair, and gave the word we knew —
"Ferrah! for bonnie Falad and the blue skies laughing o'er!"
And through the Fair that slogan swelled like the tempest's maddening roar.

III.

And soon there was nor gold nor pearls nor diamonds sparkling gay,
Nor gilded mail, nor sword, nor steed, that was not Butler's prey;
Like questing hawks we reached the town on the noon of that wild day,
And with rare spoil ere twilight fell o'er the hills we swept away!

IV.

But I — what booty did I bring when Butler gave the word?
From nigh that maid, through all the fray, one foot I never stirred;
The booth went down, old Mark the Jew was slain, but not by me,
And from the town his child I bore to Falad's mountains free!

V.

I nursed her in my mountain cot, to soothe her grief full fain,
I tried to raise her drooping heart for many a month in vain,
Till autumn with his withered garb forsook our mountain plain,
And winter died, and springtide suns called forth the flowers again.

VI.

Ah, love, it is a wondrous thing — the love that's fond and true,
It woke my prize from sorrow's trance, brought back the rose's hue
To her young cheeks, and lit her eyes with glorious brilliancie,
And turned her to a Christian maid, and conquered well for me.

VII.

Last May-day at Saint Mary's shrine that stands beside the shore,
Our bridal vows we plighted fond to love for evermore;
And Dublin swords will ne'er win back that well-won prize, I ween,
For she is now my bonnie bride, the flower of Falad Green!

THE LADY OF THE SEA.

I.

It was the fairest maiden in Kerry's broad domains
Her faith did plight to an Irish knight by the shore where Cleena reigns;
She was a Saxon maiden — 'twas to her father's foe —
And ah, that leal but hapless love did cause her bitter woe!

II.

For her dark sire had sworn that both their lives should be
The forfeit of their meeting by Cleena's murmuring sea;
And oft she wept her sister's scorn and her black brother's ire,
And oft the stern reproval of her lordly Saxon sire!

III.

She sits beside the greenwood, the lady Jane, alone,
To think upon her hapless love, and make her mournful moan;
But grief was gone, and joy soon shone, when by her side stood he,
Her banished knight, her Conal Dhuv, the Rover of the Sea!

IV.

" I've come to thee, my lonely love, back from the main sea wave,
An outlawed man, a landless knight, thy hand once more to crave:
The grass grows in my castle hall — but fly, my love, with me,
And thou shalt reign within my bark, the Lady of the Sea!"

V.

Ah! other ears than his have heard the low consent she gave
To fly with him next eventide out on the main sea wave;
A captain of a pirate bark was lurking in the screen,
And he hath sworn to cross their love — a truthful oath I ween.

VI.

It was a golden sunset, a gorgeous eve of May,
And sea and stream beneath the beam in calm resplendence lay,
And all alone where towered the crags like giants huge and
    still,
A bonnie page stood pensively by tall Saint Brandon's Hill.

VII.

A belt all bright with ruddy gold was o'er his shoulders flung,
A dagger and a silver horn from that glittering belt were hung,
And long he gazed upon the deep where sank the golden day,
Till round the rock there sudden peered a small sail far away.

VIII.

He put the horn unto his mouth, he blew a blast full clear,
And to its sound along the waves that light boat danced a-near;
But soon he drew his dagger bright — he drew, alas! in vain,
For strange dark men around him sprang, and forced him o'er
    the main!

IX.

Scarce vanished was the pirate boat the sunset billows o'er,
When from the sea-beat island crags another sought the shore;
It waited long, it moved a-near, it donned a snow-white sail,
But never sound of bugle horn came whispering on the gale.

X.

At length there leapt upon the strand a youth with eagle eye,
With stately form, and kingly face, and bearing bold and high;
There found the page's blood-stained dirk, and cried, "Ah, woe
    is me!
Some ruffian band have slain my love, my Lady of the Sea!"

XI.

He rowed his boat full furiously, he gained his bark ere night,
And told the sad tale to his crew in the sunset's waning light.
They sailed away through twilight gray, through midnight drear
    . and dark,
And when the red morn lit the spray they found the pirate bark.

XII.

An old man stood by Conal Dhuv, his foster-sire was he:
"Now give me speech with yon brave ship; perchance they guiltless be!"
Soon stood he on their deck, and asked for the page so young and fine:
"Nor page, nor maid, we've seen," they said, "upon the salt sea brine!"

XIII.

The old man looked around their deck: he saw the page's horn:
"Now, liars all, mark this!" he cried, with looks of hate and scorn;
Then drew his sword and cleared a path, and leapt into the sea,
And to his chief, despite their shot, he swam right gallantly!

XIV.

O! loud and long the cheer they gave, young Conal's gallant crew,
As on the pirate's deck they sprang for vengeance stern and true;
Revenge is ta'en, the foe they've slain, though fought he fierce and well,
But in that hour of victory their brave young chieftain fell!

XV.

A coronach,* a coronach upon the ocean sheen;
They've brought the lady from the hold, no more a page I ween;
They've placed her by her Conal Dhuv, they raise the funeral wail,
And ever as they vent their grief they fly before the gale.

XVI.

A coronach, a coranach by Cleena's fairy shore;
The lady died by her lover's side ere th' eve came blushing o'er.
A ruin crowns a wave-worn crag; there sweetly slumbers he,
Young Conal Dhuv, with his faithful love, his Lady of the Sea!

* A caoine, or lament.

THE PRINCE OF THE NORTH COUNTRIE.

I.

One evening bright, by Termon's Height,
    Under the shadow of Termon's tree,
I saw a young maid and a handsome knight,
    And fondly courting they seemed to be.

II.

The cloak he wore was of velvet so green,
    Pearled all with gold, hanging down to his knee,
And he said, "Pretty maiden, I'll make you a queen,
    If you are but willing to fly with me!"

III.

"To make me a queen my birth is too mean,
    And you will get ladies of high degree, —
I know not your name, nor the land whence you came,
    And therefore I'm not willing to fly with thee!"

IV.

"My heart and hand shall be at your command,
    And my name and land I will tell unto thee.
Hugh Raynach*'s my name, from Tir Conail I came,
    And the queen of that country my love shall be."

V.

"If I were to go with one I don't know,
    My parents and friends would be angry with me,
When I'd come back again in shame and disdain,
    And therefore I'm not willing to fly with thee."

VI.

"Castles and forths† you shall soon reign o'er,
    Flower-blooming valleys and halls of glee,
And a far-stretching shore, where the breakers roar,
    If you are but willing to fly with me."

VII.

"I love to live in my Munster home,
    Where the sun shines bright, and the winds blow free —

---

* Hugh of the wild, ferny places.   † Forth, a fort, or Dun.

From my loving mother I ne'er could roam,
  And therefore I'm not willing to fly with thee."

VIII.

"In every forth from this to the North
  We'll dance with Queen Una's * companie,
And the cares of this earth shall be drowned in mirth,
  If you are but willing to fly with me!"

IX.

"I fear to dance in the fairy hall,
  And I fear Queen Una's companie;
To Mary, our Mother, I cry and call,
  And, Sir Knight, I'm not willing to fly with thee!"

X.

"I've twenty wounds on forehead and breast,
  Got all in the front for my own countrie;
And again shall the foe see my conquering crest,
  If you are but willing to fly with me!"

XI.

"If you've twenty wounds on forehead and breast,
  And ail for the love of your own countrie,
On that gallant breast I fain would rest,
  And, Sir Knight, I am willing to fly with thee!"

XII.

"I've wandered long under fairy thrall,
  Till a maid's consent would set me free,
But never could find a maid to my mind,
  Till fortune proved kind, and sent you to me.

XIII.

"In the gladsome hall of Donegal
  Will be harping, and dancing, and revelry,
And thou shalt be mistress and queen of all,
  For I am the Prince of that North Countrie!"

* Una, one of the fairy queens of Ireland.

CLONTARF; OR, THE KING'S LAST BATTLE.

A returning Dalcassian soldier, wounded, relates what he has seen of the battle to the warders at the gate of Kincora, who had just before heard rumors of the defeat of the Danes.

I.

Quench ye the hearth-fires blazing —
 The beacon on the hill;
Hush ye your songs victorious,
 And let your harps be still;
For triumph comes too dearly,
 As you shall shortly know,
Stern guardians of Kincora's gate,
Who look upon my deadly strait,
Rent side and riven armor plate,
 And list my tale of woe.

II.

Good Friday morning early,
 All burning for the fray,
Upon the broad plain of Clontarf,
 By Liffey's shore, we lay;
For, with loud boast, King Broder's host
 The power of God defied,
And chose their battle flag to raise
On the Great Day of grief and praise —
The mighty, mournful Day of days,
 On which our Saviour died!

III.

And there came many a pirate
 From the coasts of Normandie,
To aid MacMurrogh * 'gainst the king,
 In his woful treachery;
And many a jarl from Orkney's isles,
 And Iceland, cold and dark,
From Shetland's rocks and moorlands gray,
From Faroe's strands of thundering spray,
From Sweden's shores, and Norroway,
 And the Sounds of Dannemarke.

---

* MacMurrogh, brother-in-law of Brian, and King of Leinster. He brought the Danes to his aid, and was killed in the battle.

IV.

As we looked through the blood-red morning,
  We heard a murmur loud —
Dark glimpses caught we of the foe,
  Beneath the rolling cloud
Of dust, that spread wide, wide o'erhead, —
  A dark and threatening line, —
'Neath whose voluminous, dim wings,
Like far-off lightning glimmerings,
Bosses, and scales, and brazen rings
  Of mail shirts 'gan to shine!

V.

And ever as spread that war-cloud,
  And ever nearer came,
From its dim womb of dusky gloom,
  In myriad points of flame
Glittered the Norland lances,
  Like a world of waving corn;
When o'er Momonia's * broad domains
Of fertile hills and fruitful plains,
Through fleeting clouds and summer rains,
  Shine the slanting beams of morn.

VI.

Then a light wind rose from the westward,
  And blew that cloud away,
And in barbarous pride, extending wide,
  We saw their huge array
Of men and horse, of flags and shields,
  And all their braverie,
Advancing 'neath the morning's glow,
Rank after rank, like waves that flow,
Topped with white spray, when March winds blow
  O'er the wild Ulidian † sea.

VII.

Loud was the roar and tumult,
  As to our arms we sprung,
And weapon clank from rank to rank
  In rattling discord rung;
Till forward rode our aged king,
  In glittering mail bedight —

---

* Momonia, Munster.   † Ulidia, Ulster.

Sternly our ordered lines he scanned,
His white hair by the breezes fanned,
His golden cross in his left hand,
   And his good sword in the right!

VIII.

"Be not dismayed, my children!"
   He said, and held on high
The holy cross. "O. look on this!
   'Twill teach you how to die;
And doubt ye not but the good sword —
   I still can wield it well —
That gleamed triumphantly of yore,
Through Limerick's streets, by Scattery's shore,
By far Macroom, that day of gore,
   When Mahon's murderers fell!

IX.

"Fear not for this day's battle;
   Though Donogh's * far away,
With the third part of our gallant host,
   He's at his work to-day,
Spreading through false MacMurrogh's fields
   The terror of our ire,
From Ross to wild Kilmantan's † lands,
From Barrow bright to Wexford's strands,
Plundering with his victorious bands,
   And burning corn and byre!

X.

"Long have you felt their tyranny,
   The woes that slavery brings;
These raiders fierce, these pirates dark,
   These murderers of your kings:
Then may His Son, who died for us,
   Scatter their strong array,
As, like a fierce, destroying flame,
You rush on them, to wash the shame
Of slavery, that clouds your name,
   In their false blood out to-day!"

XI.

Then loudly rose our war-cry,
   And loud clashed spear and shield,

---

* Donogh, second son of Brian.   † Kilmantan, Wicklow.

As on the Danish lines we sprang,
  Across the echoing field;
Brightly their burnished hauberks gleamed
  In the clear morning's glow,
Till, 'neath the rising war-cloud lost,
In battle's tide together tossed,
Sword clanged on sword, and spears were crossed,
  And the red blood 'gan to flow.

XII.

And ever as to our nostrils
  Rose the maddening steam of gore,
Fierce and more fierce grew the hearts of the brave,
  And louder the conflict's roar.
Breastplate to breastplate, knee to knee,
  Fought the Norsemen, stern and bold,
Till the hot blood flowed like the Shannon tide,
And the dead lay scattered thick and wide,
And many a crest and head of pride
  On the sweltering greensward rolled!

XIII.

But vain their might and their splendor,
  For still we slew and slew —
Some clutched we by the flowing beards,
  And pierced them through and through;
Some stamped we o'er in blood and dust,
  By our conquering spears impaled;
Some slew in many a ghastly row,
Over the wide field to and fro,
Where our arrows darkened the morning glow,
  And our rattling javelins hailed!

XIV.

Soon round our front Prince Murrogh,*
  In a dust-cloud riding came;
His brows were grim as we looked on him,
  And his fierce eyes shone like flame;
With arméd hand before our band
  His mail-clad breast he smote —

---

* Murrogh, eldest son of Brian, and heir to the throne. After pinning the Danish Prince Sitric to the ground with his sword. and wounding him mortally, Murrogh was himself stabbed fatally by Sitric, who, snatching the dagger from Murrogh's belt, pierced his side beneath his jack-piece, or corselet.

With martial ring his harness rang,
As gallantly to earth he sprang,
And his loud voice rose o'er the battle clang
  Like the brazen trumpet's note!

XV.

"Brave Dalgais! Meath is false to us *—
  From the field ignobly gone;
Think not of them, for you must stem
  This battle's tide alone;
Bright laurels now shall deck each brow
  As we trample down the Dane;
Rich be the kite-feast now we'll spread!"
And that mighty, clangorous field of dead
Trembled beneath our sounding tread,
  As we rushed on the foe again!

XVI.

We clove them down full vengefully;
  We smote them hip and thigh,
While the morning sun his course did run
  High up the eastern sky;
Still as he sank, our good blades drank
  Of their blood a crimson tide,
Till Sitric, pierced by Murrogh's glaive,
With Murrogh's dirk the death-wound gave—
Till dead these bravest of the brave
  On the field lay side by side!

XVII.

Then rose on our left a tumult,
  War-cries and trumpets' blare;
So busy were we, we could not see
  Who fought so fiercely there;
But ever it rose, like the sound that flows
  From Burren's storm-beat shore
Of wave-scarred, sea-confronting rock,
O'er the javelin's hiss and the sabre stroke,
O'er the crash of axe, and the horseman's shock,
  And the wide-spread battle's roar!

XVIII.

Down from that point a horseman
  Dashed over friend and foe —

* It is said that Malachi, then only King of Meath, betrayed Brian, his conqueror, and drew his forces off the field after the first onset.

Reckless of life, through the tangled strife,
    As it surgéd to and fro,
Till he gained the spot where the Dalgais * fought,
    With the whirring javelin's speed:
I looked on him, strong Lord of Feale —
His face with battle's rage was pale,
Gory his sword, gory his mail,
    Gory his steaming steed!

XIX.

"Alas! alas! and woe is me!
    Brian the Great is slain!
In Erin's land we ne'er shall see
    A king like him again —
The soldier's friend, the dauntless heart,
    The giver of rich meeds,
Of the herds and flocks of snowy white,
Of the royal feasts of gay delight,
Of the purple robes and the collars bright,
    And the golden-bitted steeds.

XX.

" He fell as falls the bravest:
    Ere his mighty spirit fled,
Broder the Dane, and henchmen twain,
    'Neath his sword lay stark and dead —
His body to Armagh's shrine he gave,
    His blessing to us all;
Then level lance, and poise the targe,
And follow me in one brave charge,
Deep through them to the ocean marge,
    To avenge our great king's fall!"

XXI.

As a herd sweeps, madly snorting,
    Of wild Momonian steeds,
From the hot ravine, with deafening din,
    Through the marsh's crackling reeds;
As the swollen floods rush through the gorge
    Of Lora's blasted pines,
As the loosened rock down Ballar Pass,
As the whirlwind through the autumn grass,

---

  * Dalgais, or Dalcassians, the great military tribe to which Brian belonged.

So, thundering loud, one raging mass,
  We burst through the Danish lines!

XXII.

And they were few of the pirates
  Who found their ships again,
For the ravens croaked, and the gray wolves yelled
  That night, o'er their countless slain;
But they played not weak or tamely
  The battle's dreadful game —
Red is each vanquished sword and hand,
Red with the best blood of our land,
For many a high prince, on that strand
  Sleeps the hero's death of fame!

XXIII.

And many an age in Banba,*
  When our bones lie in the clay,
Shall Banba's sons and daughters
  Tell of that bloody fray;
Many a sigh shall heave the bosom,
  Many a bitter tear shall fall,
For the mighty king who royally
Died with his chieftains brave, to free
Fair Banba's isle, from sea to sea,
  From the Norseman's iron thrall.

BALLAD OF BARNAKILL.†

I.

By Barnakill, full warm and bright
  Shone the sun on the birchen grove,
When out walked the Lady Una,
  Sighing for her own true love.

II.

"My love so fond, my knight so brave,
  Has left me long to mourn —

---

* Banba, one of the ancient names of Ireland.
† In this ballad are incorporated some lines and two or three verses, which seem to be the rude fragments of some ancient ballad of the Pale.

I fear by Barrow's wave he has found a bloody grave,
O never, never more to return!"

III.

In Barnakill, when cold and clear,
  Shone the moon on the birchen grove,
In her chamber sat Lady Una,
  Still sighing for her own true love.

IV.

"He said, this very night and hour,
  He would come back to me!"
The bandogs waked and whined, came a weird sound on the wind,
  And there in the moonlight stood he!

V.

"My knight, my love, where be your bed,
  That the red mould soils your mail?
And where are your serving-men, O darling?" she said,
  "And why look so grimly and pale?"

VI.

"The battle-field's my cold, cold bed;
  There my slumber is sound and deep;
And the worms are my serving-men, O darling," he said,
  "To wait on me while I am asleep!"

VII.

"My lord, my love, I'll warm thee here
  In my bosom all the night,
Till the lively song of Chanticleer
  Brings the gladsome morning light!"

VIII.

"To living man, at break of morn,
  Full blithe that song may be,
But its sound will come like the voice of doom
  To part my love and me!"

IX.

"Thy heart is cold, my husband dear,
  And rayless are thine eyes,

Yet I wish for very love of thee
That the morn would ne'er arise!

x.

"O Chanticleer, so blithe and bold,
Do not crow until 'tis day,
And your comb shall be made of the very beaten gold,
And your wings of the silver so gray!"

xi.

O, cruel, faithless Chanticleer!
Why came thy song so soon?
Alone weeps the Lady Una
In the light of the setting moon!

SIR DONAL.

i.

Afar in the vales of green Houra my heart lingers all the day long,
'Mid the dance of the light-footed maidens, with the music of Ounanar's song,
Where the steep hills uprise all empurpled with the bloom of the bright heather bells,
Looking down on their murmuring daughters, the blue streams of Houra's wild dells.
In the hush of a calm summer sunset, where sing these sweet streams as they flow,
As I sat with the bright-eyed young maidens, they made me their bard long ago;
Then I told of each valley some story, some tale of each blue mountain crest,
But they loved of all wild tales I sang them, the lay of Sir Donal the best;
So I'll sing once again of his deeds in my boyhood's rude measures and rhymes, —
Then, gentles, all list to the story, this lay of th' old chivalric times : —

II.

Nigh the shores of the loud sounding Bregoge, high towering o'er
　　valley and wold,
Walled in by the rough steeps of Houra, there standeth a gray
　　feudal hold;
It is worn by the hard hail of battle, decay is at work on its
　　hill,
Yet it stands like a sorrow-struck Titan, high, lone, and uncon-
　　querable still!
The green ivy clingeth around it, the blast is at play in its
　　halls,
The weasel peeps forth from its crannies, the black raven croaks
　　on its walls;
The peasants who pass in the even will hurry their steps from
　　its height,
For they tell fearful things of its chambers, and call it the Tower
　　of the Sprite! *
But though lone be its halls, they rang merry with wassail and
　　minstrel's wild lay,
When it sheltered the youthful Sir Donal, its lord in the good
　　olden day!

III.

O, he was a brave forest knight! As each morning upsprang
　　from the sea,
He was out by the fay-haunted streams, with his falcons, in
　　woody Fear-muighe;
Or away, far away 'mid the mountains, with stag-hound, and
　　bugle, and steed,
O'ermatching the gray wolf in boldness, outstripping the red
　　deer in speed!
And his heart and his strong hand were bravest; when high rose
　　the trumpet's wild strain,
When the war-fires blazed red on the hill-tops, and the horse-
　　men rode hard on the plain,

---

* Along the northern confines of Fear-Muighe-Feine run the Houra mountains, in the midst of which the Ounanar River rises, and flowing through a magnificent glen — Glean-an-awr, or the Valley of Slaughter — falls into the Oubeg, or Mulla, below Doneraile. The Bregoge, another tributary of the Oubeg, has its source also in these mountains; and near its banks, a few miles north-east of Doneraile, stands the ancient Castle Phooka — the " Tower of the Sprite."

He was dight in his harness, and spurring to the Desmond's
bright banner away,
His mountaineers dashing behind him, with sabres athirst for the
fray!
In bower and in hall he was welcomed, and the dames of the crag
castles brave
Were proud when he smiled on their daughters at eve, by the
Avonmore's wave.

IV.

'Tis noon on the broad plain of Limerick, and down by the calm
Lubach's tide,*
The sunbeams smite hot on the meadows, and burn by the green
forest side;
And brightly they glint from a helmet, and broadly they gleam
from a shield,
Where a knight rideth up by the river, in brave shining panoply
steeled.
Kerne crouch on his path in the greenwood, with pikes ready
raised for a foe;
But they know the high mien of Sir Donal, and stay for some
Saxon the blow;
And the galloglass scowls from his ambush; but he, too, remem-
bers that plume,
And wishing good luck to its owner, strides back to his lair in
the gloom.
But why rides Sir Donal so lonely? and why is his gladness all
fled?
On a field by Lough Gur's lonely water the friend of his bosom
lies dead.

V.

Away, then, away to the mountains, he giveth his war-horse the
rein,
While he longs for the clangor of battle to drown his dejection
again;
The blest Hill of Patrick † slopes green with its tall Guebre tower
on his way,
But the good monk who waits in the abbey in vain looketh out
for his stay;

---

* The crooked or winding river—the stream that runs by Kilmallock.
† *Ard Patrick*—the Height of St. Patrick—is a beautiful green hill at the Limerick side of the Houras. On its summit is an ancient church, the time of whose foundation is unknown. Near the church are the remains of a round tower which fell nearly half a century ago.

And anon the black Rock of the Eagle frowns down on his path
    by Easmore,
Till he crosseth the bright Oun-na-Geeraith, and windeth away
    by its shore.
Now nigh him Suidhe Fein riseth proudly o'er wild Glenisheen's
    ancient wood,
And yawns like a gate in the mountains Red Shard's Gap of
    conflict and blood;
As he turns by the crags of Sliav Fadha, and on by a flat moor-
    land side,
Till he lights nigh a clear fairy fountain at length by the Ou-
    nanar's tide.

VI.

It is on a small shrubby islet, with huge forest cliffs all
    around,
Save where the bright stream from the blue hills outleaps with a
    lone, lulling sound,
And it seems as if step of nought human did e'er on its low
    strand alight;
Yet a lady peers out from the thicket, beyond the good steed of
    the knight!
She is old, yet there's fire in her dark eye, but sorrow is stamped
    on her mien,
And she knows the tall crest of Sir Donal, and comes to his side
    from the screen;
She waveth her hand to him sadly; he follows her steps by the
    flood,
Till they enter a hut of thick brambles, concealed in the dark
    spreading wood,
And there, on a couch of green fern, an old dying chieftain is laid,
And o'er him in wild, bitter weeping, there bendeth a golden-
    haired maid.

VII.

He turns to the knight as he enters, and thus in weak accents of
    woe: —
"Thy sire was my friend, good Sir Donal, in the days of our
    youth long ago;
The Saxon hath slaughtered my people — alas! for that gloom-
    darkened hour,
When he forced me to fly, weak and wounded, thus far from Du
    Aragail's tower! *

---

* Du Aragail, an ancient castle in the parish of Dromagh, near Kanturk,
was one of the principal seats of the O'Keeffes. *Kilnamulloch*, — the

A friend, ah! a friend false and hollow, hath tracked me to Ounanar's grove,
And he swears on his sword to betray me, or have this young
maid for his love;
Black Murrogh, stern lord of Rathgogan! soon, soon from thy
wiles I am free;
But alas, for the wife of my bosom! alas, my fair daughter, for
thee!"
He died on that eve, and was borne away to the age-honored
spires
Of gray Kilnamulloch next noontide, and laid down to rest with
his sires.

VIII.

There was feasting that night in Kilcoleman, and all in their
bright martial gear,
Black Murrogh, and fearless Sir Donal, and many stout champions are there;
And there speaks Sir Donal, uprising, and bends on black Murrogh his gaze: —
"Ho! freres of the feast and the battle, a tale of the wild forest
maze!
As I rode by the Ounanar's water, Du Aragail's chieftain I
found;
He was driven from his home by the Saxon, and said, ere he died
of his wound:
'A friend, ah! a friend false and hollow, has tracked me to Ounanar's side, —
A friend who has sworn to betray me, or have my young daughter his bride!'
By my faith! but the traitor was knightly, to woo her with ardor
so brave;
Now, there lies my gauntlet before him; thus proof of his passion I crave!"

IX.

Then up starts the lord of Rathgogan, and fierce is the flash of
his eye,
As he glares on the dark brows around him with bearing defiant
and high:

" Church of the Curse," — the ancient name of Buttevant. An extremely
wild legend is connected with this name. Rathgogan is the ancient name
of Charleville.

"False knight of a falser young maiden, thy gauntlet I take
 from the board,
And soon on thy crest, in the combat, I'll prove my good name
 with my sword;
For I see but one path to my glory — a path o'er that false heart
 of thine,
But fired by the love of young damsels, but steeled by the red
 gushing wine;
And close be the palisade round us, and short be the distance
 between,
Where a liar's black life-blood shall poison the bloom of the bright
 summer green!"
"And fair shine the sun," quoth Sir Donal, "the clear sunny
 sheen on my blade,
When I close with the lord of Rathgogan, avenging Du Aragail's
 maid!"

X.

Calm eve on the fair hills of Houra, and down by the Mulla's
 green marge,
The red beams are burning in glory from hauberk, and sabre,
 and targe,
And the warriors are circling around it, that smooth listed green
 by the wave,
Where the two mailéd champions are standing with keen axe,
 and target, and glaive!
Flash lances around them in brightness, gleam banners along by
 the shore,
Fierce Condon's from Araglin's water, De Rupe's from the towers
 of Glenore;
And the Barry's wild pennon is waving, and the flags of the chieftains whose towers
Defy from their crag-seats the foeman by Avonmore's gorges and
 bowers;
Yet still the two champions stand moveless, all silent and darkly
 the while,
Like the panoplied statues that frown round the walls of some
 gray abbey aisle!

XI.

But hark! how the wild martial trumpets outroll the fierce signal for strife!
And see how these motionless statues outstart from their postures
 to life!

The mailed heels go round on the greensward, the mailed hands
 ply weapons amain,
Till the targes are battered and cloven, and the axes are shivered in twain!
Wide and deep are the wounds of Sir Donal, but wider the gash
 of his foe,
As their sabres cross, gleaming and clashing — two flames in the
 red sunny glow —
One thrust through the blood-spattered hauberk, one stroke by
 the crest waving o'er,
And the lord of Rathgogan lies fallen, to rise to the combat no
 more;
And there, for a space, swaying, reeling, and faint from his
 wounds' gushing tide,
Sir Donal looks down on the vanquished, then sinketh to earth
 by his side!

XII.

They bear one away to his tower, and they bear one away stark
 and cold;
One ne'er may awake, and one waketh, a bright, blessèd scene
 to behold;
For the maid of Du Aragail bendeth above the dim couch where
 he lies,
With love as her spirit immortal, and joy like the morn in her
 eyes!
O, sweet are the dreams of his slumbers, o'erflowing with fairy
 delight,
But sweeter the dreams of his waking each day in the Tower of
 the Sprite.
And now 'tis the fullness of summer, — a fair breezy morning in
 June, —
And the streams of green Houra are leaping along with a sweet
 gushing tune,
And thy bells, Kilnamulloch, are ringing — no knells of the
 bloom-footed hours,
But the sweet bridal chimes of Sir Donal and the maid of Du
 Aragail's towers!

THE WELL OF THE OMEN.

I.

At morn up green Ard-Patrick the Sunday bell rang clear,
And downward came the peasants with looks of merry cheer,
With many a youth and maiden by pathways green and fair,
To hear the Mass devoutly, and say the Sunday prayer;
And the meadows shone around them where the skylarks gay
    were singing,
And the stream sang songs amid the flowers, and the Sunday
    bell was ringing.

II.

There is a well sunk deeply by old Ard-Patrick's wall;
Within it gaze the peasants to see what may befall:
Who see not there their shadows shall die within the year;
Who see their shadows smiling, O, they'll have merry cheer!
There staid the youths and maidens, where the soft green grass
    was springing,
While the stream sang songs amid the flowers, and the Sunday
    bell was ringing.

III.

Out spoke wild Rickard Hanlon: " We'll see what may befall," —
'Twas to young Bride Mac Donnell, the flower among them
    all, —
" Come see if ours be sorrow or merry wedlock's band!"
Then took the smiling maiden all by the lily hand,
And there they knelt together, their bright looks downward
    flinging,
While the stream sang songs amid the flowers, and the Sunday
    bell was ringing.

IV.

They looked into the water: no shadows shone below:
The dark, dark sign of evil! Ah! could it e'er be so?
Full lightly laughed young Rickard, although his heart was chill,
And with fair Bride Mac Donnell and all went down the hill,
To hear the Mass devoutly, with the soft airs round them wing-
    ing,
While the stream sang songs amid the flowers, and the Sunday
    bell was ringing.

V.

Sweet months, despite the omen, in sunny bliss flew o'er,
And sometimes thinking on it but made them love the more;
But when across Ard-Patrick they sought the lowland plain,
Into the well's dark waters they never looked again;
There never with the maidens they sat, fair garlands stringing,
While the stream sang songs amid the flowers, and the Sunday
    bell was ringing.

. . . . . .

VI.

The storm and flood were over — they left us wild dismay,
The Ford's great rocks were loosened 'neath Easmor's torrent
    gray,
And clasped in death together — O, sad the tale to tell! —
Were found young Bride and Rickard drowned by the Robber's
    Well!
O, false and cruel water, so merry downward flinging,
How canst thou sing amid the flowers while the death bell loud
    is ringing?

VII.

From old Ard-Patrick's ruins loud sounds the piercing keen;
By the sad Well of the Omen a deep, deep grave is seen,
Where side by side together they've laid the early dead,
And the Mass they've chanted o'er them, and the requiem
    prayer is said.
There was woe and bootless sorrow in many a bosom clinging,
But the stream sang songs amid the flowers, while the death bell
    loud was ringing!

MARY LOMBARD.

I.

My iron gyves were rusty grown,
    So long I lay in thrall,
Down in my dungeon dark and lone,
    'Neath Kilnamulla's wall.

II.

My heavy chains at first were bright,
    But rust had dimmed them o'er,

When an angel came in the dead of night,
    And opened my dungeon door!

III.

Was never face so heavenly fair,
    As hers who let me go,
The lady of the sun-bright hair,
    The daughter of my foe.

IV.

She came as if from Heaven to me, —
    In the dead of night to my lair, —
And sped me to my own countrie,
    My Mary Lombard fair!

V.

When next where Kilnamulla rears
    Her towers now black and stern,
'Twas hosting with broad Thomond's spears,
    With Murrogh of the Fern.*

VI.

Through Desmond's plains with vengeful swords
    We carried war and flame,
And woe to all the Norman hordes,
    Where'er great Murrogh came.

VII.

And all around that fated town
    Our warriors thronged full fain,
Till turret-stone and gate went down,
    Before their charge amain.

VIII.

Like a great flood, with flame and blood,
    We rushed through the breach's bound,
While roof and spire were wrapped in fire,
    Lighting the carnage round!

---

* In the year 1367 Murrogh na Ranagh, or Murrogh of the Fern, king of Thomond, issued from his fastnesses and destroyed nearly all the Norman strongholds in Munster; and, after proclaiming himself king of the province, again crossed the Shannon. Buttevant, or, as it was anciently called, Kilnamulla, was burnt and sacked by his forces in this war.

IX.

'Twas the gloom of night on the far-off height,
    'Twas the glare of hell round me,
As I stood before my foeman's door,
    His daughter fair to see.

X.

My foeman lay in the burning way,
    His fond wife dying there,
And my Mary dear, wild with woe and fear,
    I found on the great hall stair.

XI.

I clasped her in my arms, and then
    Quick bore her down the street,
Through the rushing men, to the eastward glen,
    Where I left my war-horse fleet.

XII.

A sudden madness seized my brain,
    And away I dashed, away,
With my trembling love towards my native plain,
    By castle and mountain gray!

XIII.

Kilmallock's wall rose stark and tall
    On our course so wild and fast,
And the Castle of Brugh frowned grimly through
    The darkness as we passed.

XIV.

At the morning's beam fair Shannon's stream
    A long length spread before:
I cared not its length, for love gave me strength,
    And I swam my war-horse o'er!

XV.

Away again, by valley and wild plain,
    Away through each torrent's foam,
Where the mountains rise, with my glorious maiden prize,
    Till I reached my castled home.

XVI.

One clasp I gave to my sad and sorrowing love,
    One word to my mother said,

And back, my loyalty to prove,
  To Murrogh's host I sped.

XVII.

Many a day and many a weary night,
  And many a battle tough and stern,
I saw far, far from my true love bright,
  With Murrogh of the Fern.

XVIII.

And when he wore the crown of each plain and town,
  To my home at length I bore,
But my mother made her moan in its sad hall alone,
  For my Mary was sleeping evermore!

XIX.

O, my bright, tender flower ever sat within her bower,
  Her mother and slain sire to mourn,
Till sorrow quenched love's light, though it flamed up so bright,
  And she died, O, she died ere my return!

XX.

We laid her in her grave, where moans the mournful wave,-
  O, my long-loved and hard-earned bride!
There each day my watch I keep, and forever long to sleep
  By my Mary Lombard's side!

THE ENCHANTED WAR-HORSE.

I.

Doon hangs above the ocean clear,
  A tower of towers the hoarest,
And rears its gray head, stern and drear,
  O'er inland vale and forest,
Deserted all for many a year,
  While the sun shone on the roses;
And the laugh of man shall never more
Resound within its chambers hoar,
While the wave rolls by with thundering force,
  Or at its base reposes;
While the linnet sings on the golden gorse,
  And the sun shines on the roses.

II.

The fairies dance on Doon's gray hill,
    When the midnight moon shines brightly,
But they foot it, too, by its forest rill,
    With many a prank full sprightly;
They foot it round, and dance their fill,
    When the sun shines on the roses,
Within its weird-like, forest maze,
Where the flowers with light are all ablaze,
Where the stream along its glittering course
    Full many a charm discloses,
And the linnet sings on the golden gorse,
    And the sun shines on the roses.

III.

With light clouds over Doon arrayed
    In summer skies serenest,
The fairies danced within a glade,
    The loneliest and the greenest,
Where rolled 'neath shimmering sun and shade,
    A forest brook the sheenest,
And many a laugh rang to the sky,
And many a breeze went warbling by,
Gathering sweet perfumes in its course
    For all these fairy noses,
While the linnet sang on the golden gorse,
    And the sun shone on the roses.

IV.

And there danced Blanaid of the Wood,
    And there danced Maiv the Merry,
And Meergal Ban, the gay and good,
    With red lips like a cherry,
And Banba, of the Snowy Hood,
    With cheeks like rowan berry,
And many another elf-maid bright,
And many a gallant fairy knight;
And loud and sweet the green trees o'er,
    Up rang their laughter ever,
Where frowned that castle, grim and hoar,
    And sang the woodland river.

V.

A heavy tramp sounds through the copse,
    Upon their sport advancing,

And now their gleesome laughter stops,
    And now their merry dancing;
And treading down the lusmore tops,
    A steed comes outward prancing —
A great, gray steed, with glossy back,
With crested mane, of midnight black,
With archéd neck and mighty limb,
    And bold eyes glittering ever;
Where frowned that castle, hoar and grim,
    And sang the woodland river.

VI.

They look into his great, black eyes,
    That gaze on them with wonder,
And now they talk in wild surprise,
    And now they pause and ponder;
At length a gallant elf-knight cries,
    "Out from the castle yonder,
We'll bring the armor that we found
Deep in the chamber under ground,
And with it send this steed of might,
    A master seeking ever!"
Where frowned that castle on the height,
    And sang the woodland river.

VII.

With laugh and shout, away they go,
    And up the steep rocks clamber;
They heed not that the sea below
    Lies stretched like golden amber;
They were too busy, far, I trow,
    For, from the haunted chamber,
They've brought the armor forth, and braced
The saddle bright with silver chased,
The haunch-plates, breast-plate, forehead boss,
    And rein of golden glory,
Where the woodland stream sang through the moss,
    And frowned that castle hoary.

VIII.

They hung beside the saddle sheen
    A helm and lance, of lances
The best that e'er in war was seen,
    Or heard of in romances;

And then they capered round the green,
   And then, with merry glances,
Upon the steed strange spells they laid,
And, dancing round him in the glade,
Said, "Go thou forth, thou gallant horse,
   And find what fate discloses;
While the linnet sings on the golden gorse,
   And the sun shines on the roses!"

IX.

The steed sped down the forest straight,
   Came by a lordly castle,
Where all were, noon and night, elate
   With wine and roaring wassail;
A jolly knight came from the gate,
   Bedecked with plume and tassel,
And sprang upon his back, but there
Soon went he flying through the air,
And down on earth, with broken bones,
   In grief and woe to languish,
And found that sermons lie in stones *
   Of bitter pain and anguish!

X.

Next, by a castle prim and bare,
   That great steed's hoofs came clanging
Where rose the hypocritic prayer,
   And hymns with nasal twanging;
Its lord came down the castle stair,
   His godly bosom banging,
And sprang upon the horse's back,
But soon went prone into the black
Deep moat, where oft his holy steel
   Strewed poor malignants' corses,
And found his hypocritic zeal
   Was most unfit for horses!

XI.

By tower and street, the country round,
   By many a hall of pleasure,
He sped, but every rider found
   Wanting in some sad measure;

---

* "Sermons in stones, and good in everything."—*Shakespeare.*

THE ENCHANTED WAR HORSE. — Page 176.

One was a miser, whom he drowned,
    With all his bags of treasure;
One was a knave, that sold his cause,
And one a bloody tyrant was;
Another was a false, mean hack,
    Of false men's views the ranter;
But all, as each one gained his back,
    He hurled to earth instanter!

XII.

At length by lone Cragbarna's side,
    A region Ossianic,
Where none but outlaws dared abide,
    'Mid horrid rocks volcanic:
As gayly on the great steed hied,
    Down from a crag Titanic,
A young knight sprang — 'twas John the Brown,
The banished lord of Barnaloun —
Upon his back, and stuck thereon
    As firm as any Persian
That ever rode beneath the sun,
    In battle or diversion!

XIII.

The great steed plunged and reared amain,
    To cause some dire disaster,
And 'cross the crags did wildly strain,
    And down the steep gorge faster;
But every ruse he tried in vain,
    For faith he'd found his master;
He'd found a knight full brave and true,
Whose heart no foul dishonor knew,
Whose sword was drawn to sweep each curse
    Away that wrong imposes,
While the linnet sang on the golden gorse,
    And the sun shone on the roses!

XIV.

And gayly cried Sir John the Brown,
    As like a lamb, or tamer,
The steed at last trode mildly down:
    "O, now I'm free to name her, —
My ladye love of bright renown, —
    To worship and to claim her

To be my bride, for with this fine
Brave steed I'll win what should be mine,
My native hall, my broad domain,
   That every charm discloses,
While the linnet sings his merry strain,
   And the sun shines on the roses!"

XV.

Then rode he round full furiously,
   And called up friend and vassal,
And drew them on the enemy
   That held his native castle;
And there all were eternally
   Immersed in wine and wassail,
And knew not, heard not, till they saw
Sir John the Brown his good sword draw
Before the gate, on that great horse,
   To slit their traitorous noses,
While the linnet sang on the golden gorse,
   And the sun shone on the roses!

XVI.

Sir John the Brown his home hath won,
   And thrashed the foemen fairly:
His ladye love of bright renown
   He made his bride full early;
Brave lord and lady both are gone;
   Their castle looms all drearly,
A ruin stark and lone, but still
The peasant hears upon its hill
The tramp of that great wizard horse,
   And will, as evening closes,
While the linnet sings on the golden gorse,
   And the sun shines on the roses!

SARSFIELD'S RIDE; OR, THE AMBUSH OF SLIAV BLOOM.

The generally received historical account of the exploit related in the following ballad differs in several points from the traditionary version. And yet the latter should not be despised, for the peasantry of Limerick and Tipperary have stories of the incident, all agreeing with regard to the ride of Galloping O'Hogan. The songs also of the time preserve the name of that celebrated horseman and outlaw in connection with the affair. For instance, after mentioning the way in which the outlawed inhabitants of the surrounding country hung on the track of King William's convoy, one of these old songs represents O'Hogan as saying, —

"We marched with bold Lord Lucan before the break of day,
Until we came to Kinmagoun where the artillery lay;
Then God He cleared the firmament, the moon and stars gave light,
And for the Battle of the Boyne we had revenge that night!"

It may be also stated that in every song and story of the time, King William is always nicknamed "Dutch Bill," a cognomen by which he is even to the present day remembered in many parts of Munster.

Part the First.

I.

Come up to the hill, Johnnie Moran, and the de'il's in the sight
 you will see;
The men of Dutch Bill in the lowlands are marching o'er valley
 and lea;
Brave cannon they bring for their warfare, good powder and
 bullets *go leor*,
To batter the gray walls of Limerick adown by the deep Shannon shore!

II.

They girded their corselets and sabres that morning so glorious
 and still,
They leapt like good men to their saddles, and took the lone
 path to the hill;
And deftly they handled their bridles as they rode through each
 green, fairy coom,
Each woodland, and broad, rocky valley, till they came to the
 crest of Sliav Bloom!

III.

"Look down to the east, Johnnie Moran, where the wings of
 the morning are spread;
Each basnet you see in the sunlight it gleams on an enemy's
 head;

Look down on their long line of baggage, their huge guns of iron
  and brass,
That, as sure as my name is O'Hogan, will ne'er to the Wil-
  liamites pass!

IV.

"Spur, then, to the green shore of Brosna — see Ned of the
  Hills on your way —
Have all the brave boys at the muster by Brosna at close of the
  day;
I'll ride off for Sarsfield to Limerick, and tell what I've seen from
  the hill —
If Sarsfield won't capture their cannon, by the Cross of Kildare
  but we will!"

V.

Away to the north went young Johnnie, like an arbalist bolt in
  his speed,
Away to the west brave O'Hogan gives bridle and spur to his
  steed;
Through the fierce highland torrent he dashes, through copse
  and down greenwood full fain.
Till he biddeth farewell to the mountains, and sweeps o'er the flat
  lowland plain!

VI.

You'd search from the gray Rock of Cashel, each side to the blue
  ocean's rim,
Through green dale, and hamlet, and city, but you'd ne'er find
  a horseman like him;
With his foot as if grown to the stirrup, his knee with its rooted
  hold ta'en,
With his seat in the saddle so graceful, and his sure hand so
  light on the rein!

VII.

As the cloud-shadow skims o'er the meadows, when the fleet-
  wingéd summer winds blow,
By war-wasted castle and village, and streamlet and crag doth
  he go;
The foam-flakes drop quick from his charger, yet never a bridle
  draws he,
Till he baits in the hot, blazing noontide, by the cool fairy well
  of Lisbui!

VIII.

He rubbed down his charger full fondly, the dry grass he heaped
    for its food,
He ate of the green cress and shamrock, and drank of the sweet
    crystal flood;
He's up in his saddle, and flying o'er wood-track and broad heath
    once more,
Till the sand 'neath the hoofs of his charger is crunched by the
    wide Shannon's shore!

IX.

For never a ford did he linger, but swam his good charger
    across,—
It clomb the steep bank like a wolf-dog — then dashed over moor-
    land and moss;
The shepherds who looked from the highland, they crossed them-
    selves thrice as he passed,
And they said 'twas a sprite from Crag Acivil * went by on the
    wings of the blast!

Part the Second.

I.

Dutch Bill sent a summons to Limerick — a summons to open
    their gate,
Their fortress and stores to surrender, else the pike and the gun
    were their fate.
Brave Sarsfield he answered the summons: "Though all holy
    Ireland in flames
Blazed up to the skies to consume us, we'll hold the good town
    for King James!"

II.

Dutch Bill, when he listed the answer, he stamped, and he
    vowed, and he swore
That he'd bury the town, ere he'd leave it, in grim fiery ruin and
    gore;
From black Ireton's Fort with his cannon he hammered it well
    all the day,
And he wished for his huge guns to back him, that were yet o'er
    the hills far away.

---

* Acivil, the Fairy Queen of North Desmond.

III.

The soft curfew bell from Saint Mary's tolled out in the calm
    sunset air,
And Sarsfield stood high on the rampart, and looked o'er the
    green fields of Clare;
And anon from the copses of Cratloe a flash to his keen eyes
    there came;
'Twas the spike of O'Hogan's bright basnet glistening forth in
    the red sunset flame!.

IV.

Then down came the galloping horseman, with the speed of a
    culverin ball,
And he reined up his foam-flecked charger, with a gallant gam-
    bade by the wall;
And his keen eye searched tower, fosse, and rampart — they lay
    all securely and still, —
And then to the bold lord of Lucan he told what he'd seen from
    the hill!

V.

The good steed he rests in the stable, the bold rider feasts at the
    board,
But the gay, laughing revel once ended, he'll soon have a feast
    for his sword;
And now he looks out at the window, where the moonbeams
    flash pale on the square,
For Sarsfield, full dight in his harness, with five hundred bold
    troopers is there!

VI.

He's mounted his steed in the moonlight, and away from the
    North Gate they go,
Where the woods cast their black spectral shadows, and the
    streams with their lone voices flow;
The peasants awoke from their slumbers, and prayed as they
    swept through the glen,
For they thought 'twas the great Garodh Earla,* that thundered
    adown with his men!

---

* Garret, the great Earl of Desmond, who is still believed by the peasantry to arise from his enchanted cave beside Lough Gur in Limerick, on the Saint John's night of every seventh year, and sweep, at the head of his mail-clad barons and knights, through the surrounding country.

VII.

The gray, ghastly midnight was round them, the banks they
    were rocky and steep;
The hills with one sullen roar echoed, for the huge stream was
    angry and deep;
But the bold lord of Lucan he cared not, he asked for no light
    save the moon's,
And he's forded the broad, lordly Shannon with his galloping
    guide and dragoons!

VIII.

The star of the morning out glimmered as fast by Liscarley they
    rode,
As they swept round the base of Comailte the sun on their
    bright helmets glowed.
Now the steeds in a valley are grazing, and the horsemen crouch
    down in the broom,
And Sarsfield peers out like an eagle on the low-lying plains
    from Sliav Bloom.

Part the Third.

I.

O'Hogan is down in the valleys, a watch on the track of the foe;
Johnnie Moran from Brosna is marching, that his men be in
    time for a blow;
All day, from the bright blooming heather, the tall lord of Lucan
    looks down
On the roads where the train of Dutch Billy on its slow march
    of danger is bowne.

II.

The red sunset died in the heavens; night fell over mountain
    and shore;
The moon shed her light on the valleys, and the stars glimmered
    brightly once more;
Then Sarsfield sprang up from the heather, for a horse tramp
    he heard on the waste, —
'Twas O'Hogan, the black mountain sweeping, like a spectre of
    night in his haste!

III.

"Lord Lucan, they've camped in the forest that skirts Bally-
    neety's gray tower;
I've found out the path to fall on them, and slay in the dread
    midnight hour;

They have powder, pontoons, and great cannons — Dhar Dhia,
    but those great guns are bright!
They have treasure *go léor* for the taking, and their watchword
    is 'Sarsfield' to-night!"

IV.

The star of the midnight was shining when the gallant dragoons
    got the word;
Each sprang with one bound to his saddle, and looked to his pis-
    tols and sword;
And away down Comailte's deep valleys the guide and bold
    Sarsfield are gone,
While the long stream of helmets behind them in the cold
    moonlight glimmered and shone.

V.

They staid not for loud brawling river, they looked not for
    togher or path,
They tore up the long street of Cullen with the speed of the
    storm in its wrath;
When on old Ballyneety they thundered, the sentinel's challenge
    rang clear —
"Ho! Sarsfield's the word," cried Lord Lucan, "and you'll
    soon find that Sarsfield is here!"

VI.

He clove through the sentinel's basnet, he rushed by the side of
    the glen,
And down on the enemy's convoy, where they stood to their can-
    nons like men;
His troopers, with pistol and sabre, through the camp like a
    whirlwind they tore,
With a crash and a loud-ringing war-cry, and a plashing and
    stamping in gore!

VII.

The red-coated convoy they've sabred, Dutch Bill's mighty guns
    they have ta'en,
And they laugh as they look on their capture, for they'll ne'er
    see such wonders again;
Those guns, with one loud-roaring volley, might batter a strong
    mountain down —
Wirristhru for its gallant defenders, if they e'er came to Limer-
    ick town!

VIII.

They filled them and rammed them with powder, they turned
 down their mouths on the clay,
The dry casks they piled all around them, the baggage above
 did they lay;
A mine train they laid to the powder, afar to the greenwood out
 thrown, —
"Now give it the match!" cried Lord Lucan, "and an earthquake we'll have of our own!"

IX.

O'Hogan the quick fuse he lighted — it whizzed — then a flash,
 and a glare
Of broad blinding brightness infernal burst out in the calm midnight air;
A hoarse crash of thunder volcanic roared up to the bright stars
 on high,
And the splinters of guns and of baggage showered flaming
 around through the sky!

X.

The firm earth it rocked and it trembled, the camp showed its
 red pools of gore,
And old Ballyneety's gray castle came down with a crash and a
 roar; *
The fierce sound o'er highland and lowland rolled on like the
 dread earthquake's tramp,
And it wakened Dutch Bill from his slumbers and gay dreams
 that night in his camp!

XI.

Lord Lucan dashed back o'er the Shannon ere the bright star of
 morning arose,
With his men through the North Gate he clattered, unhurt and
 unseen by his foes:
Johnnie Moran rushed down from Comailte — not a foe was
 alive for his blade,
But his men searched the black gory ruin, and the de'il's in the
 spoil that they made!

---

* The explosion split the old castle of Ballyneety, shivering one half in
fragments to the ground.

THE DYING WARRIOR.

I.

Brightly on the crest of Darra
Fell the day's last golden arrow,
  And the moon smiled radiantly,
  Calmly, lonely, mournfully,
On a leafy dell and narrow,
  Opening out towards green Fear-muighe.

II.

Low young Dermuid there is lying,
Listening to the foemen flying,
  For the close and bloody fray
  In the Red Gap raged all day.
Ah! that hapless youth is dying
  In the pale moon's mournful ray.

III.

There his rushing comrades left him,
When the struggling foemen cleft him—
  Cleft him through his helmet bright,
  As he swept upon their flight—
Ah! that fatal blow has reft him
  Of the joy he hoped that night.

IV.

For beside his native forest,
In the abbey old and hoarest,
  Wife he was that night to call
  The fairest maid in cot or hall;
And that thought afflicts him sorest,
  On the brink of bliss to fall!

V.

"Death," he cries, "doth point his arrow—
Make my bed so cold and narrow,
  Where the sunlight falls in gold
  On Glenroe's bright stream and wold,
'Neath the haunted Peak of Darra,
  In the abbey gray and old!

VI.

"Thou, thy bridal dress adorning,
When the war-scout gave the warning, —
  When thou find'st thy Dermuid slain,
  Kiss his cold brow once again, —
Thou wilt have at dawn of morning
  Face of woe and heart of pain!"

VII.

In that dell, like fairies glancing,
Wildly the young fawns are dancing,
  And the limping hares out-tread,
  All their daylight terrors fled;
But none scares their bold advancing,
  For the warrior youth is dead!

VIII.

In that dell, at morn's first peeping,
Mad with sorrow, worn with weeping,
  Mary bends the dead above;
  He died in war — she soon for love;
And side by side the twain are sleeping,
  'Neath the abbey's haunted grove!

PETER CROWLEY; OR, THE WORTH OF A DEAD MAN.

"I have heard some great warriors say, that in all their services, which they had seen abroad in foreign countries, they never saw a more comely man than an Irishman, or that cometh more bravely in his charge." — *Spenser's View of Ireland.*

I.

God bless you, Peter Crowley,
  For the holy work you wrought;
God rest your soul in heaven's bright bowers
  For the lesson you have taught;
Fair Freedom, to the end of time,
  Shall fondly point to it,
That LESSON in your heart's best blood
  For trampled nations writ! —
That in their struggles to be free
  And gain their rights again,

One True Man, dead for liberty,
   Is worth a thousand men!

II.

The beacon fires enkindled
   By Emmet and by Tone,
Bright have they glowed on Freedom's road
   To lead our footsteps on, —
O Martyr, on that dangerous way
   A flame gleams now from thine
As high and clear, but still more near
   To Freedom's holy shrine,
Where graved above the gate we see,
   By Freedom's trenchant pen,
"One True Man, dead for liberty,
   Is worth a thousand men!"

III.

'Twas down in wild Kilcluny,
   At the dawning of the day,
The red-coats circled round the wood
   To catch their gallant prey,
Young Kelly, and the brave McClure,
   And Crowley, stout and bold, —
He slept as sleeps the lion king
   In his rocky mountain hold, —
Perchance he dreamt that vision free
   Within his woody den —
One True Man, dead for liberty,
   Is worth a thousand men!

IV.

Hark! 'twas the foeman's summons
   That on their slumbers broke,
And answering quick that hostile call
   The outlaws' rifles spoke,
Till captured Kelly and McClure
   Saw fearless Crowley stand,
With a bullet wound on his forehead fair,
   And a broken trigger hand!
And they heard him shout full lustily
   Adown that woody glen,
"One True Man, dead for liberty,
   Is worth a thousand men!"

BALLADS.

V.

A brave dash at the foemen,
    And through their frightened ranks,
And down the shaggy mountain side
    To Oun-na-Geerait's * banks, —
With pistol in his good left hand,
    And the red blood on his right;
There turned he with a dauntless heart
    To fight his last brave fight!
And well he knew, that soldier free,
    That Irish hero then,
One True Man, dead for liberty,
    Is worth a thousand men!

VI.

A volley from the red-coats,
    From him one pistol ball
That brought a foeman to the earth —
    And then 'twas silent all.
He tottered for a moment's space,
    Then fell into the tide
That round the hero foamed and whirled,
    With his heart's blood crimsoned wide.
"God's mercy on my soul!" cried he;
    And gasped he forth again,
"One True Man, dead for liberty,
    Is worth a thousand men!"

VII.

To the town upon the Funcheon †
    The hero's corse they bore,
And never such a sight was seen
    By Funcheon's winding shore;
The women gathered all around
    To join his sister's wail,
And the men with stern eyes sadly bent
    On the Martyr's corse so pale.
They felt that lesson of the free,
    Their proud hearts warming then,

---

* The *Stream of the Champion*, the old name of Kilcluny River, never more appropriate than now, after Crowley's death.
† Mitchelstown.

　　　　One True Man, dead for liberty,
　　　　　Is worth a thousand men!

　　　　　　　　VIII.

　　From the town upon the Funcheon
　　　On stout shoulders went his bier,
　　With laurels decked, and the fairest flowers
　　　Of the spring-time of the year;
　　Unto the ancient churchyard,
　　　Where lay his sires full low,
　　The mighty concourse wound along
　　　With mournful pace and slow, —
　　His country's tyrants shook to see
　　　The lesson taught them then,
　　One True Man, dead for liberty,
　　　Is worth a thousand men!

　　　　　　　　IX.

　　In his red grave lies our Martyr,
　　　With his glorious laurel crown,
　　In the pride of youth, and manliness,
　　　And unforgot renown.
　　And could you see the looks I saw
　　　Around his clay-cold bed,
　　With swelling breast you'd proudly say,
　　　"Old Ireland is not dead!"
　　With clinchéd hands you'd cry with me
　　　In voice of thunder then,
　　"One True Man, dead for liberty,
　　　Is worth a thousand men!"

　　　　　　　　X.

　　We'll build him up a monument
　　　With Emmet, Sheares, and Tone,
　　And with all our country's martyrs,
　　　When Ireland is our own;
　　We'll build it on some old green hill,
　　　Where the Irish winds shall blow
　　Their histories round admiring earth
　　　To the nations in their woe;
　　And with our swords the legend free
　　　We'll carve upon it then —
　　"One True Man, dead for liberty,
　　　Is worth a thousand men!"

THE SPALPEEN.

I.

When comes across the mountains the winter of the year,
With merry jokes and laughter the spalpeens gay are here;
I love the first of autumn, but more sweet hallowe'en,
For it brings back my Johnnie, my rattling, gay Spalpeen.*

II.

His hair is like the raven that flies above Knockrue,
And stately is his form; his heart is kind and true, —
O, he's kindest, best, and bravest of all I've ever seen,
And until death I'll love him, my rattling, gay Spalpeen!

III.

There's something in my Johnnie that pains my secret mind;
He's statelier than his comrades, his manners more refined;
I fear he's some rich rover, fit husband for a queen;
And yet I can't but love him, my rattling, gay Spalpeen!

IV.

The first night that I met him, I found him fond and leal;
I took him for my partner, and tripped a mazy reel, —
It was the "New-mown Meadows" and then the light Moneen †
We danced — until I loved him, my rattling, gay Spalpeen!

V.

The leaves of dying autumn by chilling winds were tost,
The corn was stacked securely, the hills were gray with frost,
When by the turf-fire blazing, were met at Hallowe'en
The farmers' sons and daughters, and many a gay Spalpeen.

VI.

The old man in the corner sat in his elbow-chair;
At all his jokes the laughter rose free from grief or care;

---

* A wandering laboring man. The circumstance related in the ballad happened in the county Limerick. It was not at all an uncommon thing for wild young sons of the higher class of farmers to go off on their adventures, in the palmy days of potato-digging, with the spalpeens; and many a wild prank they played in their peregrinations.

† *Moneen*, a kind of jig — the wildest, most athletic, and **spirited of all** the Irish dances.

The *Bean-a-thee** sat smiling, and said she ne'er had seen
A dancer like young Johnnie, the rattling, gay Spalpeen.

VII.

They've laughed round many an apple, they've burned the nuts in glee,
"And some will soon get married, and some will sail the sea!"
They've danced for th' ancient piper, they've joked and sung between,
And told their wondrous legends, each rattling, gay Spalpeen!

VIII.

Then Johnnie took the daughter, the eldest, by the hand, —
It was his own Bawn Ellen, the fairest in the land;
He led her towards her parents, with fond and manly mien,
While all stood hushed around him, the rattling, gay Spalpeen!

IX.

"I've come across the mountains far, far from home, to find
A wife above all others, both simple, fair, and kind;
She's standing now beside me, the loveliest I have seen!"
Up spoke, with manly bearing, the rattling, gay Spalpeen.

X.

"I know she's good and constant — for me would lose her life;
I have a home to give her, and ask her for my wife!"
He's doffed the old gray garment — before them all is seen
The lord of many a town-land, that rattling, gay Spalpeen!

XI.

Old Father James came early, and blessed the loving pair;
She's off with her dear bridegroom towards Kerry's hills so fair;
O'er many a fertile valley she reigns just like a queen,
Loving, and loved by, Johnnie, her rattling, gay Spalpeen!

* *Bean-a-thee*, the woman of the house.

THE SACK OF DUNBUI.*
A. D. 1602.

I.

They who fell in manhood's pride,
They who nobly fighting died,
  Fade their memories never, never;
    Theirs shall be the deathless name,
  Shining brighter, grander ever
    Up the diamond crags of fame!
Time these glorious names shall lift
Up from sun-bright clift to clift,
    Upward! to eternity!
    The godlike men of brave Dunbui!

II.

Glorious men and godlike men,
Well they stemmed the Saxon then,
  When he came with all his powers,
    Over river, plain, and sea,
  'Gainst the tall and bristling towers
    Of the Spartan-manned Dunbui —
Traitor Gael and Saxon churl,
Burning in their wrath to hurl
    Ruin on the bold and free
    Warrior men of brave Dunbui.

III.

Thomond with his traitors came,
Carew breathing blood and flame;
  First he sent his message in
    To the Southern gunsmen three,

---

* The Castle of Dunboy, or Dunbui, is situated on the shore of Bantry Bay, opposite Beare Island. It belonged to O'Sullivan Beare, and was the great military depot of, and the last fortress that held out for, the Catholics of the South in the year 1602. It was defended, almost successfully, in the summer of that year, by one hundred and forty-six men, under their commander, Captain Richard Mac Geoghegan, against an army of nearly six thousand English, commanded by President Carew. Every man of the one hundred and forty-six, together with their heroic commander, fell in its defence, except nine or ten who laid down their arms on condition of their getting quarter, *and were hanged a few minutes afterwards.* — Vide *Mac Geoghegan,* and *Annals of the Four Masters,* &c.

Message black as Hell and sin,
  Sin and Satan e'er could be;
Would they trusting freres betray,
Would they this for golden pay?
    Demon, no! foul treachery
    Never dwelt in strong Dunbui.

IV.

Onward then that sunny June,
On they came in the fiery noon,
  On where frowned the stubborn keep,
  O'er the rock-subduing flood,
  First they took Beare's island steep,
  And drenched its crags in helpless blood.
Nought could save — child's, woman's tears —
Curse upon their cruel spears!
    O, that sight was Hell to see,
    By thy bristling walls, Dunbui!

V.

Nearer yet they crowd and come,
With taunting and yelling, and thundering drum,
  With taunting and yelling the hold they environ,
  And swear that its towers and defenders must fall,
  While the cannon are set, and their death-hail of iron
  Crash wildly on bastion, and turret, and wall;
And the ramparts are torn from their base to their brow —
Ho! will they not yield to the murderers now?
    No! its huge towers shall float over Cleena's bright sea,
    Ere the Gael prove a craven in lonely Dunbui.

VI.

Like the fierce god of battle Mac Geoghegan goes
From rampart to wall, in the face of his foes;
  Now his voice rises high o'er the cannons' fierce din,
  Whilst the taunt of the Saxon is loud as before,
  But a yell thunders up from his warriors within,
  And they dash through the gateway, down, down to the shore.
With their chief rushing on, like a storm in its wrath,
They sweep the cowed Saxon to death in their path;
    Ah! dearly he'll purchase the fall of the free,
    Of the lion-souled warriors of lonely Dunbui!

VII.

Leaving terror behind them, and death in their train,
Now they stand on their walls 'mid the dying and slain,
   And the night is around them — the battle is still —
     That lone summer midnight, ah! short is its reign;
For the morn springeth upward, and valley and hill
     Fling back the fierce echoes of conflict again.
And see how the foe rushes up to the breach,
Towards the green, waving banner he yet may not reach,
     For look how the Gael flings him back to the sea,
     From the blood-reeking ramparts of lonely Dunbui!

VIII.

Night cometh again, and the white stars look down
From the hold to the beach, where the batteries frown;
   Night cometh again, but affrighted she flies,
     Like a black Indian queen, from the fierce panther's roar,
And morning leaps up in the wide-spreading skies,
     To its welcome of thunder and flame evermore;
For the guns of the Saxon crash fearfully there,
Till the walls, and the towers, and the ramparts are bare,
     And the foe make their last mighty swoop on the free,
     The brave-hearted warriors of lonely Dunbui!

IX.

Within the red breach see Mac Geoghegan stand,
With the blood of the foe on his arm and his brand;
   And he turns to his warriors, and "Fight we," says he,
     "For country, for freedom, religion, and all:
Better sink into death, and forever be free,
     Than yield to the false Saxon's mercy and thrall!"
And they answer, with brandish of sparth and of glaive,
"Let them come: we will give them a welcome and grave;
     Let them come; from their swords could we flinch,
       could we flee,
     When we fight for our country, our God, and Dunbui?"

X.

They came, and the Gael met their merciless shock —
Flung them backward like spray from the lone Skellig rock;
   But they rally, as wolves springing up to the death
     Of their brother of famine, the bear of the snow —
He hurls them adown to the ice-fields beneath,
     Rushing back to his dark norland cave from the foe; —

So up to the breaches they savagely bound,
Thousands still thronging beneath and around,
   Till the firm Gael is driven — till the brave Gael
     must flee
   In, into the chambers of lonely Dunbui!

XI.

In chamber, in cellar, on stairway and tower,
Evermore they resisted the false Saxon's power;
   Through the noon, through the eve, and the darkness of
     night,
   The clangor of battle rolls fearfully there,
Till the morning leaps upward in glory and light;
   Then, where are the true-hearted warriors of Beare?
They have found them a refuge from torment and chain:
They have died with their chief, save the few who remain,
   And that few, O fair Heaven! on the high gallows tree
   They swing by the ruins of lonely Dunbui!

XII.

Long, long in the hearts of the brave and the free,
Live the warriors who died in the lonely Dunbui —
   Down Time's silent river their fair names shall go,
   A light to our race towards the long-coming day;
   Till the billows of time shall be checked in their flow,
   Can we find names so sweet for remembrance as they?
And we will hold their memories forever and aye,
A halo, a glory that ne'er shall decay;
   We'll set them as stars o'er Eternity's sea,
   The bright names of the warriors who fell at Dunbui!

CROSSING THE BLACKWATER.
A. D. 1603.

I.

WE stood so steady,
  All under fire,
We stood so steady,
Our long spears ready
  To vent our ire —

To dash on the Saxon,
Our mortal foe,
And lay him low
  In the bloody mire!

II.

'Twas by Blackwater,
  When snows were white,
'Twas by Blackwater,
Our foes for the slaughter
  Stood full in sight;
But we were ready
With our long spears,
And we had no fears
  But we'd win the fight.

III.

Their bullets came whistling
  Upon our rank,
Their bullets came whistling,
Their spears were bristling
  On th' other bank:
Yet we stood steady,
And each good blade,
Ere the morn did fade,
  At their life-blood drank.

IV.

"Hurrah! for Freedom!"
  Came from our van,
"Hurrah! for Freedom!
Our swords — we'll feed 'em
  As best we can —
With vengeance we'll feed 'em!"
Then down we crashed,
Through the wild ford dashed,
  And the fray began!

V.

Horses to horses,
  And man to man —
O'er dying horses,
And blood and corses,
  O'Sullivan,

Our general, thundered,
And we were not slack
To slay at his back
   Till the flight began.

VI.

O, how we scattered
   The foemen then —
Slaughtered and scattered,
And chased and shattered,
   By shore and glen; —
To the wall of Moyallo,
Few fled that day, —
Will they bar our way
   When we come again?

VII.

Our dead freres we buried, —
   They were but few, —
Our dead freres we buried
Where the dark waves hurried,
   And flashed and flew :
O! sweet be their slumber
Who thus have died
In the battle's tide,
   Inisfail, for you!

THE BATTLE OF THE RAVEN'S GLEN.*
A. D. 1603.

I.

From his turrets that look to the silver Kinmera,
From the halls of his splendor by Bantry and Bearra,
With his band of brave warriors, O'Sullivan bore him,
Till the mountains of Limerick rose darkly before him;

---

* O'Sullivan, Prince of Bearre and Bantry, during his flight to Tyrone, in the winter of 1603, was attacked by the De Barrys of Buttevant, with the septs of the surrounding baronies, in the mountains of Ballagh Abhra, now Ballyhoura. He defeated them with great slaughter, as he did all that came in his way during that memorable flight, and encamped for three days and nights in the scene of the battle, the Raven's Glen, near the old church of Ardpatrick.

There he camped 'mid the rocks, where the deep pools were paven
By the white stars of night, in the Glen of the Raven!

II.

In that glen was no sound, save the murmur of fountains,
And the moonbeams were silvering the thunder-split mountains,
When a horse-tramp rang wildly from Ounanar's water,
Rolling up from the gorge of the dark Vale of Slaughter,
And the rider ne'er reined till his long plume was waven
By the breezes that sighed through the Glen of the Raven!

III.

Up sprang to their saddles the chieftains around him,
And they asked where the foe 'mid the forests had found him;
For they knew he had passed through the battle's fierce labor,
From the foam o'er his steed and the blood on his sabre,
While the rocks with the hoofs of their chargers were graven,
As they pranced into lines 'mid the Glen of the Raven!

IV.

'Twas the scout of lone Bregog: he'd heard in the gloaming
Fierce yells o'er that wild torrent's thunder and foaming,
Then a dash, and a roar, and a rushing did follow,
For the foe burst around him from moorland and hollow;
But a road to his chief through their ranks he had claven—
Now he stood by his side in the Glen of the Raven!

V.

Up started Black Hugh from his couch in the fern,
The outlaw of Dara, and Brona the stern;
"There's a passage," he said, "over Ounanar's water,*
Where Clan Morna of old were defeated with slaughter;
There bide we the steps of the traitor and craven,
And he ne'er shall come down through the Glen of the Raven!"

VI.

The ambush was set in the Passage of Lightning,
And now in the moonlight sharp weapons came brightening,
The lance of the Saxon, from Mulla and Mallow,
And the pike of the kern, from the wilds of Duhallow—

---

* There is a tradition that the Clan Morna were defeated here by the Clan Baskin; hence the name of the glen — Glenanar, or the Valley of Slaughter. There is a ford across this glen, near its upper extremity, called Aha Suillish, or the Ford of the Light. Mulla, the Aubeg, a beautiful stream flowing by Buttevant and Doneraile.

Soon they clashed with the swords of the men of Berehaven,
Till the echoes rolled back through the Glen of the Raven!

VII.

But back was the ambush now scattered and driven —
Yet the ranks of their foe were as fearfully riven!
And onward, and round them, the foemen came pouring,
With the wild torrent's speed, and its strength and its roaring,
Till the ambush were swept where the Druid had graven
His god on the crags, by the Glen of the Raven!

VIII.

Then O'Sullivan burst, like the angel of slaughter,
On the foe by the current of Geerath's wild water,
And the brave men of Cork, and of Kerry's wild regions,
Were his rushing destroyers, his death-dealing legions —
And onward they rode over traitor and craven,
Whose bones long bestrewed the lone Glen of the Raven!

IX.

All silent again over forest and mountain,
Save the voice in that gorge of Oiseen's ancient fountain;
While O'Sullivan's crest, with its proud eagle feather,
And broadswords and pikes glitter now from the heather;
For where the dark pools with the white stars are paven,
Secure rests the clan in the Glen of the Raven!

MAUD OF DESMOND.

I.

Maud of Desmond ne'er again,
  Ne'er again shall wake to love:
She hath fled from grief and pain
  Away to Heaven's bright fields above —
Never more shall wake to love,
  Dreams a knight by a torrent narrow;
'Tis far down in the summer grove,
  By the dancing tide of the murmuring Carrow.

II.

Who is he, so fraught with pain,
  That dreams 'neath summer branches there?

The dark-haired knight of Castlemain,
  Of the stalwart frame and the stately air.
His brow is clouded now with care;
  They pierce his heart, these dreams, and harrow,
And he starteth up from his mossy lair
  By the dancing tide of the murmuring Carrow.

III.

Maud of Desmond loved him true,
  But, ah, her princely father smiled
On a stranger lord, who came to woo
  That bonnie maid so pure and mild.
Grim was the smile the young knight smiled;
  This touched his heart like a poisoned arrow,
As he dashed away on his charger wild
  From the dancing tide of the murmuring Carrow!

IV.

Maud of Desmoud makes her moan
  For her hapless love in her native bowers:
The grand eve from its golden throne
  Is marshalling its crimson powers:
The fields beneath are starred with flowers,
  The stream runs calm where the aspens quiver;
It is where Crom's embattled towers
  Are mirrored in the Maig's bright river.

V.

She sees a knight come from the West
  Down the woody valley in fiery speed,
And well she knows his helmet crest,
  And the stately step of his gallant steed;
It is her own true knight, I rede,
  That comes his loving vows to give her,
And he sits beside her in the mead,
  That summer mead by the Maig's bright river.

VI.

And soon the young knight's vows are told,
  And soon he turns to the hills away:
But who, advancing from the wold,
  Bars his path to their summits gray?
It is the stranger lord, — all day
  He'd chased the roe where the wild woods quiver

To the bugle's note and the staghound's bay,
  In the summer dells by the Maig's bright river.

VII.

He stands within the woodland path,
  Glowering grim on the western knight,
And meeting in their hate and wrath,
  They close in stern and deadly fight;
There, in the reddening sunset light,
  Their keen swords into fragments shiver,
And they draw their daggers sharp and bright
  For that lady's love, by the Maig's deep river.

VIII.

Full short and deadly is the strife:
  The stranger lord is down, and there,
With outstretched hands, he begs for life, —
  The young knight listens to his prayer,
And speaks with a calm and lordly air:
  "Ho! take thy life, but shun the giver,
Shun the paths of this lady fair
  Forevermore by the Maig's bright river!"

IX.

"By the towers of Crom!" Earl Desmond cries,
  For he saw the strife from his castle wall —
"Such valor still my heart must prize,
  Till death upon its throbbings fall;
Ho! spread the banquet in the hall;
  The brave must have their meed forever!"
And he brings the knight to his festival,
  In castled Crom, by the Maig's bright river!

X.

There was a mighty feast that e'en,
  A bridal train next morning tide,
And gladsome was the young knight's mien
  With Maud of Desmond at his side;
And O, she was a happy bride,
  With all that power and love could give her, —
The fairest bride 'mid that region wide,
  In castled Crom by the Maig's bright river!

TYRRELL'S PASS.
A. D. 1579.

I.

By the flowery banks of Inny the burning sunset fell,
In many a stream and golden gleam on hill, and mead, and dell,
And from thy shores, bright Ennel, to the far-off mountain crest,
O'er plain and leafy wildwood there was peace and quiet rest.
O, sunset is the sweetest of all the hours that be
For musing lone, or tale of love, by glen or forest tree;
But its radiance bringeth saddening thoughts to him whose good right hand
Must guard his life in the coming strife 'gainst the foe of his fatherland;
For he knows, when thinking lonely by his small tent on the plain,
The glories of the sinking sun he ne'er may see again!

II.

Brave Tyrrell sat that summer eve amid the forest hills
With Captain Owen at his side, by Inny's fountain rills —
Brave Tyrrell of the flying camps, and Owen Oge of Cong —
And round them lay their warriors wild the forest glade along.
Four hundred men of proof they were, these warriors free and bold;
In many a group they sat around the green skirts of the wold;
Some telling of their early loves, and some of mighty deeds,
In regions wide by Shannon side, in Galien of the steeds —
Some cursing the Invader's steps, and wishing for the fray,
That they might sate their burning hate ere the close of that bright day.

III.

Ah! well and deeply they might hate the dark Invader then;
His steps were seen in valley green, in fertile plain and glen;
The gory field, the rifled town, the hamlet burned and lone, —
These were the marks by which he made his demon footsteps known!
He came with all his legions in their new-made light and zeal, —
He came with robber heart and hand and with the murderer's steel;
He came to root the ancient faith from out their native land,
And plant his godless temples where her fanes were wont to stand —

He came to sweep their race away, in hatred hot and keen,
That future lands might never know where such a race had
 been!

IV.

The sun had set upon their camp, the stars were burning bright,
All, save the chief and Owen Oge, were sleeping in their light;
And they sat downward where the stream was singing its deep
 song,
Planning fierce raid and foray bold that starry twilight long.
" By my good faith," said Tyrrell, " we have wandered far and
 wide,
And on no foe, still, high or low, our good swords have we tried;
There's many a keep around us here, and many a traitor town,
And we will have a town, or keep, before two suns go down!"
Said Owen Oge, " No! Heaven send our banded foemen here,
A pleasant fight in the cool of night, 'neath the starlight still and
 clear!" —

V.

With flashing sabres to their feet both warriors instant sprang,
And down the little streamlet's bed their challenge fiercely
 rang! —
They'd heard a sound beside the stream, as if some forest bird,
Awakening from his twilight dreams amid the leaves had stirred;
Another stir like the stealthy step of a wolf from out his lair,
And their trusty spy of the falcon eye stood right before them
 there!
"The foe, with Baron Trimblestown high boasting at their head,
Will find ye here in these green glades at morning light," he
 said,
Then vanished silent as he came beneath the forest shade,
And the clank of sabres followed him on his pathway through
 the glade.

VI.

For his comrades at their leader's call beside the streamlet's
 bank
Were filing from their ferny beds in many a serried rank,
And now along their ordered lines Fertullagh's accents came :
" The foeman o'er our native fields speeds down with sword and
 flame;
We'll meet him as we ever met, — the same red welcome still, —
We'll meet him in the eastward pass, and sweep him from the
 hill!"

They gained that pass ere morning leapt above the eastern wave,
And half his band to Owen Oge the hardy chieftain gave:
"Now lie ye here in ambush close till we may turn below,
And when ye hear my trumpet call, spring out upon the foe!"

VII.

There came no sound from that deep pass, — e'en from the mountain fern
No deep breath of the gallowglass, or whispering of the kern, —
No sounding, save the raven's voice around the jutting crags,
Hoarse croaking for the morrow's feast upon their flinty jags.
And now along the mist-clad hills out shone the morning ray
On Barnwell's bright and serried files all burning for the fray;
A thousand men of might they were from fat Meath's fertile plain,
And when they saw Fertullagh's files they laughed in high disdain —
"Two hundred men to stem our charge! We'll chase them till they stand!"
Then poured them in to that deep glynn upon the flying band.

VIII.

Now Tyrrell wheels his warriors round, out rings his trumpet note;
'Tis answered by the drum's deep sound from the gorge's hollow throat;
The frighted wolf leaps up the hill: "Ha, ha!" the ravens shriek,
"We'll soon have food for each famished brood — rider and warhorse sleek!"
And down like wolves from their forest glades on a herd of startled deer,
The brave four hundred fiercely rush on the foeman's van and rere!
The kerne go darting in the first, with their guns and gleaming pikes, —
Ah! woe the day for the struggling foe where'er that weapon strikes! —
The giant gallowglass strides down with vengeance in his eye,
Wild yelling out his charging shout like a thunder-clap on high!

IX.

Now up the woody mountain-side the battle rolls along;
Now down into the valley's womb the tugging warriors throng;

As hounds around a hunted wolf some forest rock beneath,
Whence comes no sound save the mortal rush and the gnash of
　many teeth,
Their charging shouts have died away — no sound rolls upwards
　save
The volley of the murderous gun, and the crash of axe and
　glaive!
O, life it is a precious gem, yet many there will throw
The gem away in that mortal fray for vengeance on their foe,
And thus they tug more silent still, till the glen is covered wide
With war-steed strong, and sabred corse, and many a gory tide.

x.

Hurrah! that shout it rolleth up with cadence wild and stern;
'Tis the triumph roar of the gallowglass, and the sharp yell of
　the kern!
The foeman flies before their steel — not far, not far he flies;
In the gorge's mouth, in the valley's womb, by the mountain foot
　he dies;
Where'er he speeds, death follows him like a shadow in his
　tracks —
He meets the gleam of the fearful pike, and the sharp and gory
　axe!
Their leader of the boasting words, young Trimblestown, was
　ta'en,
And his champions all, save one weak man, in that bloody gorge
　were slain:
They sped him on, unchased by kern, unsmote by gallowglass,
That he might tell how his comrades fell that morn in Tyrrell's
　Pass!

THE RED ROSE AND THE WHITE.

I.

The Red Rose to the White Rose spake,
　Within the garden fair: —
" O, sister, sister, I shall make
　A garland for her hair —
A garland for my lady gay,
　In spring-time of the year,
And she shall bloom, ere next blithe May,
　A bride without a peer!"

II.

"O, list ye, list ye," said the White,
  "Perchance 'tis I may rest
Among her locks of golden light,
  And on her gentle breast, —
Her breast that's like my pearly leaves
  In spring-time of the year,
For Nature also works and weaves
  Sad garlands for a bier!

III.

"When last she came to this sweet bower,
  A little bird sang by,
A sad song of a glorious flower
  He knew in spring would die.
And aye with woful grief I burn,
  In spring-time of the year,
That thou'lt ne'er grace her bridal morn,
  That I must deck her bier!"

IV.

"Now, cease thy boding voice of woe!"
  The Red Rose cries again;
"See where, in pride of beauty's glow,
  Forth walks she with her train;
Bright as the morn all glittering
  In spring-time of the year —
Can death e'er strike so fair a thing,
  That maid without a peer?"

V.

When flowers were smiling through the land,
  In glen and forest tall,
Young Lady Ann looked down the strand
  From Mallow's castle wall,
And there she saw Lord Thomas stand,
  In spring-time of the year,
Her own young knight, with hawk on hand,
  That morning mild and clear.

VI.

"Come down, come down, O, lady sweet,
  We'll range the greenwoods fair,

With hawk, and hound, and courser fleet,
  To chase the timid hare;
To rouse the pheasant from the woods,
  In spring-time of the year,
And start the heron where he broods
  'Mid sedges tall and sere."

VII.

She's mounted on the gallant bay,
  And he upon the black;
They've hunted all the livelong day
  Through glen and forest track;
They're resting now beneath the spray,
  In spring-time of the year,
Beside Queen Cleena's rock's so gray,*
  With wild waves murmuring near.

VIII.

Across her face a cold blast blew,
  Was sent by some dark fay —
It blighted her, though no one knew,
  That sweet, sweet sunny day.
Yet glad she rode towards Mallow's wall,
  In spring-time of the year,
And blithely sat she in the hall
  Beside her lover dear.

IX.

At eve they made the altar bright
  For morning's bridal train;
But Lady Ann slept sound that night,
  And never woke again.
The Red Rose it was dead and gone
  In spring-time of the year;
The White Rose 'mid her bright locks shone,
  And decked her mournful bier.

X.

" She died not! " still the peasants say —
  " Within Queen Cleena's hall

---

* Corig Cleena, a few miles above Mallow. This wild and solitary rock is believed by the peasantry to be the principal habitation of Cleena, the Fairy Queen of South Munster.

> She lives 'mong elf-maids bright and gay,
>   The fairest of them all;
> Each night, upon her gallant bay,
>   In spring-time of the year,
> She rideth round that rock so gray,
>   In the ghostly moonlight clear!"

THE DEATH OF O'DONNELL.
A. D. 1257.

I.

RED victory smiled on thy legions, Tir Conaill,
When the Geraldine fell 'neath the sparth of O'Donnell;
But fierce was the wailing, and wild was the sorrow
That broke from thy septs ere the dawn of the morrow!
For the prince of their bosoms the champions are grieving:
He fell while their axes the fierce foe were cleaving,
And he lies in his death-wounds by Swilly's dark river,
With his nation around him, as fearless as ever;
Joy, joy in his heart, though its pulses be dying,
That he fell while the foe from his valleys were flying.

II.

The clans of Tyrone, from their forays returning,
Hear thy death strains, Tir Conaill, and joy in thy mourning,
That he whose right hand was thy true stay in danger,
Lies wounded to death 'neath the blow of the stranger;
And they well know a nation thus reft of its leader
'Neath the brands of a foe into ruin will speed her.
High hope for O'Niall! How he bands his wild kerne
From the shores of bright Neagh to the green isles of Erne!
O, round him like torrents his vassals come sweeping,
Where the waves of strong Derg down the valleys are leaping.

III.

O'Donnell he lies where the green mountain forest
In the glow of the sunlight spreads thickest and hoarest,
While up to his death-couch in frantic disorder
Rush the men of fleet coursers, the scouts of his border;
And they tell, in their fear, of the black storms looming,
How the red-handed Niall and his thousands are coming!

Then quick spreads the fear of the mighty invader,
Yet all for Tir Conaill are banding to aid her;
And their chieftain — alas! that the death-wounds have
 bound him —
Calls the men of his might from the valleys around him.

IV.

Then he raises his voice by that wild river billow,
With the gash in his breast, and the gore on his pillow —
"O'Niall," he says, "from his mountains of bleakness
Ever came in the hours of our sorrow and weakness:
He pours on our valleys, and now we will greet him
With the welcome of old on the plains where we meet him!
In the day of my strength ye have found me before ye,
Where'er your bright claymores to victory bore ye;
In the day of my weakness my soul must be longing
To see how my people to battle are thronging!

V.

"Then sound ye, my children, the war note defiant
From the gray Arran cliffs to the Pass of the Giant,
And make me a bier like the biers of my fathers;
Bear me high in your van, where the red Niall gathers,*
And we'll scatter his bands, as the storm-clouds of heaven
From Aileach's black rocks by her thunders are driven!"
Then the hearts of his warriors grow stronger and prouder,
And the shouts of their ardor swell wilder and louder,
And fiercely their war-pipes are ringing and pealing,
From the low-lying glens to the far mountain shieling.

VI.

They've made him a bier like the biers of his fathers;
They bear him afar where the red Niall gathers;
Six champions of might from that green forest alley
Bear him on through each wild glade and torrent-bound
 valley,
To a small mountain plain, by a swift river torn,
Where the May-heather gleams in the dew of the morn;
But its vernal expanse, by the fairy-rings spotted,
Ere the sheen of the evening, with gore shall be clotted;

---

* "He then directed his men to place him on the bier which should take him to the grave, and to carry him on it at the head of his forces." — *Haverty's History of Ireland.* See also *Annals of the Four Masters.*

For there, with their claymores so gallantly flashing,
The septs of Tyrone on Tir Conaill are dashing!

VII.

O, fiercely they meet! As the foam-wreathéd surges,
When some demon of midnight their black fury urges
To shatter thy cross, Ard Oilean of the prayers,
So rush and so meet the wild bands of the slayers!
Soon the septs of Tyrone in their might are prevailing,
And the strength of Tir Conaill is riven and failing —
But the bier, the black bier, with the prince of their valor, —
O, they look on his face in its last mortal pallor,
And they band them once more, and rush fiercely together
On the files of Tyrone, o'er the blood-crimsoned heather.

VIII.

Shout, shout for Tir Conaill! Hurrah, for her striving!
Now the ranks of the foeman her claymores are riving;
The hoofs of her steeds through his red blood are plashing,
And each rider's bright sparth 'mid his squadrons is crashing!
As a herd of gray wolves the O'Niall she scatters,
As the dust of the desert his legions she shatters;
But who, in her next hour of need, will defend her?
For a corse on his bier lies the prince of her splendor!
O! he died while his flags waved in victory o'er him,
With the last of his foemen far scattered before him!

IX.

He worsted the stranger, he routed O'Niall,
And long, long again ere they band for the trial;
Too well they remember the welcome he gave them,
When flight, nor the strength of their numbers could save them.
O! loud through the wild hills his coronach swelleth;
It startles the dun deer and wolf where he dwelleth;
There are eyes red with sorrow, from Erne's green islands
To wild Inishone of the wood-belted highlands;
For they'll ne'er meet his peer in the sad hour of danger
'Gainst the septs of the south, or the false-hearted stranger!

ROMANCE OF THE GOLDEN SPURS.

I.

"I am weary, I am weary of the lagging hours alway,
The wound I got last autumn, it pains me sore to-day —
'Tis burning and 'tis paining worse than when 'twas wet with gore,
And the joy of peace or battle I never shall see more."

II.

Thus spoke the brave Sir Thomas, the knight of Imokeel:
Beneath the Desmond's banner he'd drawn his conquering steel;
But out beneath that banner he never more may ride,
With that shot-maimed arm of valor, and that lance-head in his side.

III.

"My gallant boy, come hither; I give thee my brave steed,
My trusty blade I give thee to serve thee in thy need;
Then don thy battle harness, and with thy following ride
To join the noble Desmond by Imokeely's side!"

IV.

Then out and spake the mother, a fond and fair ladye,
"If I should lose my Gerald, O! what can comfort me?
If I should lose my Gerald — if slain my boy should be,
One hour of peace or happiness I never more can see!"

V.

But nathless her beseeching, and nathless sigh and tear,
Young Gerald's gone to battle with many a gallant spear;
And in the early morning, by Bride's resounding wave,
They mark the sunbeams glancing from hostile helm and glaive.

VI.

"Come hither, O! come hither, thou stripling young and gay," —
'Twas thus upon the hill-side the Desmond bold did say, —
"We'll down upon yon army: God wot, we'll give them play:
Go thou and take their castle, and win thy spurs to-day!"

VII.

It was above the bridge-end that castle proud did stand;
It was a gallant fortress as e'er was in the land;

And downward dashed young Gerald at his brave lord's command,
With his fearless ranks behind him, and his long glaive in his hand!

VIII.

He's leapt the fosse so bravely, 'mid shot, and smoke, and wrack;
He's mounted to the ramparts, his brave men at his back; —
They've ta'en the gallant fortress at the good point of the steel,
But where is he, their leader, the Boy of Imokeel?

IX.

They've searched round fosse and rampart, but cannot find him there;
They've searched the battered chambers, and up the gory stair,
Till by the turret window, with his helmet cleft in twain,
They've found their young commander 'mid a circle of the slain!

X.

It was a day of triumph to the Desmond by that shore,
And yet a day of sorrow, when young Gerald up they bore —
Up they bore unto the hill-side, where the noble Desmond stood,
With his golden banner o'er him, stained with many a foeman's blood.

XI.

Then out and spoke the Desmond: "Ho! list ye all to me!
This boy has ta'en the castle — this boy a knight shall be;
But the hue of death's upon him, and he cannot speak or kneel;
Ho! page; my spurs — unbrace them, and fix them on his heel."

XII.

I wis the sight was woful, e'en in that foughten place,
With the red gash on his forehead, and the blood on his pale face,
With the golden spurs braced on him, glittering in the sunlight clear,
Beneath that rustling banner, stretched upon his gory bier!

XIII.

Through Imokeel they bore him, 'cross many a plain and dell, —
They bore him to his father, and told him how he fell;
The old man's wound burst open, and the blood welled from his side,
And he kissed his pale young champion, and down he sank, and died!

XIV.

"Now leave me," said the mother, as wild she made her moan, —
"Now leave me in this chamber, to my great grief alone!"
And she raised her voice in wailing till the twilight gathered down
Upon her leafy forests, and her hills and moorlands brown.

XV.

It was the starry midnight ere the mother's tones sank low,
And she prayed unto Our Lady with a broken voice and slow: —
"O! thou who once wert stricken worse than I, long, long ago,
Prop me up in this great trial, give me strength to bear my woe."

XVI.

What breaks the heavy stillness? what in the chamber stirs?
Sure she hears the clank of armor, and the clink of those bright spurs!
And she looks upon her Gerald, with a thrill of joy and fear,
For he's rising, rising slowly, in his armor from the bier.

XVII.

O! not slain, not slain, but wounded! Many a field of fire and steel
Saw those sharp spurs' golden brightness dimmed with gore upon each heel;
For in aftertime for Erin never one so true and leal
As Sir Gerald of the Forest, the Knight of Imokeel!

THE BURNING OF KILCOLEMAN.

I.

No sound of life was coming
  From glen, or tree, or brake,
Save the bittern's hollow booming
  Up from the reedy lake;
The golden light of sunset
  Was swallowed in the deep,
And the night came down with a sullen frown,
  On Houra's craggy steep.

II.

And Houra's hills are soundless:
  But hark, that trumpet blast!

It fills the forest boundless,
  Rings round the summits vast;
'Tis answered by another
  From the crest of Corrin Mór,
And hark again the pipe's wild strain
  By Bregoge's caverned shore!

III.

O, sweet at hush of even
  The trumpet's golden thrill,
Grand 'neath the starry heaven
  The pibroch wild and shrill!
Yet all were pale with terror,
  The fearful and the bold,
Who heard its tone that twilight lone
  In the Poet's frowning hold! *

IV.

Well might their hearts be beating;
  For up the mountain pass,
By lake and river meeting,
  Came kern and galloglass,
Breathing vengeance deadly,
  Under the forest tree,
To the wizard man who cast the ban
  On the minstrels bold and free!

V.

They gave no word of warning,
  Round still they came, and on,
Door, wall, and rampart scorning —
  They knew not he was gone!
Gone fast and far that even,
  All secret as the wind,
His treasures all in that castle tall,
  And his infant son behind!

---

* Kilcoleman Castle — an ancient and very picturesque ruin, once the residence of Spenser, lies on the shore of a small lake, about two miles to the west of Doneraile, in the county Cork. It belonged once to the Earls of Desmond, and was burned by their followers in 1598. Spenser, who was hated by the Irish in consequence of his stringent advices to the English about the management of the refractory chiefs and minstrels, narrowly escaped with his life, and an infant child of his, unfortunately left behind, was burnt to death in the flames.

VI.

All still that castle hoarest —
  Their pipes and horns were still,
While gazed they through the forest,
  Up glen and northern hill;
Till from the Brehon circle,*
  On Corrin's crest of stone,
A sheet of fire like an Indian pyre
  Up to the clouds was thrown.

VII.

Then, with a mighty blazing,
  They answered — to the sky —
It dazzled their own gazing,
  So bright it rolled and high;
The castle of the Poet, —
  The man of endless fame, —
Soon hid its head in a mantle red
  Of fierce and rushing flame.

VIII.

Out burst the vassals, praying
  For mercy as they sped —
"Where was their master staying —
  Where was the Poet fled?"
But hark! that thrilling screaming,
  Over the crackling din, —
'Tis the Poet's child in its terror wild,
  The blazing tower within!

IX.

There was a warlike giant
  Amid the listening throng,
He looked with face defiant
  On the flames so wild and strong,
Then rushed into the castle,
  And up the rocky stair,
But alas! alas! he could not pass
  To the burning infant there!

---

* On the summit of Corrin Mór, one of the Ballyhoura mountains, is a large circle of stones, in the centre of which rises a loose conical pile of small rocks. It was most probably a Brehon circle or judgment-seat.

X.

The wall was tottering under,
   And the flame was whirring round,
The wall went down in thunder,
   And dashed him to the ground;
Up in the burning chamber,
   Forever died that scream,
And the fire sprang out with a wilder shout,
   And a fiercer, ghastlier gleam!

XI.

It glared o'er hill and hollow,
   Up many a rocky bar,
From ancient Kilnamulla
   To Darra's Peak afar;
Then it heaved into the darkness
   With a final roar amain,
And sank in gloom with a whirring boom,
   And all was dark again!

XII.

Away sped the galloglasses
   And kerns, all still again,
Through Houra's lonely passes,
   Wild, fierce, and reckless men.
But such the Saxon made them,
   Poor sons of war and woe;
So they venged their strife with flame and knife
   On his head long, long ago!

ROMANCE OF MEERGAL AND GARMON.

Fytte the First.

I.

'Tis Meergal of the Mountain that sighs so mournfully,
With tearful eyes far gazing o'er the star-bespangled sea;
All alone, alone in sorrow, by the Rock of Brananmor,
Behind her love's calm planet, and the sinking moon before.

II.

Nought beholds she as she gazes through the dim and windless west,
Save the diamond star-beams dancing o'er the sea's resplendent breast,
And the glorious changeful glitter of the shimmering splendor train,
From the shore, to where the bright moon hangs above the silent main.

III.

And she cries, " He is not coming! I have waited many a day
To see his white sail gleaming o'er the blue waves far away;
Many a midnight have I wept him with a sad heart mournfully,
But he cometh not, he cometh not, across the weary sea!"

IV.

The moon hangs o'er the water, with its face so calm and pale,
Now the lady looks beneath it, and she sees a rising sail,
And along that line of splendor comes a boat as bright as flame,
With a wondrous sheen all sparkling, as if out from Heaven it came!

V.

As a fragment from the morning is its light sail gleaming o'er,
Glow its smooth sides like the sunset, glitter diamonds on its prore;
By its mast a youth is sitting with an angel's beauty crowned,
And the lady shrieks with gladness, for her long-lost love is found!

Fytte the Second.

I.

Young Meergal of the Mountain, she sits all fond and fain,
With her own betrothéd Garmon by the star-bespangled main,
And she cries: " O, long-lost rover, O, beloved Garmon, tell
Why thou comest thus so strangely, in what bright land did'st thou dwell!

II.

" For I've searched by strand and forest, I have waited many a day
By the deep, to see thy white sail o'er the blue waves far away;
Many a midnight have I wept thee, with a sad heart mournfully
Thinking, fearing thou wert lying 'neath the weary, weary sea!"

III.

"There was silence on the forest and the wide-spread burnished deep;
To the westward I was gazing from Branammor the steep,
And I saw the Land of Glory through that sunset of the May,
O, the beautiful Hy Brasil," answered Garmon of the Bay.

IV.

"I pulled a blesséd shamrock by the old saint's carven stone,
And I took my boat and faced her to Hy Brasil all alone,
And a gentle wind 'gan blowing as I left this iron shore,
And the sea grew ever brighter as I wafted swiftly o'er,

V.

"Before me in the water, with a face like Heaven so fair,
Up rose the smiling Mermaid with her glossy golden hair,
And she gazed all gently on me, and she raised her queenly hand,
Pointing through the amber sunset to that far off heavenly land!

VI.

"Still on, and on before me went that maiden of the wave,
My soul all drunk with pleasure at each piercing glance she gave,
And my heart all wildly throbbing at the witching smiles she wore,
Till five boat-lengths scarce before me spread Hy Brasil's golden shore!

VII.

"But 'twas all a land of shadows with the rainbow's radiance wove,
From the green sky-piercing mountain, to the sunny lowland grove;
Its lovely shore receded as my boat went swiftly on,
And the maiden of the ocean with the witching smiles was gone!

VIII.

"I bethought me of the shamrock in its emerald glories drest,
With the earth still fresh upon it, and I took it from my breast;
I threw it to the breezes, and they bore it to the strand,
And it never more receded :— I trod the Enchanted Land!

IX.

"A wild ecstatic wonder fills my soul since that strange day,
For I've walked with those enchanted in the ages past away;
And I've brought this boat of glory, O, my lady love, for thee,
And we'll sail to calm Hy Brasil, and be blest eternally!"

Fytte the Third.

I.

'Tis Meergal of the Mountain that never more may weep,
For she sits beside her Garmon on the star-bespangled deep;
And in that boat of beauty are they sailing to the west,
With a love that lives eternal, towards the regions of the blest.

II.

And its many-tinted dwellers rose from out the deep's still domes,
To see what moving radiance glittered o'er their sparry homes;
And the dolphin heaved and gambolled around their glorious track,
With the sea one blaze of splendor where he showed his prismy back.

III.

Behind them rose the morning o'er a green and golden sea,
And that swift boat seemed its herald, it moved so gloriously;
And a sweet, unearthly music filled the atmosphere around,
On their ears forever falling with a soul-entrancing sound.

IV.

It was the purple sunset, when the breeze blew warm and bland,
And they saw a shore beyond them by its breath of fragrance fanned,
And within a heavenly harbor, under hills serenely grand,
They have moored that boat of wonder in Hy Brasil's golden land.

V.

Up they wandered through the mountains, from the broad cerulean sea,
Till they reached a beauteous valley decked with many a fragrant tree;
As the countless stars that glitter on a cold December night,
Shone the flowers' gay-tinted blossoms o'er that valley of delight.

VI.

There a crystal stream danced downward with a wild melodious song,
And like children of the rainbow flew the warbling birds along;
Sang they sweetly as the wild harp when a master sweeps its wire,
As they flew from shore to greenwood, like gray sparks of heavenly fire.

VII.

Like the deep-blue depths of heaven, when the April hours come on,
A lake, broad, calm and glorious, 'mid that valley's bosom shone,
With its splendor-tinted islands, and their music-murmuring groves,
With its green encircling mountains, and its fairy strands and coves.

VIII.

On shore and shining island gleamed hall and palace gay,
Where dwell the blest Enchanted in cloudless joy alway;
Where roam the Fairy People through the scenes they like so well;
And, "O, love, O, love!" said Garmon, "here forevermore we dwell!"

IX.

When the stars are on the waters, and the peasants by the shore,
Oft they see that boat of beauty, with the sparkling diamond prore,
Sailing, sailing with the lovers o'er the silent midnight sea,
To the beautiful Hy Brasil,* where they're blest eternally!

---

* *Hy Brasil*—the Island of Atlantis—the Western Land, &c., is supposed to be indentical with Tir-n-a-n Oge, the Paradise of the Pagan Irish. The peasantry believe they can still see it at sunset from the coasts of Clare, Galway, and Donegal. Brananmor is one of the highest pinnacles of the great precipice of Moher, on the coast of Clare.

SONGS, POEMS, AND SHORT BALLADS.

IN LIFE'S YOUNG MORNING.

To my Wife.

Air — "The Woods in Bloom."

I.

In life's young morning I quaffed the wine
   From Love's bright bowl as it sparkling came,
And it warms me ever, that draught divine,
   When I think of thee, dearest, or name thy name.
The night may fall, and the winds may blow
   From palace gardens or place of tombs,
Yet I dream of our Love-time long ago
   Beneath the yellow laburnum blooms.

II.

Gay was the garden, bright shone the bower,
   Like a golden tent 'neath the summer skies,
The sunbeams glittered on leaf and flower,
   And the light of heaven seemed in your eyes;
The night may fall, and the winds may blow,
   But a gladness ever my heart assumes
From that wine of love quaffed long ago
   Beneath the yellow laburnum blooms.

III.

O'er vale and forest dark falls the night,
   Yet my heart goes back to the sun and shine
When you stood in the glory of girlhood bright
   'Neath the golden blossoms, your hand in mine;

The night may fall, and the winds may blow,
  And the greenwoods wither 'neath winter glooms,
Yet it lives forever, that long ago,
  Beneath the yellow laburnum blooms.

IV.

Through the misty night to the eye and ear
  Come the glitter of flowers and the songs of birds, —
Come thy looks of fondness to me so dear,
  And thy witching smiles and thy loving words;
The night may fall and the winds may blow,
  But that hour forever my soul illumes, —
Our golden Love-time long ago,
  Beneath the yellow laburnum blooms.

SONG OF TREN THE FAIRY.

AIR — "The Fairy Companie."

I.

From flower bells of each hue,
  Crystal white or golden yellow,
Purple, violet, red, or blue,
We drink the honey-dew
    Until we all get mellow, —
    Until we all get mellow,
      And through our festal glee
    I'm the blithest little fellow
      In the fairy companie.

II.

In the fairy companie
  They call me Trén the Merry,
And no name's so fit for me,
For I love in revelry
    Each gloomy thought to bury, —
    Each dark, sad thought to bury,
      As I laugh by flower and tree,
    Hill, stream, and river ferry,
      'Midst the fairy companie.

III.

'Neath the sunset's purple ray
  Cups of purple wine we swallow;
Then I laugh, and sing, and play,
And my fairy mates are gay.
  And where'er I go they follow, —
  With laughter mad they follow,
    I dance so merrilie,
  O'er hill and flower-starred hollow,
    For the fairy companie.

IV.

Our brightest, favorite spot
  Is in a Munster wild-wood,
Where the foot of man comes not,
And the rays are ne'er too hot,
  And the stream-voice clear and mild would —
  Merry, low, and sweet, and mild — would
    Make the dead leap up in glee,
  And the flowers keep in their childhood
    For the fairy companie.

V.

There from bells of many a hue,
  Crystal white, or golden yellow,
The blissful summer through,
We drink the honey-dew,
  Until we all get mellow, —
  Laughing, quaffing, glad, and mellow,
    And through our festal glee,
  I'm the blithest little fellow
    In the fairy companie.

MY BOAT.

Air — "I'll build my Love a gallant Ship."

I.

My boat is like the sea-gull white
  That skims o'er strand and swell,
It looks so bright, and sails so light,
  And stems the tide so well;
The soft wild gale fills out its sail,
  And wafts it towards the sea,
And floats me down from Cork's fair town
  Upon the pleasant Lee.

II.

I sit within that bonnie boat
  When love o'er me has power,
When sea birds float with shrilly note
  At sunset's golden hour;
Then from the shore green towering o'er
  Love seems to pilot me,
To muse alone on my loved one
  Upon the pleasant Lee.

III.

When first my boat upon the tide
  A thing of life out came,
With conscious pride, upon its side,
  I placed my true-love's name;
And since, each day, that name the spray
  Has washed full wild and free,
But still each line undimmed doth shine
  Upon the pleasant Lee.

IV.

A trim new sail my boat shall have
  When summer days come on,
And swift and brave she'll walk the wave,
  More stately than the swan;
For then my bloom-bright maid shall come
  With love and joy to me,
And side by side we oft shall glide
  Upon the pleasant Lee.

THE MOUNTAINS HIGH.

AIR — "'Tis with my Gun I'll guard you."

I.

On lowland plains I wander
   All in the falling year,
By lowland valleys ponder
   Upon my true-love dear;
But spring will soon restore me
   The smiles of Mary's eye,
And the grand clouds flying o'er me
   Upon the mountains high.

II.

Within the lowland valley
   There stands a castle strong,
Where round in each green alley
   You'll hear the wild bird's song;
Far sweeter visions move me,
   When I hear the eagle's cry,
From the fields of God above me,
   Upon the mountains high.

III.

When autumn time is coming
   Along the hills and dells,
You'll hear the wild bees humming
   Among the heather bells;
You'll hear the gay streams singing
   Their songs to earth and sky,
Like the sounds of glad bells ringing
   Upon the mountains high.

IV.

Amid their summits airy,
   In sweet spring's blessèd reign,
I'll sit beside my Mary
   With happy heart again;
I have no wish beyond her,
   And man can ne'er descry
Two youthful lovers fonder
   Upon the mountains high.

IRELAND, OUR HOME.

Air—"Planxty Creagh."*

I.

O, mournful Isle beyond the sea,
   Ireland! our home!
With bleeding hearts we turn to thee,
   Our childhood's home!
Since that sad day of weeping sore
We saw thy green and sunny shore
Sink down beyond the breaker's roar,
   Ireland! our native home!

II.

O, lovely Isle beyond the waves,
   Ireland! our home!
Where shamrocks deck our fathers' graves,
   Our childhood's home!
In far, far climes we kneel in prayer
To Him who rules earth, sea, and air,
To end thy bondage and despair,
   Ireland! our native home!

III.

O, sunny Isle of blooming woods,
   Ireland! our home!
Of silver lakes and falling floods,
   Our childhood's home!
Of golden clouds, of skies serene,
Of purple hills and valleys green,
Thy peer, on earth, was never seen,
   Ireland! our native home!

IV.

O, sacred Isle of saint and sage,
   Ireland! our home!
Of song, and sad historic page,
   Our childhood's home!

---

* Real name of "When Johnny comes marching home," one of Carolan's Planxties.

Within our hearts the hope is born
To see the gay triumphant morn
That ends thy night of grief forlorn,
              Ireland! our native home!

V.

O, genial Isle of friendship rare,
              Ireland! our home!
Of gallant men and maidens fair,
              Our childhood's home!
What man could see thy daughters bright,
Could sun him in their looks of light,
And fail for them and thee to fight?
              Ireland! our native home!

VI.

And we, thy sons, prepare once more,
              Ireland! our home!
To hurl the tyrant from thy shore,
              Our childhood's home!
To plant upon thy plains the Tree
Of everlasting Liberty,
And rise to fame or fall with thee,
              Ireland! our native home!

WILL OF THE GAP.

Air — "Graine Weal."

I.

In castle or town was there never a man
Could handle a broadsword or empty a can, —
Could glory in danger, whatever might hap,
Like the Outlaw of Sloragh, young Will of the Gap.

II.

From his boot to his basnet was burnished so sheen,
And his arm was so strong, and his sword was so keen,
And his brain was the brightest that e'er laid a trap
To catch the proud Saxon — young Will of the Gap.

III.

Up rose in the morning the Ridderah Fionn,*
And spurred with his vassals by forest and down,
To catch Will asleep in the mountain's broad lap;
But the sleep of a fox slept young Will of the Gap!

IV.

For he'd gathered his men ere the Ridderah knew,
And he placed them in ambush by lone Rossarue:
"Now he thinks he will catch us just taking our nap,
But we'll open *his* eyes!" said young Will of the Gap.

V.

The Ridderah rode with his wild vassals in,
Till he reached the deep bosom of Rossa's lone glynn.
"Now the Ridderah's caught in his own wily trap,
So blow up the trumpet!" cried Will of the Gap.

VI.

The signal was blown, and the ambush behind
And the ambush before thundered down like the wind,
And scarcely three vassals, to tell their mishap,
With the White Knight 'scaped free from young Will of the Gap!

* Ridderah Fionn, the White Knight, lord of Kilbenny.

THE FLOWER THAT NE'ER SHALL FADE.

Air — "The Doctor tries all Remedies."

I.

The primrose and the woodbine bower
   By streams their fragrance fling,
And sweetly blooms the Drinan flower
   Amid the dells in spring;
The red, red rose full brightly blows
   In many a garden shade;
But flowers and blooms, when winter comes,
   All darkly die and fade.

II.

I know a flower that ne'er shall die,
   More dear than life to me, —
In Mary's heart that flower doth lie
   Of love and constancy;
The blooms may go, when winter's snow
   Robes hill and greenwood glade,
And storms may lower, but, O, that flower
   Shall never die or fade.

THE SONG OF LORD GOLOPTIOUS.

I.

The fatness of the land is mine:
   The swarming game my Manton kills,
The mighty herds of lowing kine,
   The white sheep dotted o'er the hills,
The meadows mown and springing new,
   The waving fields of golden corn,
The sowers and the reapers too,
   For I am Lord Goloptious born!

II.

What though the beastly peasants say
    My grandsire's sire a scullion's clout
Flourished in camp? He made his hay
    When William turned the Stuart out; —
Our title it is sound and good,
    From vanquished dogs of Irish torn,
Baptized and sealed in Irish blood,
    And I am Lord Goloptious born!

III.

My father sold his vote, they cry,
    When Ireland's wrangling Senate fell.
What then? I often heard him sigh
    He had no other votes to sell,
Such grand rewards his buyers gave,
    The titles that our name adorn;
And England wept above his grave,
    And I am Lord Goloptious born!

IV.

The peasants pass my castle gate, —
    A ragged, worthless, beggar crew, —
They hate me; but with tenfold hate
    I pay them back the interest due;
As one so high in England's trust,
    I look on them with proper scorn,
And grind them to the bitter dust,
    For I am Lord Goloptious born!

V.

They dare, betimes, with voices bold,
    To raise their discontented cries;
They dare to shiver in the cold,
    And die of hunger 'neath our eyes!
For them, the bane of Church and State,
    For all such sordid slaves, forlorn,
My maxim is, Exterminate,
    For I am Lord Goloptious born!

VI.

Monsters they are who cannot see
   Wisdom in England's ruling plan,
Who shout aloud for liberty,
   And rave about the rights of man, —
Who say they have some claim to eat
   Their country's cattle and their corn;
I'd give them cannon balls for meat,
   For I am Lord Goloptious born!

VII.

O, that the good old times were back
   Of feudal dungeons, deep and strong,
With pitch-cap, gibbet, block, and rack,
   I'd make them sing another song
Than that old strain, still unsubdued,
   About the dawn of Freedom's morn, —
I'd spill in seas their rebel blood,
   For I am Lord Goloptious born!

MARY'S SWEETHEART.

Air — "Says the Mother to the Daughter."

I.

The first time that I saw my love, I knew his heart was mine,
The next time that I saw my love, I thought he was divine;
For he said he was no rover, and would ne'er leave me to pine,
And, O, my heart is happy with this true-love of mine!

II.

I met him at the Patron by Saint Mollagga's Tree,
Where at the dance and hurling, the boldest, best was he;
O, my heart was very happy on that blissful holiday,
And I learned to love him dearly while we danced the hours away!

III.

My Brian Ban is clothed in garments of the frieze;
But 'tis not costly garments or hoarded wealth I prize;
'Tis the truthful heart he gave me, 'tis the glance of his kind eyes,
And the loving tales he tells me while the golden daylight dies.

IV.

A brave heart's in his bosom, yet he's gentle as a child;
He tells me pleasant stories till with laughter I am wild;
He'll ofttimes change to sadness, and make me sob and cry,
Then kiss my bitter tears away till none so glad as I!

V.

And now he sits beside me in the greenest dell of dells,
And the sweetest of all stories my fond, fond darling tells,
That he loves me with a constant love, that never can decay,
Till we sleep beneath the green grass in Molagga's churchyard gray!

THE CANNON.

Air — "Barrack Hill."

I.

We are a loving company
   Of soldiers brave and hearty;
We never fought for golden fee,
   For faction, or for party;
The will to make old Ireland free,
   That set each dauntless man on,
And banished us beyond the sea,
   With our brave iron cannon.
     And here's the gallant company
       That fought by Boyne and Shannon,
     That never feared an enemy,
       With our brave iron cannon!

II.

Come, fill me up a pint o' wine,
   Until 'tis brimming o'er, boys,
Our gun is set in proper line,
   And we have balls galore, boys;
Now, here's a health to good Lord Clare,
   Who'll lead us on to-morrow,
When through the foe our balls will tear,
   And work them death and sorrow!

And here's the gallant company
  That always forward ran on
So boldly on the enemy,
  With our brave iron cannon!

III.

I've brought a wreath of shamrocks here,
  In memory of our own land, —
'Tis withered like that island drear, —
  That sorrowful and lone land;
I'll hang it nigh our cannon's mouth,
  To whet our memories fairly,
And there's no flower in all the south
  Could deck that gun so rarely.
    And here's the gallant company
      That soon shall rush each man on,
    And plough the Saxon enemy
      With our brave iron cannon!

IV.

At Limerick how it made them run,
  The Dutchman and his crew, boys;
'Twas then I made this gallant gun
  To plough them through and through, boys;
And since that day in foreign lands
  It roared triumphant ever —
It blazed away, yet here it stands,
  Where foeman's foot shall never!
    And here's the gallant company
      That soon shall rush each man on,
    And break and strew the enemy
      With our brave iron cannon!

V.

'Tis dinted well from mouth to breech
  With many a battle furrow;
A fitting sermon it will preach
  At Fontenoy to-morrow.
Then never let your spirits sink,
  But stand around, each man on
This foreign slope, and we will drink
  One brave health to our cannon!

And here's the gallant company
  That soon shall rush each man on,
And plough the Saxon enemy
  With our brave iron cannon!

MY STEED WAS WEARY.

Air — "'Twas early, early, all in the Spring."

I.

My steed was weary upon the hill,
While the night came down and the winds blew chill;
But I thought of thee by the distant Nore,
And my heart was nerved for the way once more.

II.

My steed was weary beside the wood,
And I knew his weakness to swim the flood;
But I thought of thee by the distant Nore,
And I spurred him safe to the other shore.

III.

My steed was weary beside the fen;
He saw the danger and feared it then;
But I thought of thee by the distant Nore,
And safely, safely I brought him o'er.

IV.

My steed dropt down by the mountain lake,
And I slept by his side in the wild ash brake,
And I dreamt of thee by the distant Nore,
Till the morning's splendors came shining o'er.

V.

Then up I stood with my steed again,
And I reached my home in the lowland plain,
And my thoughts of thee by the distant Nore
Were sweeter and brighter than e'er before.

FAR AWAY.

Air — "I might have got an Earl."

I.

Along the winding river
  The wintry tempests blow;
The sear leaves glance and quiver
  Within the wave below;
The sun is redly sinking
  Beyond the mountains gray,
And I am ever thinking
  Of her that's far away.

II.

Her eyes are like the violets
  In some green summer dell;
The rose of Lene's bright islets
  Her lips can ne'er excel;
That wild lake of the mountain
  Its depths no man can say;
My love's as deep a fountain
  For her that's far away.

III.

O, were I like the earls
  That reigned o'er Desmond's towers,
Her hair should shine with pearls,
  Instead of fading flowers;
And robes of queenly splendor
  Her fair form should array,
My love's so true and tender
  For her that's far away.

IV.

O, could you see her golden
  Bright locks, and form so fine,
You'd think some goddess olden
  Had witched those eyes of thine;
And while the sun is sinking,
  I'm spellbound day by day,
For, O, I'm ever thinking
  Of her that's far away.

I'LL DECK HIS GRAVE WITH FLOWERS.

Air—"Ingheen's Dubh's Lament."

I.

The sun pours down his light
  On flower and blooming tree,
And heaven and earth are bright,
  But all seems dark to me;
No comfort have I known,
  But through the long day's hours
To sigh and weep alone,
  And deck his grave with flowers.

II.

Long, long I fed love's flame
  With hopeful heart and high,
Till from the wars he came—
  But, O, he came to die!
Now, hope will ne'er return,
  And dark the future lowers,
And I can nought but mourn,
  And deck his grave with flowers.

III.

'Tis at my true love's feet
  I think the rose looks best;
The shamrocks smile most sweet
  Above his Irish breast;
And at his headstone twine
  The fairest myrtle bowers,
Where still I mourn and pine,
  And deck his grave with flowers.

IV.

'Tis by yon abbey wall
  My soldier love lies low,
Where wave the yew trees tall,
  And mournful breezes blow;
And there till death I'll keep
  My watch through sun or showers,
And sigh alone, and weep,
  And deck his grave with flowers.

YOU'RE A DEAR LAND TO ME.

Air — "The Blackbird."

I.

There's a stream in Glenlara, whose silvery fountain
  Leaps up into life where the heather-bells bloom,
That steals through the moorland and winds round the mountain,
  Now laughing in sunlight, now weeping in gloom;
And by its merry dancing, a rural sight entrancing,
  From out the greenwoods glancing, my home you once could see;
Now an exile far away from that home I sigh and say, —
  O, green-hilled, pleasant Erin, you're a dear land to me! *

II.

There's a tree by that river in bright beauty shining,
  With green leaves and blossoms all brilliant and gay,
With the birds in its branches wild melodies twining,
  Where I sat with my love on each blithe summer day,
When the sunset clouds were glowing, and the gentle kine were lowing,
  And the perfumed airs were blowing round that bonnie, blooming tree;
Tree or love I'll ne'er see more by that murmuring river shore,
  O, green-hilled, pleasant Erin, you're a dear land to me!

III.

Now I sit where the camp-fire is brilliantly burning,
  A soldier, far, far from thy green shore away,
And I dream of my love at each evening's returning,
  But I think upon thee in the roar of the fray,
And of our green flags streaming, and bayonets proudly gleaming,
  Some day thy shore redeeming from the Saxon's tyranny;
Then I ne'er regret for you a freeman's sword I drew,
  Though green-hilled, pleasant Erin, you're a dear land to me!

---

* Meaning, according to the idiom, that he *paid dearly* for his devotion to Ireland.

THE WHIG'S LAMENTATION.

Air — "Granua Weal."

I.

In ermine and scarlet I sported my wig,
While Ireland was blessed by the rule of the Whig,
And if Paddy complained, then I ordered the soap
To smooth for his neck a good tenpenny rope!

II.

Now the times they are changed, and the Tory is in,
And the Whig is kicked down to the Father of Sin;
But if I had my wish, by the toe of the Pope,
I'd give Paddy and Tory both plenty of rope!

III.

Mavrone! while we could, how we feathered our nest
With sinecures, pensions, and places the best!
Now we itch for our flesh-pots — in darkness we grope
For the haft of the hatchet and coil of the rope!

IV.

They mark down the Whigs, "Bloody, brutal, and base,"
But that phrase of contempt bears the lie on its face,
For what panacea for Paddy can cope
With our poorhouse, our prison, our gibbet, and rope?

V.

I hate Irish Paddy, the Tory I hate,
May the de'il in his wisdom give both the same fate;
May both to his regions the same time elope
From a twenty-foot gibbet and tenpenny rope!

VI.

Now, to conclude and to finish my song,
May the Lord reinstate us before it is long,
And make Paddy rebel, just to give us full scope
For our famed panacea — the gibbet and rope!

(PADDY, *loquitur.*)

VII.

"Rebel!" Faith we will; soon our green flag we'll fly,
And the fires of our camps shall flash up to the sky;
Then, chips of one block, Whig and Tory, we hope
To pay back on the nail for your gibbet and rope!

THE MOUNTAIN ASH.

AIR — "The Green Ash Tree."

I.

The mountain ash blooms in the wild,
  Or droops above the wandering rill;
    You ne'er can see
    A fairer tree,
But I know one dear maiden mild
  With witching form more lovely still.

II.

The mountain ash has berries fair,
  The reddest in the woodlands green;
    Sweet lips I know
    With redder glow
Than ever lit those berries rare —
  The red lips of my bosom's queen.

III.

The mountain ash has leaves of gold
  When autumn browns the steep hill's side;
    Of locks I dream
    With brighter gleam
Of yellow in their braid and fold
  Than e'er tinged leaf in woodland wide.

IV.

The mountain ash in winter sear
  Stands bravely up when wild winds blow;
    So love shall stand,
    Serene and bland,
Between me and my Ellen dear,
  A fadeless flower in weal or woe.

THE ENSIGN AND HIS BANNER.

A Brigade Song.

Air — "The Green Flag."

I.

They said I was too young to seek
  For fame or martial glory;
They said I was too slight and weak
  To brave the battle gory;
But years have passed, and I have got
  A soldier's mien and manner,
And borne through many a storm of shot
  My conquering Irish banner.

II.

The bloody breach of strong Namur,
  It was the first I mounted,
And many a comrade's corse, be sure,
  Within that breach we counted;
There placed we high the *Fleur-de-lis*,
  And Bill,[*] the old Dutch trepanner,
As fast he fled, looked back on thee,
  Far higher still, my banner!

III.

And since that mighty day of death,
  With honor still I've borne it;
It waved in many a battle's breath,
  And many a shot has torn it;
It saw on Steinkirk's fiery plain
  Brave Sarsfield beat the planner
Of all our woe, Dutch Bill, again,
  My glorious Irish banner!

IV.

I had a sweetheart in Ireland
  Before I crossed the water;
My comrades say some Saxon band
  Has drenched her home in slaughter;

[*] The Irish nickname for King William the Third.

Ah! cold she sleeps — God rest her soul! —
  Beside the Banks of Anner,
And now I've nought, as seasons roll,
  To love, but my green banner!

V.

And now, where'er my banner wave,
  I'll think on that sad river,
Where lies my true-love's gory grave,
  And fight for vengeance ever; —
With Ireland's woes in memory,
  Some brave revenge I'll plan her,
And when I fall, my shroud shall be
  My glorious Irish banner!

THE COCK AND THE SPARROW.

AIR — "The Game Cock."

I.

ONE morn, at the sack of Cragnour,
  A cock and a sparrow were speaking,
While 'neath where they sat on the tower
  The Crop-ears their fury were wreaking —
Were wreaking in blood, fire, and smoke —
  "Ah! the castle is ta'en, bone and marrow,
And my poor Irish heart it is broke,"
  Said the brave jolly cock to the sparrow.

II.

"For the Crop-ears will have us full soon,
  And our bed will be no bed of roses:
They will starve us right dead to the tune
  Of a psalm that they'll twang through their noses;
Never more shall I crow in the hall,
  For the gloom there my bosom would harrow —
May the fiend whip them off, psalms and all,"
  Said the brave jolly cock to the sparrow.

III.

" 'Tis certain the castle they've got,
  And 'tis sure that they'll slay all that's in it;
But as victory is theirs, and what not,
  You're expected to crow like a linnet!"
Cried the sparrow, with voice sad and low: —
  But "I'd rather my grave cold and narrow,
Than at Puritan triumph to crow,"
  Said the brave jolly cock to the sparrow.

IV.

"No more," said the sparrow, "we'll see
  Irish gallants come in late and early;
No more shall they hunt o'er the lea,
  When the sweet autumn wind shakes the barley;
Never more shall they dance on the bawn,
  Or ride from the gate like an arrow!"
"Ah! no more shall I wake them at dawn,"
  Said the brave jolly cock to the sparrow.

V.

But the chief of Cragnour soon returned,
  And the Crop-ears right sorely he hammered;
Then the sparrow with gleefulness burned,
  And "Hurra for my Irish!" he clamored; —
And "Hurra for the chief of Cragnour!
  There is joy through my flesh, bone, and marrow;
For his victory I'll crow hour by hour,"
  Said the brave jolly cock to the sparrow.

MY GERALDINE.

Air — "He is Gone."

I.

He has come back the same
  To this glad heart of mine,
In his power and his fame,
  With his glances divine;
O! tell me the story
Of his triumph and glory
On the field of Knocklory,
  My brave Geraldine.

II.

Rode he up to the gate,
  This fond lover of mine,
In his armor of plate,
  And his trappings so fine;
And he looked all so grandly,
And he smiled all so blandly,
And he kissed me so fondly,
  My brave Geraldine.

III.

Sun or moon, starry sphere,
  Care I never to shine,
While my true love is near,
  With his glances divine;
Sun or moon ne'er could render
To my fond heart such splendor
As his love looks so tender,
  My brave Geraldine.

IV.

In the bright, festive hour,
  When they quaff the red wine,
I will steal to my bower,
  With this gay harp of mine,
And I'll banish all sadness,
And I'll pour out my gladness
In a strain of fond madness,
  My brave Geraldine.

V.

I will sing how he won
  By yon dark hills of pine,
Each Sassenach gun,
  And each banner so fine; —
How his foes fled before him,
How gallant he bore him,
With his Irish flag o'er him,
  My brave Geraldine.

THE MERRY CHRISTMAS FIRE.

Air — "The first night I was married."

I.

In summer time my heart is glad,
 In autumn low or gay,
But there is sweet, and nought of sad,
 When Christmas comes alway;
And never bliss more sweet than this
 Can happy man desire,
Than sit a-near his true love dear
 By the merry Christmas fire.

II.

In summer time the vales are bright
 With glancing leaf and flower,
And autumn spreads its amber light
 On many a lovely bower;
And sweetly sing the birds in spring,
 Like tune of fairy lyre;
But far more dear, my true love near,
 And the merry Christmas fire.

III.

From the Christmas fire the gay flames dart,
 And glance, and glow, and whirl,
Like the fire of love within my heart
 For my own sweet Irish girl.
O! gladdest boon, to sit full soon,
 Where young heart ne'er could tire,
All fondly near my true love dear,
 By the merry Christmas fire.

ADDRESS TO AN OLD PIPE.

I.

Old friend, thy blackened, shining bowl
Brings feelings strange, beyond control,
For memory unwinds her scroll,
   And sends to me
Sweet thoughts, that crowd my brightening soul,
  Like song-birds on a leafy woodland tree.

II.

I look across a bridge of years,
That 'tween me and the past uprears
Its arches washed by blood and tears, —
   Ireland's and mine, —
And there the land of youth appears,
  In all its life and loveliness divine!

III.

I see the path the mountains through,
Where first thy solace sweet I knew,
And rolled a cloud of vapor blue
   Up to the sun;
And talked with my companion true
  Of wealth, and love, and honors to be won.

IV.

Again on me his honest eyes
Look kindly thought serene, and wise;
Again the lark sings in the skies,
   And high and hoar
Old Gaultee's summits towering rise,
  O'er mead, and wood, and glittering streamlet's shore.

V.

And now our fortune's still the same;
We've won but little wealth or fame,
Yet we can boast an honest name,
   Hearts free from guile,
And comrade, I at least can claim
  A woman's faithful heart and loving smile.

VI.

Old friend, since first thy blackened clay
Was white as daisies of the May,
I've spent full many a rueful day
   Of care and grief;
Yet oft you charmed my cares away,
  And soothed my soul, and brought my heart relief.

VII.

When early love first falsely broke
Its promise, from the dream I woke —
Keen though I felt its cruel stroke,
   I drowned despair
In warm wreaths of thy curling smoke,
  And banished from my heart corroding care.

VIII.

When fortune whelmed her thunder loud,
Malignant on my head, I vowed
To face the tempest, fearless, proud,
   And found a balm,
Old friend, within thy perfumed cloud,
  Till fortune smiled again, and all was calm.

IX.

When friendship's counterfeit grew rust,
And rotten hearts betrayed their trust,
And he whom once I loved the most
   Paid back to me
Fraternal love in dross and dust,
  A refuge still, old friend, I found in thee.

X.

When manhood's blood coursed through my veins,
I roamed o'er Ireland's hills and plains,
I loved her well, I mourned her chains,
   Her cruel lot;
Your vapor soothed a patriot's pains,
  And calmed my heart a while, but cured it not.

XI.

For who that deemed himself a man,
Since this old troublous earth began

To roll through space its mighty span
    Of changeful years,
Could see his country 'neath the ban
    Of tyranny, and feel not at her tears?

XII.

But come, old friend, I've preached too long,
And mine should be another song,
A freeborn pean, loud and strong,
    Of happier times,
When right shall be where all is wrong,
    And sorrow cease, as I now end my rhymes!

MY TRUE LOVE BRIGHT.

Air—"The Summer is come."

I.

The winds were stayed in their endless flight,
O'er storied valley and mountain height,
As I sat me down with a wild delight,
To think an hour on my true love bright,

II.

My true love bright dwells far away;
My true love hears not her minstrel's lay;
Yet I know, O! I know that she ne'er will stray
From the love she plighted that winter day.

III.

The glittering stars that hang on high
Have beams like the beams of my true love's eye;
When I speak to my love, her words reply
Like an angel's song in the crystal sky.

IV.

The lily flower by the wave-lit strand
Is white, like the white of my true love's hand,
And a rose doth smile in some golden land
Like the smiles of my love, so sweet and bland.

V.

In Paradise, by a blest stream's shore,
The amaranth bloometh forevermore;
That flower will wither and die before
I cease to love, or my maid adore.

VI.

And golden noon and starred midnight
Go my thoughts to her like the fleet wind's flight;
For evermore with a wild delight
I fondly think on my true love bright.

THE PETTICOAT.

Air — "I am a Roving Doctor."

I.

Since the days of Trojan Paris,
  When beauteous Helen was the toast,
O'er lords and mighty monarchs,
  The women, they have ruled the roast;
And why should Croppies hang behind
  In gallantry such men of note?
On Irish ground, in Irish wind,
  We spread our flag — a Petticoat!
For we were Croppy heroes,
  With pike in hand and flag afloat,
Who fought and bled for freedom
  Beneath that flag — the Petticoat!

II.

This Petticoat was broidered
  By fingers fair as fair could be,
And once its folds fell over
  A gleaming ankle gracefully;
A milk-white foot, that stept the glades
  As light as fairies of the moat, —
Young Nora's, pride of Wexford maids,
  This tyrant-conquering Petticoat!
And we were Croppy heroes,
  With pike in hand and flag afloat,
With stains of blood upon it —
  This flag — the conquering Petticoat!

III.

'Twas on a summer morning,
  As we marched down the dewy hill,
We found our bright-haired Nora
  Upon the wayside, stark and still;
A yeoman's bullet in her breast,
  A sabre wound across her throat —
'Twas then we made, with vengeful zest,
  Our banner of her Petticoat!
    For we were Croppy heroes,
      With pike in hand and flag afloat,
    Determined to avenge her
      Beneath that flag — the Petticoat!

IV.

The blood-spots scarce were faded
  Ere we their crimson did renew;
Upon the hill of Oulart,
  Her murderers, every man we slew;
From field to field, from town to town,
  In England's reddest blood we wrote
The story of that Kirtle Gown,
  The blood-stained, conquering Petticoat!
    For we were Croppy heroes,
      With pike in hand and flag afloat —
    The terror of our tyrants,
      Beneath that flag — the Petticoat!

V.

And if great lords and monarchs
  Are so polite to womankind,
The world for our devotion
  To Nora's skirts no fault can find, —
If England's king her life could take,
  Could condescend to cut her throat,*
Brave boys, it was no shame to make
  Our banner of her Petticoat!
    For we were Croppy heroes,
      With pike in hand and flag afloat,
    And bravely we avenged her,
      Beneath that flag — the Petticoat!

---

* The warlike old Croppy means that the king cut her throat by deputy, which was all the same to poor Norah. Theig the Croppy's relation will be received, I suppose, only as tradition, but the Petticoat banner is mentioned in the histories of the period.

VI.

Then all you roving heroes,
 Attend to Theig the Croppy's song;
May God preserve old Ireland,
 And Freedom's rule therein prolong!
May tyrants there who spoil the land
 All sink in black perdition's boat,
And may it rise to great command
 The influence of the Petticoat!
 And we were Croppy heroes,
  With pike in hand and flag afloat,
 Who taught our blood-stained tyrants
  The Lesson of the Petticoat!

MARJORY LE POER.

Air—"Marjory."

I.

I BEAR my fortune on my back,
A soldier's belt, a soldier's jack,
And, cloud or sunshine on my track,
 I ride by mount and shore;
And ever as my hawk I fly,
Or chase the stag o'er mountains high,
I think upon the laughing eye
 Of Marjory le Poer!

II.

I wander through the mountain cooms,
And lie amid the heather blooms,
Where 'mid the flowers the wild bee hums,
 With gay skies laughing o'er,
And gaze into the blue, and there
Build golden castles in the air,
Where reigns my queen of beauty rare,
 My Marjory le Poer!

III.

With plume and baldrick bright displayed,
With musketoon and flashing blade,
In deadly war's stern ranks arrayed,
 I dash through dust and gore;

And ever as the surging fight,
Loud thundering rolls from height to height,
I think upon the glances bright
    Of Marjory le Poer!

IV.

And thus in peace, and thus in war,
In joy at home, or wandering far
Beneath some lonely foreign star,
    By plain or mountain hoar,
All Nature sings one ceaseless tune,
In winter wild or summer noon —
My gem of gems, my rose of June,
    My Marjory le Poer!

I SIT BENEATH THE SUNSET SKIES.

Air — "Come, come with me."

I.

I sit beneath the sunset skies,
    Within the woodlands fair,
And look into my Mary's eyes
    For true love shining there;
I clasp her hand till daylight dies
    O'er hill and golden sea,
And moonlight shines through th' ancient pines
    Upon my love and me.

II.

In winter wild dark gleams the sloe
    Upon the whitened bough;
Her raven locks as darkly flow
    Around her lovely brow;
The morning star's soft virgin glow
    Within her eyes I see,
While moonlight shines through th' ancient pines,
    Upon my love and me.

III.

I stray through wildwood glades **afar**
    To think on her alone;

I sit me where the bright flowers are,
  And make my heart her throne;
And I will love while gleams the star,
  Or leaves grow on the tree,
While moonlight shines through th' ancient pines,
  Upon my love and me.

A REAPING WE WILL GO.

Air — "The Jolly Companie."

I.

It was a man of Wexford,
  With valor in his eye,
That sat upon a tumbril,
  And that raised his voice on high,
And sang this song of Freedom,
  With his brown face all aglow: —
"The autumn it is coming,
  And a reaping we will go!
  And a reaping we will go
Where the drums and trumpets play,
And the cannons roar from shore to shore,
  And rifles flash! — hurrah!

II.

"Amid the Irish mountains,
  In Irish vale and glen,
Say what shall be the harvest
  Of the brave, united men?
The scarlet Saxon soldiers,
  All rangéd in a row,
Shall be our swaths of corn,
  When a reaping we will go!
  And a reaping we will go
Where the drums and trumpets play,
And the cannons roar from shore to shore,
  And rifles flash! — hurrah!

III.

"And who shall smile upon us,
  And bless our flashing arms?

And who shall be our Queen of hearts
  In battle's loud alarms?
Our dear, belovéd Ireland,
  No other queen we'll know.
And we'll die for her or conquer,
  When a reaping we will go!
    And a reaping we will go
  Where the drums and trumpets play,
And the cannons roar from shore to shore,
  And rifles flash! — hurrah!

IV.

"And where shall be the harvest-home
  On our last reaping morn,
When the shamrock wreaths of victory
  Our happy brows adorn?
In Dublin's Royal Castle
  We'll make a gallant show,
With our Green Flag o'er it flying,
  When a reaping we will go!
    And a reaping we will go
  Where the drums and trumpets play,
And the cannons roar from shore to shore,
  And rifles flash! — hurrah!

V.

"Then all through holy Ireland
  Shall never more be seen
The gibbet, rack, and prison
  For the wearing of the Green;
So we'll strike the heated iron
  While we find it in a glow,
And we'll soon win back our freedom
  When a reaping we will go!
    And a reaping we will go
  Where the drums and trumpets play,
And the cannons roar from shore to shore,
  And rifles flash! — hurrah!"

THE RED LUSMORE.

Air — "The blooming Meadow."

I.

The snow is on the mountains high,
    The bloom has left the heather,
But laughing spring will soon be nigh,
    And summer's golden weather;
Then many a vale we'll wander o'er,
    Whose streams leap glad and fleetly,
And many a glen of red lusmore,*
    That shines in June so sweetly.

II.

What makes me love the lusmores gay,
    With all their bright bells round them?
My dear one's lips are red as they,
    And sweet as bee e'er found them;
And O! it shines by torrents hoar,
    In haunts of sprite and fairy,
Where many an hour, in days of yore,
    I dreamt of one like Mary.

III.

While purple decks its gorgeous bells
    I'll never seek a new love;
In summer time, where'er it dwells,
    I'll wander with my true love;
And aye I'll kiss her o'er and o'er,
    And vow my fond vows meetly,
In fairy glens of red lusmore,
    That shines in June so sweetly.

* *Lusmore*, i. e., the great herb, the Foxglove.

THE PEOPLE.

AIR—"All the way to Galway."

I.

A MIGHTY Voice sang in mine ear,
With tone prophetic, sweet and clear,—
"Bright Freedom's happy day is near
    For Ireland and her People!"
      The People! The People!
      God bless the Irish People!
      Through all their years
      Of blood and tears,
    Old Ireland's gallant People!

II.

With gibbet, fire, and fetter girth,
With bloody wars and famine dearth,
Our tyrants strove from off the earth
    To blot old Ireland's People!
      The People! The People!
      But firm as Shandon steeple
      Upon its rock,
      They stood each shock,
    Old Ireland's gallant People!

III.

For as the oak tree by the glen,
Shorn by the axe, springs up again
From deepest roots beyond our ken,
    So flourished Ireland's People!
      The People! The People!
      Though wars cut down the People,
      Each springing root
      Bore tenfold fruit,—
    Old Ireland's gallant People!

IV.

Then, brothers, here's to our dear land!
With freemen may her shores be manned!
And down with England's gory hand,

And up with Ireland's People!
The People! The People!
Like bells from Shandon steeple,
With ringing chime,
Sing out sublime
Hurrah! for Ireland's People!

THE BANKS OF ANNER.

Air — "The leaves are green in Aherloe."

I.

In purple robes old Sliavnamon
  Towers monarch of the mountains,
The first to catch the smiles of dawn,
  With all his woods and fountains; —
His streams dance down by tower and town,
  But none since Time began her
Met mortal sight so pure and bright
  As winding, wandering Anner.

II.

In hillside's gleam or woodland's gloom,
  O'er fairy height and hollow,
Upon her banks gay flowerets bloom,
  Where'er her course I follow.
And halls of pride tower o'er her tide,
  And gleaming bridges span her,
As, laughing gay, she winds away,
  The gentle, murmuring Anner.

III.

There gallant men, for freedom born,
  With friendly grasp will meet you;
There lovely maids, as bright as morn,
  With sunny smiles will greet you;
And there they strove to raise above
  The Red, Green Ireland's banner —
There yet its fold they'll see unrolled
  Upon the banks of Anner.

IV.

'Tis there we'll stand, with bosoms proud,
  True soldiers of our sireland,
When Freedom's wind blows strong and loud,
  And floats the flag of Ireland.
Let tyrants quake, and doubly shake
  Each traitor and trepanner,
When once we raise our camp-fire's blaze
  Upon the banks of Anner.

V.

O God! be with the good old days,
  The days so light and airy,
When to blithe friends I sang my lays
  In gallant, gay Tipperary;
When fair maids' sighs and witching eyes
  Made my young heart the planner
Of castles rare, built in the air,
  Upon the banks of Anner!

VI.

The morning sun may fail to show
  His light the earth illuming;
Old Sliavnamon to blush and glow
  In autumn's purple blooming;
And shamrocks green no more be seen,
  And breezes cease to fan her,
Ere I forget the friends I met
  Upon the banks of Anner!

GRA GAL MACHREE.

AIR — "Ne'er wed an old Man."

I.

WHEN morning discloses its light on the roses,
  Upon them reposes the sweet honey dew;
Like buds of their fairest, thy lips, O, my dearest!
  Have honey the rarest to sweeten them too:
Thine eyes they are brighter than stars of the night, or
  Than April skies' light, or than gems of the sea;
Thy neck's like th' illuming bright lily, assuming
  Its first tender blooming, sweet Gra Gal Machree.

II.

I went to the greenwood, that streamlets serene would
 Make music, and sheen would enliven me more :
Sweet visions they wrought me, sweet memories they brought me,
 Of thee, who first taught me love's passion and lore ;
The birds round me winging, their carols were singing,
 Their voices outringing with rapture and glee ;
My heart then enchanted, by dearer tones haunted,
 For thy loved words panted, sweet Gra Gal Machree.

III.

O Love! I am thinking of thee, from the blinking
 Of morn till the sinking of day in the west,
And thus each fair creature, and bright, blooming feature,
 And aspect of nature, brings joy to my breast ;
Each night through the airy, sweet dreamland of fairy,
 My soul still unweary, is wandering to thee,
And dream or reflection, is one recollection
 Of thy fond affection, sweet Gra Gal Machree.

ALONG WITH MY LOVE I'LL GO.

AIR — "The Roads they are wet and wintry, Love."

I.

My love has an eye of brightness,
 An arm of valor free ;
My love has a heart of lightness,
 But ever true to me ; —
The pride of my heart unchanging,
 His black locks' martial flow,
And away to the wild wars ranging,
 Along with my love I'll go.

II.

They tell me of the strangers
 Who waste our island fair ;
That war has toils and dangers
 Too stern for me to bear ; —
The stranger's gory rieving
 May lay our dwellings low ;
Yet to my fond froth cleaving,
 Along with my love I'll go.

III.

The woods wear winter sadness,
   White falls the icy shower,
There's shelter, peace, and gladness
   Within my father's tower;
I bore the summer's burning;
   I heed not winter's snow;
And thus, through joy or mourning,
   Along with my love I'll go.

IV.

O! ne'er for once to leave him
   In tented field or hall,
To smile if joy receive him,
   Or die if he should fall!
And ever thus unchanging,
   Through want, and toil, and woe,
Away to the wild wars ranging,
   Along with my love I'll go.

THE SPRING OF THE YEAR.

AIR — "The Spring of the Year."

I.

WE sat by the verge of the forest,
   Where flowers shone like stars in the ray,
Where steep rocks towered highest and hoarest,
   'Mid those hills of the east far away;
And sweet was the fond love that bound us,
   Undimmed by all doubting and fear,
And young, like the fresh flowers around us,
   In the soft, blooming spring of the year.

II.

The breeze brushed the stream into splendor,
   And murmured down valley and lea;
The wild birds sang songs low and tender
   To none but my darling and me;

And sweet were the smiles of my true love,
   And bright were the eyes of my dear,
A-sparkling with warm rays of new love
   In the soft, blooming spring of the year.

III.

The bronzed nuts in autumn that cluster,
   The golden-leaved sprays drooping down,
Are dim near the amber-bright lustre
   That gleams in her long locks of brown;
Her cheeks like the rose of the morning,
   Her neck like the blooms of the brere,
That smile all the woodlands adorning,
   In the soft, blooming spring of the year.

IV.

What vows of affection we plighted,
   What dreams 'mid those high hills we wove,
Of glory and bliss, ever lighted
   And warmed by the gay lamp of love!
Those vows live by doubt still unhaunted,
   The gay lamp shines steady and clear,
Still brightening those dreams that enchanted
   In the soft, blooming spring of the year.

V.

The future for us may be laden
   With grief, 'stead of bliss and of fame,
But I and my dear Irish maiden
   Shall love to the end still the same.
So sure to that love we'll be clinging,
   As flowers in our wild woods appear,
Or birds in green Ireland are singing
   In the soft, blooming spring of the year.

THE OUTLAW OF KILMORE.

AIR — "The wicked Kerryman."

I.

FAR in the mountains with you, my Eveleen,
I would be loving and true, my Eveleen;
  Then climb the mountains with me.
Long have I dwelt by the forest river side,
Where the bright ripples flash and quiver wide;
There the fleet hours shall blissful ever glide
  O'er us, sweet Gra Gal Machree.

II.

There on my rocky throne, my Eveleen,
Ever, ever alone, my Eveleen,
  I sit dreaming of thee;
High on the fern-clad rocks reclining there,
Though the sweet birds their songs are twining fair,
Thee I hear — and I see thy shining hair,
  Still, still, sweet Gra Gal Machree!

III.

Hunted and banned I've been, my Eveleen,
But my long sword is keen, my Eveleen,
  To keep all danger from thee:
The flash of this sword is my foeman's warning light,
And I live 'mid the wild hills, scorning might,
While my love grows eve and morning bright
  For you, sweet Gra Gal Machree!

IV.

Deeply in broad Kilmore, my Eveleen,
Down by the wild stream's shore, my Eveleen,
  I've made a sweet home for thee;
Yellow and bright, like thy long, long flowing hair,
Flowers the fairest are ever blowing there, —
Fairer still with thy clear eyes glowing there,
  Fondly, sweet Gra Gal Machree!

V.

Then come away, away, my Eveleen;
We will spend each day, my Eveleen,
  Blissful and loving and free.
Come to the woods where the streams are pouring blue,
Which the eagle is ever soaring through;
I'll grow fonder, each day adoring you,
  There, there, sweet Gra Gal Machree.

AN IRISH MORNING.

Air — "I built my Love a gallant Ship."

I.

Within the wood the wild bird wakes,
  And sings his wintry song;
With dreary light the morning breaks
  The snow-clad hills along;
Ah! once to me the early sun
  Brought light and joy each morn; —
Now, would that I were dead and gone,
  Or never had been born!

II.

Rise up, rise up, my husband dear,
  Rise up, my children, too;
This is no hour to linger here,
  No time to sleep for you.
The bailiff he is here — *Mo bron!*
  To cast us forth forlorn;
Ah! would that we were dead and gone,
  Or never had been born!

III.

They say the laws are good and wise,
  To even-hand justice true,
Equal to poor and rich: Arise,
  And see what they can do!
They cast us forth, they trample on
  Our rights, with hate and scorn;
Far better were we dead and gone,
  Or never had been born!

IV.

Awake, awake! All silent there;
   They'll never more arise!
She looks. Death answers in the stare
   Of their cold, stony eyes;
Famine had slain sire, daughter, son,
   And left her there forlorn,
Crying, " Would that I were dead and gone,
   Or never had been born!"

V.

Thus British Law shall scourge the land
   From town to rural glen,
Till the crushed People understand
   The God-made rights of men.
Till come that day, they'll cry " *Mo bron!*"
   Noon, night, and early morn,
And wish that they were dead and gone,
   Or never had been born!

I'LL STAY AT HOME.

AIR — " Paddies evermore."

I.

THE coat is rough that covers me;
   My hands are hard as horn;
The great ones mock my poverty,
   And look on me with scorn,
And sneer, and say, I'll sail away —
   A wretch obscure and banned!
No; I'll be true for life to you,
   And stay at home, dear land!

II.

I have a wife as summer bright,
   My loving Eileen Bawn;
A little son with locks of light,
   And smiles like May-day's dawn;
And could I leave them here to grieve,
   And seek some foreign strand?
No; I'll be true to them and you,
   And stay at home, dear land!

III.

And could I leave the grand old hills,
  And never see them more,
The green woods and the sparkling rills
  That deck my native shore,
To sweat and slave, then fill a grave
  Delved by some foreign hand?
No; I'll be true for life to you,
  And stay at home, dear land!

IV.

'Tis hard with tyranny to bear,
  With poverty to cope;
But still the stout heart laughs at care,
  And while there's life there's hope.
Yes, hope with me a day to see
  Of Freedom great and grand;
So I'll be true for life to you,
  And stay at home, dear land!

V.

I mind me of my sires who bled
  For Freedom long ago;
Who 'gainst each host our tyrants led,
  Dealt gallant blow for blow.
I hold to-night their memory bright,
  Each brave and patriot band,
And I'll be true, like them, to you,
  And stay at home, dear land!

THE LOCKS OF AMBER.

Air—"Nora an cul ombra."

Her eyes beamed so clearly
  With love's sunny ray,
When I told her how dearly
  I loved her alway,
As she sat in the chamber,
  'Mid gladness and light,
With her long locks of amber
  All glossy and bright.

II.

There are shells by the sea-side
  Of brown golden hue,
There are flowers by the lea-side
  To mate with them, too:
The high rocks I clamber
  With gold-moss are dight,
Like my love's locks of amber,
  All glossy and bright.

III.

When clouds gold and dun set
  O'er ocean and strand,
The deep hues of sunset
  Look glorious and grand!
O! they make me remember
  With endless delight
My love's locks of amber,
  All glossy and bright.

IV.

One dear lock, I wear it,
  My fond maiden gave;
Nigh my heart I will bear it
  Till cold in my grave:
Should life lower like December,
  They'd give my heart light,
Those long locks of amber,
  All glossy and bright.

ALLISDRUM'S MARCH AT THE BATTLE OF KNOCKINOSS.

A. D. 1648.

Air—"Allisdrum's March."

I.

Blow up the pipes with the brave battle chorus,
Look to your banner, the foe is before us,
Steady your guns, but when wanting to slay more,
There's nought like the rush and the slash of the claymore!

Follow me, follow me, dauntless and steady,
Shoulder to shoulder; the battle is ready;
Many a foeman will ne'er see a day more,
When we blow up the pipes and fall on with the claymore!

II.

Up Knockinoss comes he, Murrogh the Burner,*
The scourge of his race, of the Old Faith the spurner;
Black be the day he returned into Ireland,
To change her from peace to a woful and dire land!
Follow me, follow me, dauntless and steady,
Shoulder to shoulder; the battle is ready:
Look to your guns, but when wanting to slay more,
Blow louder the pipes and fall on with the claymore!

III.

On down the hill, and ne'er fire till you're near them,
Then try from your path with one volley to clear them;
Down with your guns then, and up with your claymore,
And fast from our onset they'll soon clear the way more!
Follow me, follow me, dauntless and steady,
Shoulder to shoulder; the battle is ready;
For God and our country we'll never delay more
To blow up the pipes and fall on with the claymore!

IV.

Crash through the foe went that chief and his brave men,
With bosoms the stoutest that ever God gave men;
But curst be the day when Lord Taafe grew faint-hearted,
And stood not, nor charged, but in panic departed!
Leaving that chief with his comrades to die there,
Leaving their corses for th' eagles to lie there;
But the foeman he rued and remembered each day more,
Stout Allisdrum's march, and the sweep of his claymore!

* Baron of Inchiquin.

THE LITTLE BIRD.

Air — "As I was riding out one Day."

I.

A LITTLE bird with golden wings
   Flies past from bloom to blossom:
'Tis like the memory that springs
   Of you within my bosom;
He flies unto the woodland tree,
   The tree he best loves only:
And thus that memory comes to me,
   Where'er I wander lonely.

II.

That little bird, some magic power,
   Some spell, has surely found him,
For when he warbles in his bower,
   The woods seem glad around him;
And when I hear his dulcet voice,
   I think of yours each day, love,
And memory makes my heart rejoice,
   And I am glad and gay, love.

III.

I miss him now the woods among,
   'Mid dewy leaves adorning:
The wild hawk heard his lonely song,
   And killed him in the morning;
But nought can kill the memory
   Of you, now sweetly shining
Within my heart so constantly,
   Till life that heart's resigning.

GARRYOWEN.

I.

They say a dead man tells no tales,
That silence o'er his tomb prevails,
However blow blind Fortune's gales
    In peace or battle gory;
But we can give that phrase the lie,
For dead men's voices fill the sky,
And float from Limerick's towers on high,
    O'er Garryowen in glory!

II.

O, mighty dead! O, unforgot!
O, heroes of the glorious lot!
Your deeds they sanctify each spot,
    Your names each legend hoary!
From charnel crypts of mouldered bones,
From fosses, walls, and graven stones,
Your voices sound in thunder tones
    O'er Garryowen in glory!

III.

They name great names, great battles won,
Great deeds by Irish heroes done,
They cry, "Unite! Be one! Be one!"
    From ancient graves and gory;
They bid us, brothers, all prepare
For th' hour when we can do and dare,
When Freedom's shout shall rend the air
    O'er Garryowen in glory!

IV.

And we can dare and we can do,
United men and brothers true,
Their gallant footsteps to pursue,
    And change our country's story;
To emulate their high renown,
To strike our false oppressors down,
And stir the old triumphant town
    With Garryowen in glory!

V.

And when that mighty day comes round,
We still shall hear their voices sound —
Our tramp shall roll along the ground,
    And shake the mountains hoary;
We'll raise the Sunburst as of yore,
And Limerick's streets and Shannon shore
Shall echo to our shout once more
    Of Garryowen in glory.

THE LESSON.

TO MY SON.

I.

Boy, you are come of gentle blood,
  Though now of poor degree, —
Where'er you go, may God the Good
  Smile on your destiny;
Whate'er your future, dark or bright,
  Through life's becheckered span,
In fortune's glow, or blackest night,
  Still prove yourself a MAN!

II.

While toiling up life's mountain rude,
  O'er pathways insecure,
A kindly bond of brotherhood
  Should bind you to the poor;
Whome'er you see misfortune grip
  And wither 'neath her ban,
Go, grasp his hand in fellowship,
  And prove yourself a MAN!

III.

Whate'er you sow in heedless youth,
  In manhood you will reap;
Then walk in virtue's path of truth,
  And God's commandments keep,
For virtue is the surest friend
  Since life and time began;

Then with her arms your soul defend,
  And prove yourself a MAN.

IV.

Whene'er you see some coward slave
  To foreign rule incline;
For foreign gold, the sordid knave,
  His native land malign;
From peasants born, or nobly sprung,
  Howe'er his life-stream ran,
Go, curb the dastard's villain tongue,
  And prove yourself a MAN!

V.

His native land! Our native land!
  I hear the warning hum,
Along the plains, from strand to strand,
  Of dangerous days to come;
But soldier poor, or general high,
  To lead her battle's van,
On danger look with steady eye,
  And prove yourself a MAN!

VI.

For Ireland oft your fathers dreed
  Misfortune's doomful wrath,
But yet in Ireland's darkest need
  Still tread the patriot's path;
A day shall come, whose glorious wind
  Her victor flags will fan,
With Christian soul and patriot mind,
  Then prove yourself a MAN!

VII.

O! wealth it is a faithless thing,
  And false are pride and fame;
For death may snap the human string
  While loudest throats acclaim;
Then ne'er let wealth, or fame, or pride,
  Your youthful heart trepan, —
Let Christian honor be your guide,
  And prove yourself a MAN!

DIARMID MOR.

Air—"Says the Mother to the Daughter."

I.

The wintry sun, with cheerless gleam
  Gilds Limerick's battered towers,
But far away down Shannon's stream
  A cloud of darkness lowers;
And there they glide upon the tide,
  The ships that bear him o'er
The stormy wave, with Sarsfield brave,
  My gallant Diarmid Mor.

II.

One summer eve, long, long ago,
  He said by wandering Lee,
Its rushing waves should backward flow
  Ere he would part from me;
But war came down, with darkest frown,
  And called from Shannon shore —
He left his bride that eventide,
  My gallant Diarmid Mor!

III.

He heard its call, and sped away
  To aid his native land.
Can Aughrim's field, or Limerick say
  They saw a truer hand?
Heart, arm, and glaive he freely gave,
  As did his sires before —
And now he flees across the seas,
  My gallant Diarmid Mor.

IV.

By Lee's green banks the flowers shall bloom,
  When summer decks the grove,
But when unto my heart shall come
  The smiles of my true love?
O! oft and drear shall flow the tear,
  Till some glad bark has bore
My love again back o'er the main,
  My gallant Diarmid Mor.

PADDY'S PROPOSAL.

Air — "No, Mr. Gallagher."

I.

I HAD a young sweetheart, and asked her to marry me;
She frowned that my impudence so far could carry me,
Said, to ask her to marry a poor serf in slavery
Was nothing but meanness, and all kinds of knavery!
She told me to handle a pike ere she'd list to me,
And vowed if I didn't, by that and by this to me,
She'd join for a rebel, to vex and to harry me,
Or remain an old maid, and she never would marry me!

II.

Her fingers I squeezed in the big, brawny hand o' me,
And went with a captain who took the command o' me
Off to the hill-side to practise the drilling there
The pike, and the rifle, and all kinds o' killing there;
I came back again when I thought he'd perfected me, —
She said I returned long before she expected me,
And bade me be off with the devil may carry me,
And till Ireland was free that she never would marry me!

III.

Then I kicked my caubeen for relief to my devilment,
And thought for a time what her words so uncivil meant —
"Begor! she has spirits," said I, "like the queen o' hearts,
And bates to tarnation whate'er I have seen o' hearts!"
I took up my pike, and its handle I kissed again,
And practised the drill till I half sprained my wrist again,
And thought with the bayonet no soldier could parry me,
And the next time I asked her she surely would marry me!

IV.

I took to the hills with our roving and airy boys,
And 'tis we that manœuvred like gallant Tipperary boys;
But we had no provisions, no tents for to cover us,
But the snow, and the rain, and the fogs rolling over us.
We had a smart skirmish one day as a feeler there,
To make out the strength of the soldier and Peeler there —

"Och!" says I, when 'twas over, "now nothing need worry me,
'Tis so easy to kill them, she surely will marry me!"

V.

But the sleet and the rain kept incessantly pouring there,
And the floods rattled down and the tempest was roaring there;
'Twas these, not the soldiers nor Peelers could sunder us,
For when they stood before us we soon brought them under us.
Now she comes to my cave in the hills where I'm hiding here,
And she gives me such courage, so gay and confiding here,
That I'm sure Fortune's wheel to the topmost will carry me,
That we'll soon free old Ireland, and Mary will marry me!

MARY EARLEY.

AIR — "The little fairy Moat."

I.

THERE is an island on the lake,
   Where dwelt my Mary Earley,
My modest maid, with smile so sweet,
   And teeth so white and pearly,
With graceful form, and heart so warm,
   And eyes that shone so clearly,
And wild I loved, and wild adored
   My sweet young Mary Earley.

II.

There is a boat upon that lake,
   With sails of snowy whiteness,
That floats across the silent tide,
   From shore to shore in brightness;
And oft within that swan-like boat,
   While morn was shining fairly,
I've basked me in the sunny smiles
   Of loving Mary Earley.

III.

And oft upon the silent eves
   Of golden summer weather,

We've sailed away to some bright bay
　　With joyful hearts together;
The wild birds seemed to haunt that shore,
　　To sing around us rarely,
And many a song of love they sang
　　For me and Mary Earley.

IV.

One autumn day, to bar my way
　　To love and that green island,
The storm swept down the moorlands brown,
　　And roared o'er glen and highland;
I plunged me in the surging tide,
　　And soon I clasped her dearly,
And kissed her by the island's side,
　　My loving Mary Earley.

V.

And now, beside Lough Deirgert's shore,
　　I sigh for Mary Earley,
And song birds all unheeded pour
　　The strains they sing so rarely;
There is a ruin lone and hoar,
　　Where sigh the sad winds drearly,
And there she sleeps forevermore,
　　My loving Mary Earley.

TO IRELAND.

I.

LAND of hills and wildwoods blooming,
Heaven's own tints from heaven assuming,
Queen of valor, old and hoary,
Thou shalt shine in song and story,
Radiant yet with Freedom's glory!

II.

Long we've bowed in slavish sorrow,
Hoping vain for Freedom's morrow;

Long before the foeman quailing,
Rang thy harp with plaintive wailing,
Groaned thy children unavailing.

III.

Land of beauty! Land of promise!
Rise, and hope thou all things from us;
Freedom wakens like a giant, —
We are now no slaves compliant,
We confront thy foes defiant!

IV.

Pass from brother unto brother, —
Pass the word, beloved mother! —
Pass the word in tone of thunder,
Freemen stand thy blue skies under,
Sworn to rend thy chains asunder!

V.

May no foul dissension harm us;
May thy wrongs resistless arm us;
May thy bright smile beaming o'er us,
True fraternal love restore us,
For the Battle Day before us!

MY FLOWER OF FLOWERS.

Air — "Slan Beo."

I.

Far, far away where the valleys are fair and green,
And the Suir murmurs down its castles and wildwoods between,
And the beautiful hills shine grand in the sunset hours,
With a heart full of sorrow I first met my flower of flowers.

II.

With grief in my heart — yet sorrow is ne'er so sad
But fondness can lighten and true love can make it glad;
And fondness and true love I found by the Suir's green bowers,
When I pledged her my troth and worshipped my flower of flowers.

III.

O! fair is the rose that smiles in Anner's green dale,
And modest and pure is the lily so pearly and pale,
And the eyebright shines like a star from Heaven's blue towers:
But fairer to me is my beautiful flower of flowers.

IV.

My heart's like a golden temple of fairyland,
Since I first saw my love with her face so bright and bland,
And the world seems a path where never a dark cloud lowers —
For the sun that shines o'er is my beautiful flower of flowers.

FINEEN THE ROVER.

Air — "You'd think, if you heard their Pipes squealing."

I.

An old castle towers o'er the billows
  That thunder by Cleena's green land,
And there dwelt as gallant a rover
  As ever grasped hilt in the hand;
Eight stately towers of the waters
  Lie anchored in Baltimore Bay,
And over their twenty score sailors,
  O! who but that Rover holds sway?
    Then ho! for Fineen the Rover,
    Fineen O'Driscoll the free,
    Straight as the mast of his galley,
    And wild as a wave of the sea!

II.

The Saxons of Cork and Moyallo,
  They harried his lands with their powers;
He gave them a taste of his cannon,
  And drove them like wolves from his towers;
The men of Clan London brought over
  Their strong fleet to make him a slave;
They met him by Mizen's wild highland,
  And the sharks crunched their bones 'neath the wave!

Then ho! for Fineen the Rover!
    Fineen O'Driscoll the free,
With step like the red stag of Beara,
    And voice like the bold, sounding sea!

III.

Long time in that old battered castle,
    Or out on the waves with his clan,
He feasted, and ventured, and conquered,
    But ne'er struck his colors to man.
In a fight 'gainst the foes of his country
    He died as a brave man should die,
And he sleeps 'neath the waters of Cleena,
    Where the waves sing his *caoine* to the sky!
Then ho! for Fineen the Rover,
    Fineen O'Driscoll the free,
With eye like the osprey's at morning,
    And smile like the sun on the sea!

SNOWING.

AIR—"An gun gal ban."

I.

'Tis snowing—'tis drifting and snowing;
    Will the snow freeze my heart to-night?
'Tis blowing—'tis drearily blowing;
    Will the cold blast make love less bright?
O! the bleakness my heart may enter,
    And the world's dark misery;
But through summer or coldness of winter,
    'Twill brighten with thoughts of thee!

II.

There's a summer that sweetly bloometh,
    Whose freshness can ne'er depart;
In the footsteps of love it cometh,
    And it reigns in the constant heart!
'Tis snowing—'tis drifting and snowing,
    And the wind howls drearily,
But that gay summer's splendor glowing
    Lights my bosom with thoughts of thee!

THE YELLOW HAIR.

Air—"As I went forth one evening."

I.

You'd know my gentle true love 'mid five hundred maidens fair,
By her smiles of pleasant sweetness and her wondrous golden hair,
By her step of airy lightness, like a fawn's in forest lone,
And her gushing, loving laughter, like a sweet flute's golden tone.
   O! the yellow, yellow hair! O! the glittering, yellow hair!
   Sweetly flowing, brightly glowing, o'er her neck and shoulders fair!

II.

With a violet-tinted ribbon, and a ribbon all of green,
Doth she bind those glossy tresses at the pleasant morning's sheen;
And all day they gleam and glitter, like a young queen's golden crown,
But she lets them flow at sunset in their yellow brightness down.
   O! the yellow, yellow hair! O! the glittering, yellow hair!
   Sweetly flowing, brightly glowing, o'er her neck and shoulders fair!

III.

Beyond the tall, great mountains, where sing the wild streams' tides,
Amid the airy greenwoods, my lovely maid resides;
And she'll give, when next I meet her, of that hair one ringlet band,
And I'll wear it in my bosom, ever wandering through the land.
   O! the yellow, yellow hair! O! the glittering, yellow hair!
   Sweetly flowing, brightly glowing, o'er her neck and shoulders fair!

A HYMN TO ENGLAND.

Air — "The Boys of Wexford."

I.

Hail to the English government,
  By right divine our own;
May quiet consciences be theirs,
  From ministers to throne;
For what they do throughout the land
  Give praise unanimous,
For sure 'tis all by God's command
  They slay and torture us!
    Then hail to England's government,
      Our own by right divine,
    And starve 'mid plains where plenty reigns,
      And die and make no sign!

II.

There once were gallant Irishmen,
  Long deemed to Ireland true,
Who thought their heritage their own,
  Church, creed, and conscience too;
Poor, blinded slaves, untaught, unjust,
  To clash with England's will;
England has trampled them to dust,
  And shall we weep them still?
    O, no! we'll praise the government,
      Our own by right divine,
    And starve 'mid plains where plenty reigns,
      And die and make no sign!

III.

Up spoke the holy Wexford priest,
  "Give England up your arms;
What have poor clods like us to do
  With war and war's alarms?
Leave war to kings and princes great,
  We want but only peace,
To save our souls, and for the state
  Our crops and herds increase.

      So let us hail the government,
        Our own by right divine,
      And starve 'mid plains where plenty reigns,
        And die and make no sign!"

IV.

They yielded: then great England fell,
    Of course by God's command,
With murder, rape, and sacrilege
    Upon the bleeding land;
They slew him and his flock like brutes,
    They hacked him part by part,
They fried his fat to grease their boots,
    And supped upon his heart! *
    For this, we hail the government,
      Our own by right divine,
    And starve 'mid plains where plenty reigns,
      And die and make no sign!

V.

When Famine spread his banner pale,
    And shook his spectral spear
O'er the doomed land, and every wind
    Brought Plague, and Death, and Fear,
The voice that ever filled our ears
    Was, "Yield ye Cæsar's due;
What right to think, what right to eat,
    Have wicked dogs like you?" †
    Then let us hail the government,
      Our own by right divine,
    And starve 'mid plains where plenty reigns,
      And die and make no sign!

VI.

We have no memories to sear
    Our hearts, of blood and pains,
Of massacres of child and man,
    Of dungeons and of chains;

---

* See the several histories of the Rebellion of 1798 for an account of the career and death of Father Murphy, the heroic priest alluded to in this hymn. An English yeomanry corps, the "Ancient Britons," used his body exactly in the manner given in the above text.

† I saw, myself, when a boy, the people of a district daily dying of hunger, where there was as much corn, cattle, and food of every kind within its bounds as would be sufficient to feed the whole population for a year or two.

Of hero heads on castle towers,
  In many a ghastly row,
Of pitchcaps, thumbscrews' torture powers,
  Of pillage, ruin, woe!
    O, no! Then hail the government,
      Our own by right divine,
    And starve 'mid plains where plenty reigns,
      And die and make no sign!

VII.

And all you sons of wickedness,
  Kneel down and pray with me
For newer tortures, heavier chains,
  And deeper misery;
And thank your blessed stars on high
  For each soul-saving meed,
But keep your arms and powder dry
  For England's hour of need!
    And hail our holy government,
      Our own by right divine,
    And starve 'mid plains where plenty reigns,
      And die and make no sign!

O, FAIR SHINES THE SUN ON GLENARA.

Air — "Glenara."

I.

O, fair shines the sun on Glenara,
And calm rest his beams on Glenara;
  But O! there's a light
  Far dearer, more bright,
Illumines my soul in Glenara,
The light of thine eyes in Glenara.

II.

And sweet sings the stream of Glenara,
Glancing down through the woods like an arrow;
  But a sound far more sweet
  Glads my heart when we meet
In the green summer woods of Glenara, —
Thy voice by the wave of Glenara.

III.

And O! ever thus in Glenara,
Till we sleep in our graves by Glenara,
  May thy voice sound as free
  And as kindly to me,
And thine eyes beam as fond in Glenara,
In the green summer woods of Glenara!

THE GIRL I LEFT BEHIND ME.

A PRISON SONG.

I.

I sat beneath a withered tree
  When winter winds blew keenly,—
As soon such winds might bring to me
  The red rose blushing sheenly,
As fate return life's jovial morn,
  And smiling gay re-find me,
The hopes all crossed, the loved and lost,
  The girl I left behind me!

II.

Like that sear tree whose leaflets shone
  Last spring with dewdrops pearly,
My hopes outbloomed at manhood's dawn,
  In love's light shining early;
The leaves are dead, my joys are fled,
  The tyrant's shackles bind me,
And never more may fate restore
  The girl I left behind me!

III.

But sure a man hath other ties
  Than love's light flame pursuing,
To dry his country's tearful eyes,
  The tyrant's work undoing;
I sowed the seed of that bright creed,
  And scorn the doom assigned me,—
For her alone I make my moan,
  The girl I left behind me!

IV.

They tell me that her early bloom
  Is dimmed with constant weeping,
Like Ireland, o'er her woful doom
  A tearful vigil keeping;
But spite of fears and patriot tears,
  My better hopes remind me
I'll see her face, and yet embrace
  The girl I left behind me!

V.

Yes, sometimes to my prison cell
  Hope comes in arms all gleaming,
In fancy brings the battle yell,
  And green flags proudly streaming;
In fancy shows our tyrant foes
  Retreat, no more to bind me,
And Freedom's reign restores again
  The girl I left behind me!

THIS MAID OF MINE.

AIR — "Costly were her robes of gold."

I.

My Mary is not wondrous fair,
  As other maidens are,
Yet she's to me a jewel rare,
  A clear, bright, shining star;
No glorious form that can surprise,
  No Grecian face divine —
The beauty of her soul-bright eyes
  That marks this maid of mine.

II.

No vain pursuit, no idle thought,
  No art its charm bestows;
No smiles with honeyed treachery fraught
  My darling true-love knows;

A bashful mien, a modest face,
  Where sunny health doth shine,
A form of sweet and simple grace
  That mark this maid of mine.

III.

She dwells not in the lordly halls
  Where Fashion loves to blaze,
But where the rocks, like giant walls,
  And hills their green sides raise;
And there no guile her heart has known,
  No proud charms false and fine —
There trusting love for me alone
  That marks this maid of mine.

SHAWN DHAS OF TULLYELMER.

Air — "The old Astrologer."

I.

Shawn Dhas,* of Tullyelmer,
  He was a nice young man,
With squinting eyes and turned-up nose,
  And a mouth spread half a span;
The flesh was lank upon his limbs,
  But mighty were his bones,
And his feet were like two wooden rams
  That drive the paving stones!
    Sing de'il may care how others fare,
      I'm born a beauty bright,
    And a princess I will marry,
      Who'll be my heart's delight!

II.

As Shawn he went a-courting,
  One pleasant morn in May,
He met an old Astrologer
  Upon the king's highway,

---

* *Shawn Dhas.* John the Handsome. By antiphrasis, John the Ugly, — its sense in the song.

With thin-cut lips, and piercing eyes,
   And long, hooked nose between —
You'd travel all old Ireland's ground
   To find a blade more keen!
      Sing de'il may care, &c.

III.

He sidled up and simpered,
   And thus to him did say,
"I hear you can tell fortunes,
   Will you tell mine, I pray?"
"O, I can tell good fortunes
   But for a golden fee,
Then whip me out a guinea bright,
   And cross my palm!" said he.
      Sing de'il may care, &c.

IV.

Out hopped his golden guinea,
   And crossed the old man's palm,
Who said, "From south to polar star
   This is man's only balm;
The moon is in her tantrums now,
   With the Crab and Gemini,
And to smile down good luck on you
   Requires the guinea fee!
      Sing de'il may care, &c.

V.

"So I'll put it in my pocket,
   And I'll tell your fortune soon —
Brian Aireach and his Reaping Hook
   They both command the Moon;
Bold Leo and young Virgo bright
   Hold Libra's scales on high,
Which shows that you some princess grand
   Will wed before you die!"
      Sing de'il may care, &c.

VI.

And now on the fine ladies
   Shawn Dhas will always leer,
With a sidelong look in his great eyes,
   And his mouth from ear to ear:

But at the pleasant country girls
 He'll sneer, and pass them by,
With his leaden poll thrown proudly back,
 And his chin cocked to the sky,
  Singing, "De'il may care how others fare,
   I'm born a beauty bright,
   And a princess I will marry,
    Who'll be my heart's delight!"

MY ANNA'S EYES.

Air — "The Summer is come."

I.

Where shines the sun on Cummeragh's dells,
Far, far away my Anna dwells,
And there her eyes first beamed on me,
And chained my heart eternally.
 I sit alone, that memory rise
 Of sunny hopes and golden ties,
 Of smiles that beam like morning skies
 Within her large, blue, loving eyes!

II.

Saint Anne's lone well is bordered round
With golden moss and fairy mound;
There harebells glow like sapphire gem:
My Anna's eyes are blue like them.
 I sit alone, that memory rise
 Of sunny hopes and golden ties,
 Of smiles that beam like morning skies
 Within my Anna's loving eyes!

III.

Where'er she walks, by hill or stream,
On all those eyes of glory beam,
With sweet and gentle rays that are
Like splendors of the evening star.
 I sit alone, that memory rise
 Of sunny hopes and golden ties,
 Of smiles that beam like morning skies
 Within my Anna's loving eyes!

IV.

And there is more than common light,
Far dearer still, to make them bright, —
Fond rays, that pure and freshly dart
From sinless soul and sunny heart.
  Then lone I sit, that memory rise
Of sunny hopes and golden ties,
Of smiles that beam like morning skies
Within her large, blue, loving eyes!

THE BLIND GIRL OF GLENORE.

AIR — "The Summer shines around me."

I.

THE summer shines around me,
  With its blooms and shady bowers,
But I cannot see the glory
  Of the meadows and the flowers;
Once to me the golden summer
  Was all one lapse of light,
Till the red, red lightning struck me,
  And withered up my sight.
    Ah! Donall, Donall,
      Donall of Glenore,
    Give me back the heart I gave you
      In the sunny days of yore.

II.

Do you mind the sunlit meadow
  Where the Funcheon murmurs past,
Where you vowed one silent even
  That your love should ever last?
I have now no friends to love me —
  In Molagga's yard lie they —
And the blindness, O! the blindness
  Is upon me night and day!
    Ah! Donall, Donall,
      Donall of Glenore,
    Give me back the heart I gave you
      In the sunny days of yore.

III.

They tell me in the village
  That your heart to me is changed;
But your words have never told me
  That you wish to be estranged;
Yet I will not cloud the gladness
  Of a heart so kind and free —
O, this blindness! O, this blindness!
  Sad the doom it brought to me!
    Ah! Donall, Donall,
      Donall of Glenore,
    Give me back the heart I gave you
      In the sunny days of yore.

IV.

Place your hand upon my temples,
  Feel the hot blood pulsing through; —
Is it pain of bitter sickness,
  Or pain of love for you?
'Tis the bitter, bitter fever
  That is burning in my brain,
While I strive that love to banish
  Till my heart-strings crack and strain.
    Ah! Donall, Donall,
      Donall of Glenore,
    Give me back the heart I gave you
      In the sunny days of yore.

V.

Donall took the hand of Nora
  On that lovely morning-tide,
He led her to the chapel,
  And he made her there his bride.
O! to find a pair so happy
  You should travel far and wide,
As the blind maid and her Donall
  By the Funcheon's flowery side!
    Ah! Donall, Donall,
      Donall of Glenore;
    Still he loved her, as he loved her
      In the sunny days of yore!

FAIR KATE OF GLENANNER.

AIR—"Fair Kate."

I.

THE sunlight is sleeping on Cummeragh's wild mountain,
And gay shine the blossoms by dingle and fountain;
Sweet murmurs the stream where the soft breezes fan her,
And bright at my side sits fair Kate of Glenanner.

II.

The boughs of the elms in the cool breeze are swaying,
With the clear waves beneath towards the wide ocean playing,
And the tall ferns wave like a green sunlit banner,
While I whisper my love to fair Kate of Glenanner.

III.

She smiles as she points at the sunny wave near me,
And I wish for a boat with its white sail to bear me
From that spot, from the stream where the gray arches span her,
To some green isle of love with fair Kate of Glenanner.

SONG OF THE FOREST FAIRY.

AIR — "The Fairy Man."

I.

WHERE the gold moss hangs on the mighty oak,
Where never was heard the woodman's stroke,
  In the ancient woods,
    Where the wild deer bide —
  Where the heron broods,
    By the lakelet's side,
Morn, noon, and eve, in the rosy air,
We dance full merrily there, O, there!

II.

At night, in a glade of the brightest green,
We meet with fond homage our youthful queen:
  There in revel and feast
    We spend the night,
  Or in balmy rest
    Till the morning light,
When out on the greensward, smooth and fair,
We dance so merrily there, O, there!

III.

'Tis glorious to see the globes of dew
By the red beams of morn pierced through and through;
  'Tis sweet to peer
    Where the wild-flower gleams,
  And sweeter to hear
    The birds and the streams;
And sweeter than all in the blue, bright air,
To dance so merrily there, O, there!

TO A BIRD.

I.

WHENCE art thou, O delightful bird,
  That sittest on the leafy bough?
Thy cheery note, so long unheard,
  Calms my sad soul and smooths my brow.
What sunny climes hast thou explored,
  What wide seas' foam, what deserts' dearth,
Since first thy wings resplendent soared
  Up from thy native spot of earth?

II.

Thou need'st not at my greeting start,
  For, comrade, who could work thee harm?
Could fright thy little trusting heart,
  Or spoil thy bright wing's painted charm?
Whence comest thou, O minstrel gay?
  Perchance far, far beyond the foam
Thou sat'st upon the wildwood spray
  To sing beside my native home!

III.

O, comrade of the tuneful craft,
  Could I but dream a song like thine,
I'd sing how summer breezes waft
  Their perfumes round that spot, — how twine
The sweetbrier and the woodland rose
  Through that blithe vale my song should tell,
And how like wreaths of fragrant snows
  The hawthorn hedge blooms up the dell.

IV.

Deep in my soul thy heavenly strain
  Lights one great flash of memory, —
I see that valley green again,
  The rural home and guardian tree,
The purple hill, the spreading wold,
  The ruined tower and village spire,
Meadow and streamlet, as of old,
  Bathed in the level sunset fire!

V.

I hear the ringdove from the wood
  Coo to his mate with plaintive call,
The skylark from his golden cloud,
  The murmuring of the waterfall;
The merry milkmaid's roundelay,
  The airy ploughboy's whistle keen,
The children at their jocund play
  Around the hawthorn on the green.

VI.

And 'neath that hawthorn's perfumed shade
  I sit again, while sunset dies,
Beside my first-loved village maid,
  And gaze into her clear blue eyes,
Till the old love-dream lights once more
  Within my breast its rapturous flame,
With warmth of life, nor foreign shore,
  Nor joy, nor grief, nor chance can tame!

VII.

And those blithe friends in life's young day
  Who danced beneath that blooming tree,

O minstrel! tell me where are they,
  And have they all forgotten me?
Farewell! Thou spread'st thy shining wing
  To visit isles beyond the foam.
Thou'rt gone — and where? Perchance to sing
  My memory into hearts at home!

THE STIRRUP-CUP.

I.

Comrades, to you I give the hand,
  Who hate with me the tyrant's rule;
Who fight with me for old Ireland,
  And learn with me in Freedom's school,
    By night and day,
    To walk the way
That leads direct to Freedom's shrine:
    Then fill me up
    A stirrup-cup;
I'll pledge you in a stoup o' wine!

II.

Long years ground down, and, passion-blind,
  Our peasants, 'neath each tyrant's reign,
Helped their false lords with darkened mind
  To clasp more firm their helot's chain;
    But now they see
    True Liberty,
A foe to every feudal line:
    Then fill me up
    A stirrup-cup;
I'll pledge them in a stoup o' wine!

III.

The hireling sells his land for pay,
  And flaunts the red of England's queen;
But, praise to Heaven! no hirelings they
  Who wear our everlasting green;
    For Ireland's good
    In brotherhood,

Self-interest nobly they resign:
  Then fill me up
  A stirrup-cup;
I'll pledge them in a stoup o' wine!

IV.

Our lords, — come, tell me who are they,
  And tell it with a freeman's tongue? —
In Cromwell's time, and William's day,
  Base churls, from scamps and scullions sprung!
    But bard and sage,
    And History's page,
Our peasants prove of noble line:
  Then fill me up
  A stirrup-cup;
I'll pledge them in a stoup o' wine!

V.

Ah! Freedom may be dearly bought,
  When bought with many a brave man's gore;
But better die like those who fought
  And fell round Ireland's flag of yore;
    Then bear the pain,
    And drag the chain,
'Neath whose fell links our brothers pine:
  Then fill me up
  A stirrup-cup;
I'll pledge them in a stoup o' wine!

VI.

Give me your hands, brave brothers round,
  Stripling and war-worn soldier keen;
In Irish hands, on Irish ground,
  The glittering pike once more is seen,
    With sword and gun,
    And Freedom's sun
Will light us to their battle line:
  So fill me up
  A stirrup-cup, —
I pledge you in a stoup o' wine!

HOW SARSFIELD DIED IN GLORY.

Air — " Rodney's Glory ; " or, " The Princess Royal."

I.

'Twas in that sad and woful year
Of war and famine, death and fear,
When Ireland lowered her banner spear
   On Limerick's turrets hoary,
We took to ship and sailed the sea
Unto the shore of Normandie,
And then once more our banner free
     Flashed to the ray
     In many a fray,
And victor saw that bloody day
   When Sarsfield died in glory!

II.

The morn rose red on Landen plain,
King William charged o'er heaps of slain,
And Frenchmen's blood poured out like rain
   Upon the field so gory;
To stem his onset vain they tried,
As on he swept in warlike pride,
Till Luxemburg, our marshal cried,
     " New force we want
     To bear the brunt,
So bring the Irish to the front!"
   Where Sarsfield died in glory.

III.

Then you should hear our slogan roar,
Loud swell the din of battle o'er,
As forward our battalions bore
   To change the Frenchman's story;
Against the foe our strength we threw,
And mixed us in the bloody brew,
While swords and spears in flinders flew,
     And grape and shot
     And bullets hot

Rained round the crimson, fatal spot
  Where Sarsfield died in glory!

IV.

There, like the bolt that from on high
Tears roaring through the storm-wracked sky,
And on the trembling ground anigh
  In thunder bursts before ye;
So our brave chieftain 'neath the ball,
In thundering clangor met his fall,
But rallying at his dying call,
    With deafening shout,
    Our foemen stout,
We swept away in bloody rout,
  Where Sarsfield died in glory!

V.

His hand upon the wound he pressed,
Sad sinking to his final rest,
Then took it from his gallant breast,
  With his hot life-blood gory —
"O, would," the dying hero cried,
"That this my heart's ensanguined tide
Had stained some native mountain side
    For old Ireland!"
    Then dropped his hand,
And midst our tearful, conquering band
  Brave Sarsfield died in glory!

VI.

Then all good men, where'er you be,
Who fought for Ireland's liberty,
Our hero brave lament with me,
  And ponder well his story;
And pray, like him, that you may die
Beneath old Ireland's genial sky,
With Saxon dead piled mountains high,
    The spot around
    Where you have found
The hero's death on Irish ground
  That Sarsfield died in glory!

DONAL O'KEEFFE'S LAMENT.

Air — "She's a dear Maid to me."

I.

My name is Donal Dhu — an outlaw bold and true,
  I ranged the country through, from Saxon bondage free,
Till I loved a maiden fair, with her glossy, curling hair,
  But she sunk me in despair — she's a dear maid to me!

II.

My sires were princes grand, within old Ireland's land:
  With many a knightly band they held their castles free,
Till the Saxon with them strove — an outlaw now I rove,
  Lamenting my false love — she's a dear maid to me!

III.

Her brow like wintry snows, her cheeks were like the rose
  That nigh Blackwater blows when summer decks the tree;
Her dark eyes glittered bright, full, full of love's delight, —
  They haunt me day and night — she's a dear maid to me!

IV.

With gems of costly sheen I decked my mountain queen,
  And glorious was her mien of beauty fresh and free;
Her step was like the fawn on Araglin's wild lawn,
  Her smile was like the dawn — she's a dear maid to me!

V.

Margaret Kelly was her name, and burning was the flame
  That o'er our bosoms came when we first loved trustingly;
But her love grew false and cold, and her outlaw's life she sold
  For the Saxon's worthless gold — she's a dear maid to me!

VI.

O! woful was the hour that revenge o'er me had power
  To slay my beauteous flower, when I knew her perfidy —
I drew my skian unblessed, and with rage and grief possessed,
  I plunged it in her breast — she's a dear maid to me!

VII.

And now I've 'scaped the chain, and now I'm free again,
  On many a battle plain I will let the Saxons see
What their traitor wiles shall prove, though an outlaw still I rove,
  Lamenting my false love — she's a dear maid to me!

FAIR HELEN OF THE DELL.

Air — "The Dark Maid of the Dell."

I.

Though joy his flowers be twining,
And thou in beauty shining,
Yet O! in joy's declining
  I'd love thee still as well;
Wherever fortune lead thee,
Or wind or wave can speed thee,
This true heart still shall heed thee,
  Fair Helen of the Dell.

II.

I've never yet beholden
A form so finely moulden,
Thy hair a sunset golden,
  Thy voice the clear harp's swell;
Thine eyes have Heaven's own brightness,
Thy neck the lily's whiteness,
Thy step the hill-stream's lightness,
  Fair Helen of the Dell.

III.

Few summers thou hast numbered;
Thy heart to this has slumbered;
Love leads it now uncumbered
  In his bright bowers to dwell;
He casts his splendor o'er thee,
He walks in light before thee,
That I may wild adore thee,
  Fair Helen of the Dell.

THE PUNCH BOWL; OR, THE CROPPY'S FINGER.

AIR — "Come all you jolly Shepherds."

I.

"Rise up, rise up, Pat Randal,
  And take the corn to town;
Our rent is due next Saturday,
  Full five and twenty poun';
The morn is breaking early,
  I hear the wild birds' song, —
Rise up, rise up, Pat Randal,
  You're waiting there too long!"
    Hey the jolly Punch bowl,
      Best on Irish ground,
    And hey the Dead Man's finger
      That stirred it round and round!

II.

Up and waked Pat Randal,
  And looked upon his bride,
Where, like a dew-bright lily,
  She stood by his bedside:
"God's blessing on you, Mary,
  This lovely summer morn."
And up and rose Pat Randal,
  And took to town his corn.
    Hey the jolly Punch bowl,
      Best on Irish ground,
    And hey the Dead Man's finger
      That stirred it round and round!

III.

"Yield up! yield up, base Croppy!
  You fought at Arklow glen,"
Up spoke the English captain,
  With all his loyal men;
"You fought at Arklow glen," he said,
  "And Oulart's bloody heath,

And for that same, false Irish dog,
  Now you shall die the death!"
    Hey the jolly Punch bowl,
      Best on Irish ground,
    And hey the Dead Man's finger,
      That stirred it round and round!

IV.

Out answered bold Pat Randal,
  "Yes, and at Wexford town;
And 'twas from Eniscorthy's gate
  I tore your red flag down!
At Ross and Tubber'neering's Pass,
  I'll ne'er deny the same —
Give me a sword, and with you all
  I'll play again that game!"
    Hey the jolly Punch bowl,
      Best on Irish ground,
    And hey the Dead Man's finger,
      That stirred it round and round!

V.

Long, long poor Mary Randal
  Her woful watch shall keep,
In heart-consuming sorrow
  Her gallant husband weep,
For by the lonesome highway
  The Murdered lies at rest,
A finger lopped from his right hand,
  Ten bullets in his breast!
    Hey the jolly Punch bowl,
      Best on Irish ground,
    And hey the Dead Man's finger
      That stirred it round and round!

VI.

It was the English captain
  Amused his guests that night,
It was his lovely daughter
  With ringlets golden bright,
That took the Croppy's finger,
  And with it stirred the draught,
While to Ireland's deep damnation
  The rousing punch they quaffed!

    Hey the jolly Punch bowl,
      Best on Irish ground,
    And hey the Dead Man's finger
      That stirred it round and round!

VII.

Like the Cross that to Constantine
    Showed victory from the skies,
May that murdered Croppy's finger
    Blaze yet before our eyes,
In the Day of Retribution
    Pointing out bright Freedom's way,
Till my country's brave battalions
    Sweep the English power away!
    And hey the jolly Punch bowl,
      Best on Irish ground,
    And the Croppy's gory finger
      That stirred it round and round.

THE DRINAN DHUN.

Air—" The Drinan Dhun."

I.

By road and by river the wild birds sing;
O'er mountain and valley the dewy leaves spring;
The gay flowers are shining, gilt o'er by the sun;
And fairest of all shines the Drinán Dhun.

II.

The rath of the fairy, the ruin hoar,
With white silver splendor it decks them all o'er;
And down in the valleys where merry streams run,
How sweet smell the blossoms of the Drinán Dhun.

III.

Ah! well I remember the soft spring day
I sat by my love 'neath its sweet-scented spray;
The day that she told me her heart I had won,
Beneath the white blossoms of the Drinán Dhun.

IV.

The streams they were singing their gladsome song,
The soft winds were blowing the wildwoods among,
The mountains shone bright in the red setting sun,
And my love in my arms 'neath the Drinán Dhun!

V.

'Tis my prayer in the morning, my dream at night,
To sit thus again by my heart's dear delight,
With her blue eyes of gladness, her hair like the sun,
And her sweet, loving kisses, 'neath the Drinán Dhun.

THE SIEGE OF LIMERICK.

Air — "Cúl awling deas."

I.

By William led, the English sped,
  With musket, sword, and cannon,
To sweep us all from Limerick's wall,
  And drown us in the Shannon;
But we bethought how well they fought,
  Our fathers there before us;
We raised on high our charging cry,
  And flung our green flag o'er us!

II.

For days on days their cannon's blaze
  Flashed by the blood-stained water;
The breach is done, and up they run,
  Five hundred to the slaughter;
They crossed the breach beyond our reach —
  New foes fresh work supplied us —
Our women brave, their homes to save,
  Soon slew them all inside us!

III.

Though through the smoke their army broke,
  With cannons booming solemn,
We would not flinch, but inch for inch
  Opposed its bristling column;

Three times we dashed them back, and smashed
  Their lines with shot and sabre,
And nought had they at close of day
  But thinned ranks for their labor.

IV.

With angry word then said their lord,
  "Our foes are better, braver!"
Then fled he straight from Limerick's gate,
  For he could not enslave her;
Then raised we high our triumph cry,
  Where battle's chances found us,
With corse, and gun, and red flags strewn,
  And blood and ruin round us!

WHATEVER WIND IS BLOWING.

Air—"Where have you been?"

I.

My heart's not made to freeze and fade
  On sorrow's stony mountains,
But aye it turns, and O! it burns
  To drink at Pleasure's fountains!
    Then I will drink what best I think
      To cool its hot thirst glowing,
    And love shall be first guide to me,
      Whatever wind is blowing.

II.

When woe calls down night's darksome frown,
  With not a star for warning,
One thought of two sweet eyes of blue
  Soon brings the glorious morning.
    Still o'er my way, with blessèd ray,
      May love's calm light be glowing,
    And honor too still guide me through,
      Whatever wind is blowing.

GLENORA.

Air — "Banalana."

I.

O, fondest and fairest!
　O, lovely Glenora!
The sweet smile thou wearest,
　Glenora! Glenora!
It pictures red roses
When summer discloses
Their bright buds the rarest —
　Glenora! Glenora!

II.

The hill-stream down flinging,
　O, lovely Glenora!
Its sweetest song singing,
　Glenora! Glenora!
Reminds me of thee, love,
Thy step light and free, love,
Thy gay laugh outringing,
　Glenora! Glenora!

III.

Like wings of the raven,
　O, lovely Glenora!
'Gainst snowy clouds waven,
　Glenora! Glenora!
Thy black tresses twine on
Thy shoulders, or shine on
Thy bosom's white heaven,
　Glenora! Glenora!

IV.

O, fragrant and bloom-bright,
　O, lovely Glenora!
The sword and the plume bright,
　Glenora! Glenora!

May win a high name, love,
On war's field of fame, love,
My life to illume bright,
  Glenora! Glenora!

V.

But never, O, never,
  My lovely Glenora!
Shall fortune dissever,
  Glenora! Glenora!
Our true hearts confiding,
In love fondly gliding
Down life's winding river,
  Glenora! Glenora!

I SIT ON THE HOLD OF MOYALLO.

AIR — "Through Mallow without my Armor."

I.

I sit on the hold of Moyallo,
  And look on the Blackwater stream,
As it bounds from the moors of Duhallow,
  And shines in the gay summer beam:
And I dream of a nation uprisen
  From its dark night of bondage and gloom —
A captive, long pining in prison,
  Restored to day's beauty and bloom.

II.

I look from the light dancing water,
  O'er steep hill, and wild wood, and mound,
Where many a dark day of slaughter
  Hath reddened the green vales around:
Of vengeance I am not a dreamer
  For the true blood there spilt long ago,
Though I dream that mere words won't redeem her,
  Green Erin, from bondage and woe.

III.

Long, long we have asked to restore us
   Our freedom, and still we are slaves:
'Twas thus with our fathers before us,
   And bondmen they went to their graves:
The wish, and the faint heart to slack it,
   Have failed, since the green earth began;
The wish, and the brave hand to back it,
   'Tis that makes the patriot man!

IV.

From the north to the blue southern water,
   Who wish for their freedom again,
Should ask no revenge for each slaughter,
   But rise up like brave, honest men;
And when by the word or the sabre
   We've righted the wrongs we deplore,
Like men, and not slaves, with our neighbor
   We'd prosper in peace evermore.

MY FIRST LOVE.

Air — " My Love is like a Summer Day."

I.

Where towers the rock above the trees,
   With heath-bells blooming o'er,
Where waves the fern in summer breeze,
   And shines the red lusmore,
In woodland nook beside the brook,
   I sit and sadly pore
On love I nursed in boyhood first
   For one I'll ne'er see more.

II.

How fair, when shines the summer beam
   Upon the mountains warm,
The lady fern beside the stream —
   As fair my Margaret's form:

The snow-white crystals shine beneath,
  The red lusmores above, —
Ah! such the bright, bright laughing teeth,
  And lips of my first love!

III.

The gorse flowers Ullair's dells illume,
  One sea of golden light;
My Margaret's hair was like their bloom,
  As yellow and as bright:
'Twill haunt me still, through joy or ill,
  Till death shall end my care,
The wondrous grace of her fair face
  Beneath that golden hair.

IV.

I loved her with a burning love
  That matched my boyhood well,
And brilliant were the dreams I wove
  While tranced in that sweet spell;
And in my breast she'll reign and rest
  Each eve while sad I pore,
Where ferns are green the banks between,
  And shines the red lusmore!

THE RAPPAREE'S HORSE AND SWORD.

AIR — "O! say, my brown drimin."

I.

My name is Mac Sheehy, from Feal's swelling flood,
A rapparee rover by mountain and wood:
I've two trusty comrades to serve me at need, —
This sword at my side, and my gallant, gray steed.

II.

Now where did I get them, — my gallant, gray steed,
And this sword, keen and trusty, to serve me at need?
This sword was my father's — in battle he died —
And I reared bold Isgur by Feal's woody side.

III.

I've said it, and say it, and care not who hear,
Myself and gray Isgur have never known fear:
There's a dint on my helmet, a hole through his ear:
'Twas the same bullet made them at Limerick last year!

IV.

And the soldier who fired it was still ramming down,
When this long sword came right with a slash on his crown;
Dhar Dhia! but he'll ne'er fire a musket again,
For his skull lies in two at the side of the glen!

V.

When they caught us one day at the castle of Brugh,
Of our black-hearted foemen the deadliest crew,
Like a bolt from the thunder gray Isgur went through,
And my sword! long they'll weep at the sore taste of you!

VI.

Together we sleep 'neath the wild crag or tree, —
My soul! but there ne'er were such comrades as we!
I, Brian the Rover, my two friends at need,
This sword at my side, and my gallant, gray steed!

THE JOVIAL CHRISTMAS DAYS LONG AGO.

AIR — "Uluchan Dhuv O!"

I.

THROUGH the murky mist of years, with a sigh and silent tears,
    I look to the days long ago,
To the gay and happy time when with story, jest, and rhyme
    We sat by the fire's ruddy glow;
When the eyes that shine no more shone around the merry hearth
Of the homestead far away in the land of my birth,
And the jolly rafters rang to the music and the mirth
    Of the jovial Christmas days long ago!

II.

From its mighty guardian hill there's a merry, murmuring rill,
    Dancing down through the valley of Glenroe;
There's a green wood smiling fair, and a lordly castle there,
    And a homestead by tyranny laid low;
My blessing on that home, and the hours of gay delight
With my friends around its hearth each returning festive night,
With the eyes of her I loved shining on me fond and bright,
    In the jovial Christmas days long ago!

III.

O! Heaven be with the day when with youthful hearts and gay,
    We longed for the blithe Christmas snow
To cast its mantle white from the towering mountain height
    To the glens and the shining dales below;
In each sad, exiled heart fond the memory remains
Of the Christmas candles burning in the glowing window panes:
Of the feasting and the dancing to the piper's merry strains,
    In the jovial Christmas days long ago!

IV.

Whate'er my fate may be, and whatever climes I see,
    Far from Erin and lovely Glenroe,
My anger red shall rise when I think how lowly lies
    Each home 'neath the tyrant's cruel blow;
And I'll pray to God on high to strike dead the tyrant's hand,
And to give the lonely exiles back again their native land,
With the merriment, the music, and the feasting high and grand
    Of the jovial Christmas days long ago!

MARYANNE.

Air — "John the Journeyman."

I.

In sweet Tipperary dwells my love,
Where Sliabhnamon stands tall above,
And from that hill to banks of Ban
There's not a girl like Maryanne!
  O, fair the face of Maryanne!
  O, warm the heart of Maryanne!
  From Sliabhnamon to northern Ban
  There's not a girl like Maryanne.

II.

My girl is artless as a child,
So fair and modest, fond and mild;
Not all the verses made by man
Could tell the charms of Maryanne.
  O, fair the face of Maryanne!
  O, fond the heart of Maryanne!
  Not all the verses made by man
  Could tell the charms of Maryanne.

III.

Her glossy hair is black as night,
And dark, deep blue her eyes of light;
Like midnight stars o'er Heaven's blue span,
The sparkling eyes of Maryanne.
  O, fair the face of Maryanne!
  O, fond the heart of Maryanne!
  Like midnight stars o'er Heaven's blue span,
  The sparkling eyes of Maryanne!

IV.

My soul is sad, my heart is sore,
To think I ne'er may see her more;
For ne'er was girl, since youth began,
So dear to me as Maryanne!
  O, fair the face of Maryanne!
  O, warm the heart of Maryanne!
  From Sliabhnamon to northern Ban
  There's not a girl like Maryanne!

THE OAKS OF GLENEIGH.

I.

O, THINK of the days when the crag's hoary masses
Bent o'er one green forest in Houra's wild passes,
   When the gray wolf was king of the forest and mountain,
   And the red deer ran free by the blue torrent's shore,
When the prey scarcely rested at eve by the fountain,
   Swept on by the spear of the wild creachadore!

II.

'Twas a brave time — a wild time — the hills seem to mourn
Till the splendor of glade and of forest return;
   Yet is there not splendor as wild and as shaggy,
   Where the huge blasted roots of that forest remain,
Wide spread o'er each deep cave and precipice craggy,
   Sending scions of strength to the blue sky again?

III.

Afar where Molama in thunder is flowing,
Afar in Gleneigh are these strong scions growing —
   They spring from the stream and they tower from the ledges
   Of the huge rocks which frown o'er that wild fairy dell;
Like young guardian giants encircling the edges
   Of the deep, silent pool and the moss-wreathéd well.

IV.

How thick in the summer their green leaves were shining!
How sear and how scattered at autumn's declining!.
   But the wild hills shall see them far greener than ever,
   When winter hath fled from the bright smiles of May;
Ah! thus should Adversity's children endeavor
   To breast the rude blasts, like the oaks of Gleneigh!

BRAVE DONALL.

AIR — "Donall's Lament."

I.

I stray alone by cove and cave,
With sad eyes looking o'er the wave,
And heart as mournful as the grave,
Since I lost my lover brave!
    O, my brave Donall!
    My bold, brave Donall!
My heart is in your foreign grave,
    My bold, brave Donall!

II.

Not all unknown his soldier sire;
Like glory did my love require;
Till fame grew in his heart of fire
A burning and a wild desire!
    O, my brave Donall!
    My bold, brave Donall!
What more than love could you require,
    My bold, brave Donall?

III.

Away to France my true love sped,
To join the bold Brigade, he said;
'Twas 'neath its flag in battle red
His only brother fought and bled!
    O, my brave Donall!
    My bold, brave Donall!
With fair, false hopes my heart you fed,
    My bold, brave Donall!

IV.

'Twas mounting on the foeman's wall
My gallant true love met his fall,
But dying, saw his banner tall
Waving in victory over all!

O, my brave Donall!
My bold, brave Donall!
For me they weave the funeral pall,
My bold, brave Donall!

v.

And thus I stray where Shannon's wave
Moans mournfully by cove and cave,
My sad heart in that far-off grave,
Where sleeps in gore my lover brave!
O, my brave Donall!
My bold, brave Donall!
My heart is withering in your grave,
My bold, brave Donall!

I STILL AM A ROVER.

Air — "Bundle and go."

I.

I still am a rover our green island over,
　A passion-fraught lover of beauty and bloom,
On wild mountains pondering, through sweet valleys wandering,
　Where soft winds are squandering the blossoms' perfume;
From all those dear places, the bland summer graces, —
　From all their fair faces my heart still doth stray,
Where clear waves are flinging, and flowerets are springing,
　And blithe birds are singing in sunny Gleneigh!

II.

There green woods wave slowly to winds breathing lowly,
　And ruin walls holy stand gray o'er the scene;
There clear fountains rally their strength in each valley,
　Where waves the wild sally and birch leaves are green;
There rocks famed in story stand silent and hoary,
　And fields in the glory of summer are gay,
And mead blossoms muster their bells of bright lustre,
　And rich berries cluster in sunny Gleneigh!

III.

Yet 'tis not the tender sweet beauty and splendor
　That dwells there can render such joy to my breast;

'Tis love has arrayed it, and decked and displayed it,
  As spring never made it, or mild summer dressed:
There Gracie is dwelling, in beauty excelling,
  Her bright looks still telling love ne'er can decay,
While clear waves are flinging, and flowerets are springing,
  And blithe birds are singing in sunny Gleneigh!

MOLL ROONE.

A Rapparee Song.

I.

There's a girl in Kilmurry, my own loved one,
The loveliest caileen that the sun shines on;
Her eyes are as bright as the Maytide moon,
And the devil a girl like my own Moll Roone!

II.

I mounted my steed in the evening brown,
And away I spurred till the storm came down;
Away over mountains and moorlands dun,
Till I came to the cottage of my own Moll Roone.

III.

I sat me down by the bogwood fire,
And I said that her love was my heart's desire.
And she gave me her love. O, she granted my boon,
And my heart was glad for my own Moll Roone.

IV.

Come, what is the use of a brave brown steed
But to spur to the doing of a gallant deed?
And what is the use of a sword or gun
But to fight for a girl like my own Moll Roone?

V.

As I rode down the mountain one Saturday night,
The valley below was one blaze of light,
And I found out its meaning full sadly and soon, —
'Twas the foe fired the cottage of my own Moll Roone!

VI.

I spurred through Blackwater, o'er brake and moor,
I spurred through the foe to her cottage door,
There my sword cleft the skull of a Dutch dragoon,
And I bore away in triumph my own Moll Roone!

THE RIGHTS OF MAN.

Air — "The Old Astrologer."

I.

Though he was born to till the soil,
  Or ply the busy trade,
To pamper tyrants by his toil
  The poor man ne'er was made;
That wondrous flame, the soul's the same
  In poor or noble clay,
And the selfsame laws will try its cause
  On the final Judgment Day!
    Then here's the son of poverty,
      Who bravely fills his can,
    And drinks with me to Liberty,
      And the God-made rights of man!

II.

The reckless despot on his throne, —
  Who gave him right to sway?
To make the suffering millions groan
  In bondage day by day?
Is he a god that with his rod
  Can fill unnumbered graves?
No! blood and bone he still must own,
  He's mortal like his slaves!
    Then here's the son of poverty,
      Who fearless fills his can,
    To pledge with me bright Liberty,
      And the God-made rights of man!

III.

When delved great Adam's progeny,
  And our primal mothers span,*
There was no difference of degree
  E'er seen 'twixt man and man;
But human might, ambition's flight
  Have set up tyrants' rule.
A lesson stern the nations learn
  In hard misfortune's school!
    So here's the son of poverty,
      Who stoutly fills his can,
    And works with me for Liberty,
      And the God-made rights of man!

IV.

There never was a law divine,
  To make the poor bow down
To mortal man, whate'er his line,
  However bright his crown:
The poor man's blood is warm and good,
  And red as his who reigns,
And why should he bend neck or knee —
  Bow silent down in chains?
    So here's the son of poverty,
      Who fills a brimming can,
    And prays with me for Liberty,
      And the God-made rights of man!

V.

On many a plain, with fire and steel,
  The poor man's cause was tried,
And many a deed of noble zeal
  That great cause sanctified;
For that good cause, for righteous laws,
  Arise, prepare, and be
Brave patriots all, to stand or fall
  Soldiers of Liberty!
    And here's the son of poverty,
      Who clinks with mine his can —
    Who'll strike with me for Liberty,
      And the God-made rights of man!

---

* "When Adam delved and Eve span,
  Who was then the gentleman?"

THERE IS A TREE IN DARRA'S WOOD.

AIR—"Barrack Hill."

I.

There is a tree in Darra's wood
  That bears the rose-red berry,
Where sweetly sings the fairy flood
  With cadence wild and merry;
O Love, like berries of that tree,
  Thy red lips smile so dearly,
And like that stream's glad minstrelsy,
  Thy laugh rings soft and clearly!
    So clearly, so clearly,
      So witching, soft, and clearly,
    That evermore I must adore
      And love thee, true love, dearly!

II.

Beneath that tree I've built a bower,
  Its roof with love-knots twining,
And there the snowy shamrock flower
  And blue-bells gay are shining;
I've built a bower within my breast,
  And placed thee on its throne, love,
And ever there I'll love thee best,
  My dark-eyed Grace, my own love!
    My own love, my own love,
      I've placed thee on its throne, love,
    And day and night, forever bright,
      There you shall reign, my own love!

III.

'Mid Darra's wood a castle tall
  Stands wrecked with age, and hoary;
A white rose tree hangs from its wall
  With blooms of star-like glory;
Thy fair brow hath that rose's hue,
  Kind Nature's own adorning:
Thy heart is stainless as the dew
  That gems its leaves at morning:

At morning, at morning,
  When dew that flower's adorning,
When out I rove through Darra's grove,
  To think on thee at morning.

IV.

O, still may wane the summer moon,
  The gay flowers follow after;
The merry birds may hush their tune,
  And glad streams cease their laughter;
The leaves may wither on the tree,
  All things grow cold and drear, love,
But that sweet bower I've built to thee
  Shall ever bloom, my dear love!
My dear love, my dear love,
  You'll reign without a peer, love,
That bower within, the glorious queen
  Of my fond heart, my dear love!

I BUILT ME A BOWER.

AIR—"Gouan gal bān."

I.

I built me a bower in life's greenwood,
  A palace of blooms for my soul,
And there on the maids all unseen, would
  I dream 'neath love's blissful control,
Till I set up the image of Alice
  Supreme on my heart's burning throne;
Then long in my flower-woven palace
  I bowed to that image alone.

II.

O, fair was my bird of the mountains,
  O, sweet as the thorn's scented spray,
O, pure as the light of the fountains
  That dance down the green hills in May.
A chapter of joy-woven story,
  A voyage o'er a bright fairy sea,
A May-tide of bloom and of glory
  Were the days of our love-time to me.

III.

But the chapter oft ends all in sorrow,
 The voyage hath its tempests and gloom,
And the May-tide, though bright be each morrow,
 Must pass, like our lives, to the tomb.
O, the dreams of my love-time are humbled,
 The blooms from my green bower are fled,
My idol lies shattered and crumbled,
 My Alice, my sweet flower, is dead!

FAIR MAIDENS' BEAUTY WILL SOON FADE AWAY.

Air—"My Love she was born in the North Countrie."

I.

My love she was born in the North countrie,
Where Antrim's wild highlands look over the sea;
My love is as fair as the soft smiling May;
But fair maidens' beauty will soon fade away.

II.

My love is as pure as the bright, blesséd well
That springs all so lonely in Gartan's green dell;
My love she is graceful, and tender, and gay;
But fair maidens' beauty will soon fade away.

III.

My love is as sweet as the cinnamon tree;
As the bark to its bough cleaves she firm unto me;
Its green leaves will wither and its roots will decay,
So fair maidens' beauty will soon fade away.

IV.

But love, though the green leaf may wither and fall,
 Though the bright eye be dimmed, and the sweet smile, and all;
O, love has a life that shall never decay,
Though fair maidens' beauty will soon fade away.

THE WATERFALL.

I.

Where the moss-bronzed oaks are towering
  'Tween the rude rocks' hoary wall,
Into a chasm with sudden spasm
    Rusheth the waterfall!
    Breaking its prison thrall,
      Bursting its rocky bar,
Its voice rolls loud from the bright spray cloud,
    Over the hills afar!

II.

All through the flame-browed summer
  'Twas but a tiny stream —
Brown autumn gave the swelling wave,
  And the fierce and fiery gleam.
  O wanderer, you would deem
    That a bright-eyed monster there
Rushed out on thee with a roar of glee,
    Mad from his forest lair!

III.

It springeth far in the hill-tops,
  That torrent wild and rude,
And rolls along, with its ancient song,
  Through the deep solitude;
  Then o'er the sedgy wood,
    Down from the torn clift,
With a sudden sweep it taketh its leap
    Into that caverned rift!

IV.

It boils, and writhes, and hisses
  As it leapeth down amain,
And its quivering roar shakes the valleys hoar
  Like a Titan's yell of pain!
  Then darting on again
    Swiftly its wild waves go,
Winding away in their azure play,
    Through the widening vales below!

THE CAILIN RUE.

Air — "An Cailin Ruadh."

I.

When first I sought her by Cashin's water,
    Fond love I brought her, fond love I told;
At day's declining I found her twining
    Her bright locks, shining like red, red gold.
She raised her eyes then in sweet surprise then —
    Ah! how unwise then such eyes to view!
For free they found me, but fast they bound me,
    Love's chain around me for my Cailin Rue.

II.

Fair flowers were blooming, the meads illuming,
    All fast assuming rich summer's pride,
And we were roving, truth's rapture proving,
    Ah! fondly loving, by Cashin's side.
O, love may wander, but ne'er could sunder
    Our hearts, that fonder each moment grew,
Till friends delighted such love requited,
    And my hand was plighted to my Cailin Rue.

III.

Ere May's bright weather, o'er hill and heather,
    Sweet tuned together rang our bridal bells;
But at May's dying, on fate relying,
    Fate left us sighing by Cashin's dells.
O, sadly perished the bliss we cherished!
    But far lands flourished o'er the ocean blue;
So as June came burning I left Erin mourning,
    No more returning, with my Cailin Rue.

IV.

Our ship went sailing with course unfailing,
    But black clouds trailing lowered o'er the main,
And its wild dirge singing, came the storm out springing,
    That good ship flinging back, back again!
A sharp rock under tore her planks asunder,
    While the sea in thunder swallowed wreck and crew!
One dark wave bore me where the coast towered o'er me,
    But dead before me lay my Cailin Rue!

THE GREEN RIBBON.

Air—"The Banks of Banna."

I.

I MET my love in the woodland screen
  With fond and sweet caresses;
I gave my love a ribbon green
  To bind her yellow tresses;
She loosed each long lock's shining fold
  O'er her neck of snowy whiteness,
And she bound the green with the yellow gold,
  In braids of glossy brightness.

II.

It was beside a murmuring rill
  That through the woods descended,
And over peaceful vale and hill
  The sun shone calm and splendid;
O, often 'mid those leafy bowers
  In sweet blooms I arrayed her;
But lovelier far than summer flowers
  That bright green ribbon made her.

III.

May summer deck that lovely wood
  With shining flowers the fairest,
And paint the rocks and light the flood
  With rainbow hues the rarest;
And still through every changing scene
  May our fond love keep glowing,
While the leaves shine as that ribbon green,
  And the wild rill's tide is flowing.

IRELAND'S FREEDOM; OR, THE DROP OF BLOOD.

I.

In Titan days of strength and youth,
With burning heart he spoke the truth,
And woke the People from their sleep
With words of thunder, loud and deep!
But, woe to us! when age came on,
When strength of frame and soul was gone,
When tighter grew the tyrant's yoke,
The slavish, cruel words he spoke, —
That Ireland's freedom is not good
If purchased by one drop of blood!

II.

Our hopes were bright; the dawning sun
Of Freedom smiled our green hills on;
With hearts elate we looked to him, —
He spoke, and made our morning dim.
Prepared were we to do the best
That men could do at his behest;
But God forgive him in his grave
Who spoke the doctrine of the slave, —
That Ireland's freedom is not good
If purchased by one drop of blood!

III.

What said the Prophets old, inspired
Of God, with freedom's sunlight fired?
Against each foreign tyrant horde
They preached the doctrine of the sword.
And if in earth's primeval youth
The God-inspired outspoke the truth,
Shall we, the noble Irish race,
With the great Lie our souls debase,
That Ireland's freedom is not good
If purchased by one drop of blood?

IV.

What did the Pagan old, untaught?
With blood his country's weal he bought.
What did the noble Winkelried?
With his own blood his land he freed.
In every region, old and young,
Where Truth eternal found a tongue,
Martyrs a hundred fold laid down
Their lives to purchase Freedom's crown.
And Ireland's freedom is not good
If purchased by one drop of blood!

V.

In other days, when to the sheen
Our sires unfurled their flag of green,
With England's power like men to cope,
Then what said cardinal and Pope?
Did they the doctrine false uphold?
They gave to Ireland men and gold,
And blessed and bade her soldiers free
Fight unto death for liberty!
And now our freedom is not good
If purchased by one drop of blood!

VI.

Race that spread'st from land to land,
For labor's field the stalwart hand,
For council sage and battle plain,
The ready tongue and fiery brain, —
Race that wadest seas of gore
For freedom of each foreign shore,
Will you perpetuate the curse?
Will you the damning Lie indorse
That Ireland's freedom is not good
If purchased by one drop of blood?

VII.

Ah, God forbid! Forbid it they
Who slumber in Thermopylæ;
And those forbid, the martyred brave
Who died our own dear land to save,
On stricken field and 'leaguered wall,
From sad Kinsale to Donegal;

And God forgive him, too, who first
With the false creed our people cursed, —
That Ireland's freedom is not good
If purchased by one drop of blood!

THE GROVES OF THE POOL; OR, THE IRISH ROVER.

I.

You may like Dodge's Glen, as a poet,
 To sit in the green, shady grove,
And if you set out upon pleasure,
 May sport it all day in the Cove;
But if you are bent on rebellion,
 And to learn in a good rebel school,
Just go courting a nice little sweetheart
 In the jolly old Groves of the Pool!
  And I am a bold Irish hero,
   Who love the fair maids as I roam,
  Who hate all oppressors, from Nero
   To the tyrants who lord it at home!

II.

'Tis there you will see the fair maidens
 Each bright morning bleaching the clothes,
With their white feet agleam in the water,
 And a blush on their cheeks like the rose;
With a flash in their eyes independent
 That would brand you a coward and fool,
If you feared to wear Green for your color
 In the jolly old Groves of the Pool!
  Chorus.

III.

I danced in the Claddagh of Galway,
 For frolics in Meath bore the bell;
For the smiles of a gay little sweetheart
 I fought in the town of Clonmel;
An heiress I courted in Mallow,
 A traitor I shot in Rathcoole, —

But I've gone through more games in one morning,
  In the jolly old Groves of the Pool!
    Chorus.

IV.

Up spoke Roisin Duv, my young sweetheart,
  With a look between earnest and jest,
"Who'll win me must handle a sabre,
  And fight for the land we love best;
Must stand in the red gap of danger,
  A soldier collected and cool —
That's the man for my love and devotion
  In the jolly old Groves of the Pool!"
    Chorus.

V.

O, all you poor cowards and dastards,
  From the fair maids of Cork keep away;
Beware! If you make their acquaintance,
  You'll be all hanged for rebels next day.
With their talk, and their tears, and their laughter,
  They'll put you 'neath petticoat rule,
And they'll make you mount Green for your color
  In the jolly old Groves of the Pool!
    Chorus.

VI.

While the Lee winds in glory and splendor
  By wildwoods, and castles, and towers,
While the slopes of Glanmire in the water
  Are mirrored with all their bright bowers —
Till Fate, with her wheel and her spindle,
  Winds up my last thread on her spool,
I'll think on my wild days of raking
  In the jolly old Groves of the Pool!
    For I am a bold Irish hero,
      Who love the fair maids as I roam,
      Who hate all oppressors, from Nero
      To the tyrants who lord it at home!

ANNIE DE CLARE.

Air — "The Merry Dancers."

I.

The rill at its fountain, how calm is its flowing!
The rill down the mountain comes rushing and glowing;
True love in my breast like its tide's ever growing,
    Since I saw the bright eyes of my Annie de Clare.

II.

O, blest be the hours that I last saw them beaming
In her home of the Crag, by the waterfall's streaming;
How I scaled the wild rocks with the red sunset gleaming,
    Up into the arms of my Annie de Clare!

III.

O, the glory that lay o'er the green earth and heaven!
O, the sweet lapse of bliss to my fond bosom given,
As I sat by the stream on that calm summer even,
    In the love-lighted smiles of my Annie de Clare.

IV.

Many and bright were the pleasures that crowned me,
And dear the enchantments since boyhood that bound me,
But dearer than all were the fond arms round me,
    And the red, rosy lips of my Annie de Clare.

V.

When the ardor of love lights the soul with its splendor,
No cares may annoy her, no sorrows can rend her;
So my soul's rapt in gladness, with visions all tender
    Of glory and love and my Annie de Clare.

VI.

And glory may crown me, of bright meeds the giver,
But love hath a guerdon more blissful forever, —
That bower where we sat by the wild Mumhan river,
    And the fond, twining arms of my Annie de Clare.

THE MARCH OUT OF LIMERICK.

Air — "The Rapparee's March."

1.

Comrades true, to dare and do,
   O, they are few who've yet denied us;
We'll not say they could betray,
   For many a day they've fought beside us;
By hill and glade, in fight and raid,
   With vengeful blade we smote the foeman,
And now till we find Ireland free,
   Our banner-tree shall droop to no man.

II.

Alas, for strife! child, parent, wife,
   More dear than life, we leave behind us;
They weep full sore, but on this shore
   O, never more in joy they'll find us:
More blest the brave in bloody grave,
   By Boyne's red wave, or Aughrim sleeping,
Than we who hear our children dear,
   And fond friends near thus wildly weeping!

III.

Sarsfield stands before our bands,
   For foreign lands his words prepare us;
By Thomond Gate the Dutchmen wait,
   Their flag elate, but to insnare us;
In serried mass our bright files pass,
   With steel cuirass and helmet gleaming,
Our brave choice said by onward tread,
   And green flag spread above us streaming.

IV.

Yon mournful train they weep in vain,
   Black woe and pain their steps attending;
And think of all who met their fall
   Brave Limerick's wall so long defending;

When we look back on war's grim wrack,
On turret black and breach all gory,
By hearthstone bare and breach we swear,
Revenge to share, come grief or glory!

V.

Farewell, ye Dead, who nobly bled!
Your blood was shed for Ireland's honor;
To change her doom, to chase the gloom,
Whose shadows loom so dark upon her.
And ye, farewell, whose wild cries swell
A mournful knell, at home to bind us;
Your hearts full sore, on th' Irish shore
Forevermore we leave behind us!

THE FAIR MAID'S LAMENT.

Air — "Each night when I slumber."

I.

Of all the glens in Ireland, Dundara's glen for me;
There first I met my sweetheart, and loved him constantly;
Yet now within Dundara each day I grieve and pine,
For I have nought to comfort this lonely heart of mine!

II.

Each night when I slumber, with dreams I'm oppressed;
Still thinking of my true love deprives me of my rest;
He's sailing now for Holland, to face his enemy —
Bright angels be his guard, and from danger set him free!

III.

I wish it were my fortune along with him to be,
To spend some pleasant hours in his sweet company,
When in rude war's alarms with courage I'd behave,
To give my love to understand that I'm no coward slave!

IV.

My father and my mother are angry with me,
And often do upbraid me, all for my constancy;
But let them all say what they will, still loyal I'll **remain**,
Until my darling true love returns home again.

V.

I might have got an earl, or young man of noble birth,
But I prefer my true love above all men on earth;
For what care I for noble birth, or for the golden store,
When I could live on desert hills with him whom I adore?

VI.

Each night when I slumber, with dreams I'm oppressed;
Still thinking of my true love deprives me of my rest;
Beneath the lonely willow each day I'll sigh and mourn,
For in grief I mean to languish till my true love's return!

FAINGE AN LAE.*

AIR—" Fainge an lae."

I.

The sun, in his splendor and glory,
  Sets over the shining main,
And island and precipice hoary
  Are swimming in gold again:
Ah! many a battle-field gory
  He lights by that ocean's spray,
The scenes of each tragical story
  Which darkened our Fainge an lae!

II.

The hill-tops of Clare are defining
  Their shapes in the golden glow;
The mountains of Kerry are shining
  Sublime on the plains below;
They look on a master still twining
  The gyves of our woe each day;
They look on a race ever pining,
  And all for our Fainge an lae!

III.

They mind me, so riven and valleyed,
  Of bownocht † and rapparee,

---

* The Ring of the Morning, or the Dawning; i. e., the dawning of the morning of Freedom.
† A foot-soldier.

Who oft round their hoar summits rallied,
  To set their green country free.
O, these were the men that ne'er dallied,
  When once set in war's array,
But fierce on the scared foeman sallied,
  And all for their Fainge an lae!

IV.

Fair Freedom soon, soon must awaken,
  With her form of sun-bright mould;
Then let her not wander forsaken,
  But armed, as in days of old.
With her green flags and banners outshaken,
  O, what could our triumph stay?
Our thirst for the right would be slaken;
  We'd soon have our Fainge an lae!

V.

When the power of the tyrant is riven,
  And swordless his blood-stained hand,
When the black clouds from Erin are driven,
  O, where is the brighter land?
And when shall that grand hour be given
  That sets us on Freedom's way?
When, like the great Dead, we have striven,
  And all for our Fainge an lae!

DONALL NA GREINE.*

Air — "Domnall na Greine."

I.

Where rolls the tide of the wandering Mulla,
  Brilliantly gleaming, gushing and gleaming,
Young Donall lay in a sunny hollow,
  Lazily dreaming, thinking and dreaming;
And thus he lay all that sweet summer idle,
  Fleeing from labor, fleeing from labor,
When his left hand should hold the skian or the bridle,
  And his right the steel sabre, the keen-cutting sabre;

* Donall of the sunshine; i. e., Donall the Lazy.

And hurrah for ease and for love's bright story,
  Sang Donall na Greine, tall Donall na Greine;
For both he dreamed of, not war and glory,
  Donall na Greine, tall Donall na Greine!

II.

There built he many an airy castle,
  Towering and gleaming, towering and gleaming,
And peopled their halls with fair maid and vassal,
  In his wild dreaming, in his wild dreaming;
And ne'er one cause could he still discover
  Why his ease should be broken, his sweet ease broken,
Till his love proved false, and his dreams were over,
  And he a rover — to sorrow awoken!
    Then hurrah, hurrah for a life of labor,
      Sang Donall na Greine, tall Donall na Greine!
    The steed, the corselet, and flashing sabre,
      For Donall na Greine, bold Donall na Greine!

III.

His steed's black mane to the winds is streaming,
  By valley and highland, by moorland and highland;
You'd stray from Bengore with the white spray gleaming,
  To Cleir's stormy island, to Cleir's stormy island,
Ere a better or doughtier man could meet you
  Than Donall na Greine, tall Donall na Greine!
Or a fiercer, haughtier smile could greet you —
  Tall Donall na Greine, bold Donall na Greine!
    And hurrah, hurrah for a life of labor,
      Sang Donall na Greine, bold Donall na Greine!
    The rushing charge and the flashing sabre
      For Donall na Greine, bold Donall na Greine!

IV.

Soon the rapparees all, his brave brothers were sworn
  Through hardship and danger, through hardship and danger;
O'Hogan to battle was never borne
  So fleet on the stranger, the false-hearted stranger —
O, to see him down on the foeman dashing!
  How fearless he bore him, how reckless he bore him!
With his sabre keen in his strong hand flashing,
  Through the Sassenaghs crashing — his green flag o'er him.

And hurrah, hurrah for a life of labor!
  Sang Donall na Greine, bold Donall na Greine;
The rushing charge and the shining sabre
  For Donall na Greine, bold Donall na Greine!

v.

Once again he loved, by the Shannon water,
  A maiden unchanging, with fond heart unchanging,
And after many a field of slaughter,
  Away they went ranging, to foreign lands **ranging**;
At Fontenoy his brave generals paid him,
  Tall Donall **na** Greine, bold Donall na Greine!
A captain fine **on** that field they made him,
  For fear never swayed him, bold Donall na Greine!
Then hurrah for love and a life of labor!
  Sang Donall na Greine, bold Donall na Greine!
Unchanging love and a conquering sabre
  For Donall na Greine, bold Donall na Greine!

THE HILLS OF SWEET TIPPERARY.

Air—"The Orange Rogue."

I.

O, MARY dear, 'tis long ago
  Since hand in **hand together**
We sat in pleasant Rossaroe,
  Amidst the blooming heather;
Your eyes were like the lustre shed
  By heaven so blue and airy,
Your cheeks were like the roses red
  'Mid green hills of Tipperary.
    O, the hills, the hills so green,
      The hills so high and airy,
    May heaven shine o'er them ever sheen,
      The hills of sweet Tipperary.

II.

We sat while evening's light illumed
  Comailthe's stately mountain,*

* Keeper Hill.

Where heather bells and gorse flowers bloomed
  Round old St. Brendan's fountain;
The redbreast's song, the thrush's lay,
  Like strains from haunts of faery,
Our vespers for the closing day
  'Mid green hills of Tipperary.
    O, the hills, &c.

III.

The bubbling well, the ruined cairn,
  Where slept some warrior olden,
The foxglove, heath, and waving fern,
  And gorse flowers gay and golden:
The sunlit tree, with shattered arm,
  That eve, true love unchary
Cast o'er them all some magic charm,
  'Mid green hills of Tipperary,
    O, the hills, &c.

IV.

What vows in that sweet spot we made
  Of true love, fond and tender,
Nor dreamed that joy could falsely fade,
  Like that gay sunset's splendor;
Nor thought death's gloom and misery
  Our happiness could vary,
So blindly rapt in love were we,
  'Mid green hills of Tipperary.
    O, the hills, &c.

V.

What hopes were doomed, what fortunes fell,
  Since you and I together
Sat by St. Brendan's sunlit well,
  Amidst the blooming heather!
I wander far from Rossaroe,
  No longer blithe and airy,
And on your grave the shamrocks grow,
  'Mid green hills of Tipperary.
    O, the hills, the hills so green,
      The hills so high and airy,
    May heaven shine o'er them ever sheen,
      The hills of sweet Tipperary.

THE COMING BRIDAL.

Air — "B'fearr liomsa ainnir gan gúna."

I.

My home stands by Funcheon's bright river,
  Where the broom blossoms shine in the spring,
Where the green beeches murmur and quiver,
  And the birds 'mid their cool branches sing;
And there, where the sky gleams so blue in
  The stream as it winds through the dells,
Adown by the old castle ruin,
  My love in her white cottage dwells.

II.

The black whortle shines 'mid the heather,
  Where the wild deer in brown autumn rove,
And dark is the strong raven's feather,
  But darker the locks of my love.
Two trees by the Fort of the Fairy,
  A red rose and white sweetly grow;
O, the lips and the brow of my Mary
  Outshine their pure crimson and snow.

III.

No flocks hath she down by the island,
  No red gold her coffers illume,
No herds over brown moor or highland,
  No meads where the sweet flowers may bloom:
The old dame hath herds by the wildwood;
  She'd give me herds, green meads, and gold,
But the young heart that loved me since childhood
  Shall find me in manhood unsold.

IV.

Next Sunday the fires will be blazing
  For the Baal-feast o'er mountain and plain;
That morn village crowds will be gazing
  With joy on our gay bridal train;

Could love half so blest ever falter,
  When placed 'mid the throng side by side,
When there, at the old chapel altar,
  The good priest will make her my bride?

THE WIND THAT SHAKES THE BARLEY.

Air — "The Old Love and the New Love."

I.

I sat within the valley green,
  I sat me with my true love,
My sad heart strove the two between,
  The old love and the new love, —
The old for her, the new that made
  Me think on Ireland dearly,
While soft the wind blew down the glade,
  And shook the golden barley.

II.

'Twas hard the woful words to frame,
  To break the ties that bound us, —
'Twas harder still to bear the shame
  Of foreign chains around us;
And so I said, "The mountain glen
  I'll seek next morning early,
And join the brave United men!"
  While soft winds shook the barley.

III.

While sad I kissed away her tears,
  My fond arms round her flinging,
The foeman's shot burst on our ears,
  From out the wildwood ringing.
The bullet pierced my true love's side,
  In life's young spring so early,
And on my breast in blood she died,
  While soft winds shook the barley!

IV.

I bore her to the wildwood screen,
  And many a summer blossom
I placed, with branches thick and green,
  Above her gore-stained bosom:
I wept, and kissed her pale, pale cheek,
  Then rushed o'er vale and far lea,
My vengeance on the foe to wreak,
  While soft winds shook the barley!

V.

And blood for blood, without remorse,
  I've ta'en at Oulart Hollow,*
I've placed my true love's clay-cold corse
  Where I full soon will follow;
And round her grave I wander drear,
  Noon, night, and morning early,
With breaking heart, whene'er I hear
  The wind that shakes the barley!

FANNY CLAIR.

AIR — "Mör Cluna."

I.

QUEENLY is thy mien and air,
Jewels sparkle in thy hair,
  And those ringlets twining,
  And thy dark eyes shining,
  Set my fond heart pining,
    Fanny Clair.

II.

Grace dwells in thy features fair,
Pride of birth sits haughty there,
  Yet in thy heart's glowing,
  Love — on me bestowing
  Fond hopes brighter glowing,
    Fanny Clair.

* The quarry on Oulart Hill, where the infamous North Cork militiamen were cut to pieces by the people.

III.

Never shall my heart despair
While that smile thy sweet lips wear;
  In it rests a token
  That thy love's awoken,
  Though it burns unspoken,
      Fanny Clair.

IV.

Then the life that else was bare
Shall find glory, spite of care,
  For thy sake shall never
  Cease each good endeavor,
  Till we're joined forever,
      Fanny Clair!

WILLY BRAND.

Air — "Blow the Candle out."

I.

My love is come of English blood,
  And was my father's foe;
But now he's all for Ireland's good,
  As once for Ireland's woe;
And now he's leal and true as steel
  When war is in the land;
So aye through blame, and O, through shame,
  I'll love my Willy Brand.

II.

My love he is a soldier free,
  So stately and so tall,
With armor shining gloriously,
  And sword, and plume, and all;
With horseman's shoon and musquetoon
  He rides by tower and strand,
And aye through blame, and O, through shame,
  I'll love my Willy Brand.

III.

My love has drawn his gallant sword
   For Ireland's cause and king,
Black Cromwell, with his blood-stained horde
   Of traitors back to fling;
And may God speed each man and steed
   The dark foe to withstand,
While aye through blame, and O, through shame,
   I'll love my Willy Brand.

IV.

Each day she waited by the hill
   Her Willy Brand's return,
And still the same, through woe and ill,
   Her love for him did burn:
And back love gave her soldier brave
   When peace swayed o'er the land;
For aye through blame, and O, through shame,
   She loved her Willy Brand!

THE LASSES OF IRELAND.

Air—"Pilib a Ceo."

I.

Here's to our dear lasses, wheresoe'er their home,
'Mid the ancient cities, or where wild streams foam;
Ne'er were hearts more constant, ne'er were eyes so bright,
So we'll pledge them fondly on this festive night.
   Then to our dear lasses,
     With their smiles divine,
   Drink, in sparkling glasses
     Of the rose-red wine!

II.

All the lovely maids that charmed our sires of yore,
Live and shine immortal in wild bardic lore;
Still the same sweet faces, still the forms so fair,
Bloom from Antrim's Pillars to the bright Kenmare.

  Then to those dear lasses,
   With their smiles divine,
  Drink, in sparkling glasses
   Of the rose-red wine!

III.

Once I was a rover through broad England's plains;
Through and through I've wandered Scotland's wild domains:
There I found fair maidens in the light of youth,
But no Irish fondness, and no Irish truth.
  So to our own lasses,
   With their smiles divine,
  Drink, in sparkling glasses
   Of the rose-red wine!

IV.

Denmark's dames are lovely, with their locks of gold;
Spanish forms are stately; France hath charms untold;
Yet that sweet, bright beauty filling glance and smile,
Dwells but with the maidens of our own green isle.
  So to our own lasses,
   With their smiles divine,
  Drink, in sparkling glasses
   Of the rose-red wine!

V.

May they live forever, as in th' olden time,
When brave warriors wooed them, and sweet bards sublime;
May their glorious faces shine for aye the same,
With the light of beauty and love's radiant flame!
  And to our own lasses,
   With their smiles divine,
  Drink, in sparkling glasses
   Of the rose-red wine!

O'SULLIVAN'S FLIGHT.

A. D. 1603.

Air — "Ca rouish anish an cailin vig."

I.

GLENGARIFF's shore could give no more
  The shelter strong we needed,
So away we trode on our wintry road,
  Its dangers all unheeded.
The snows were deep, the paths were steep,
  But worse than these soon found us —
The ruffian swords, and the traitor hordes
  That flocked like wolves around us!
    We'll shout hurrah for valor's sway,
      Each trembling coward scorning,
    For cleaving brands, in dauntless hands,
      And all for Freedom's morning!

II.

By Blarney's towers, Mac Caurha's powers
  Our good swords turned their backs on;
And Mallow's flood we stained with blood
  Of Barry, Rupe, and Saxon!
By Gailty's hill around us still
  Rushed many a fierce marauder,
Yet our path we clave to Shannon's wave,
  And all by the good *lamh laider.**
    We'll shout hurrah! &c.

III.

Mac Eggan's wrath there barred our path,
  But we gave him warning early
To clear the way, or his bands we'd slay,
  And we kept our promise fairly!
Each killed his steed in that hour of need,
  After false Mac Eggan's slaughter,

* The Strong Hand.

Corachs* unstaid of their skins we made,
 And crossed the Shannon's water!
  Then shout hurrah! &c.

IV.

O'Sullivan was the dauntless man,
 When the foe by Aughrim found us;
Black Malby's head on the sward he laid,
 And we slew all around us!
But O, how few of our brave and true
 Reached Ullad's † mountains hoary!
Yet none should weep for the brave who sleep
 On that path so rough and gory!
  But shout hurrah for valor's sway,
   Each trembling coward scorning,
  For cleaving brands, in dauntless hands,
   And all for Freedom's morning!

JOHN'S OLD WIFE OF TULLYVOE.

Air — "The Scolding Wife of Tullyvoe."

I.

John's old wife of Tullyvoe
Was crooked made, from top to toe;
In elf-locks wild her hair did flow,
John's old wife of Tullyvoe!

II.

She had a tongue would skin a flint,
A temper with the devil in't,
Always in a burning glow,
John's old wife of Tullyvoe!

---

* *Corach*, a light boat. O'Sullivan ordered his men to cut osiers by the shore, and make boat frames of wicker work. These frames they covered with the skins of their horses, and in the corachs or boats thus formed they crossed the Shannon.

† *Ullad*, Ulster.

III.

Her mouth was wide, her lips were thin,
With only six black teeth within,
In a most uneven row,
John's old wife of Tullyvoe!

IV.

Her feet and hands, and talon nails,
And squinting eyes — my courage fails
In description here to go;
John's old wife of Tullyvoe!

V.

Her laughing, bright-eyed servant girls
She banged about, and tore their curls,
From morning's light till evening's glow,
John's old wife of Tullyvoe!

VI.

As from the fair of Carragrome
John himself came *hearty* * home,
Burning gall did overflow
John's old wife of Tullyvoe!

VII.

She bit his ear, she tore his head,
She pulled his nose until it bled,
She knocked him down with one fell blow,
John's old wife of Tullyvoe!

VIII.

She flung, she flounced with devilish zest,
She danced "Shane Gow" † upon his breast,
With stamping, vicious heel and toe,
John's old wife of Tullyvoe!

IX.

If you want more verse to flow,
More particulars to know,
You yourself, not I, may go
To John's old wife of Tullyvoe!

* *Hearty*, half-seas-over; tipsy.
† A favorite jig, or *Moneen*.

SONG.

AIR — "The Handsome Face."

I.

A young, bright face, where all can trace
    The heart's pure thoughts ever shining there;
In dreamland golden there's nought beholden,
    Half so bewitching, or half so fair.

II.

Two bright eyes like the summer skies,
    Where the soul laughs out in a living ray;
What can lighten the heart, and brighten
    Its depths, when darkened, so well as they?

III.

Lips as red as the light that's shed
    By the dew-bright roses in leafy June,
With the white teeth's splendor, and voice as tender,
    And soft, and sweet, as an old love tune.

IV.

O, my love, my maid of the wildwood glade
    In the western mountains, excels in all;
And through all ranging and fortune's changing,
    With those sweet charms keeps my heart in thrall!

THE STORMY SEA SHALL FLOW IN.

AIR — "I wish I were an Earl."

I.

The stormy sea shall flow in,
    Our highland valleys through,
Ere I, my stately Owen,
    Prove false to love and you.

My heart was sad and lonely,
  Each weary night and day,
And your kind accents only
  Could chase my grief away.

II.

For O, my mother left me —
  Cold, cold in death she lies —
Ah! how drear fortune reft me
  Of all my heart could prize!
My father far would wander
  Unto some foreign zone,
And I was left to ponder
  Upon my grief alone!

III.

Then came a sure, sweet token
  Such sorrows might not last,
The love in joy unspoken,
  You spoke when joy had passed;
Then O, the sea shall flow in
  Our highland valleys through,
Ere I, my stately Owen,
  Prove false to love and you!

MARGARET.

Air — "She is gone."

I.

The woods, and the hills, and the flower-edged streams,
  Are brighter than they were wont to be,
For winter hath fled, and the sunny gleams
  Of spring-tide clothe them in radiancy;
But my Margaret is gone, and my golden dreams
  Are darkened and dead to me.

II.

All things look serene and **bright**,
  Crag and castle, and vale **and all**;

The young lambs play in their fresh delight,
    And the sweet birds sing in the forest tall:
But my Margaret is gone, and the shades of night
    Dark down in my bosom fall.

III.

The clouds from the mountain tops have rolled,
    And the woods and the valleys are clad in green;
But where is she with the hair of gold,
    And the eyes so sweetly blue and sheen?
Ah! my Margaret is gone, and those dreams of old
    Shall never come back, I ween!

I LOVED A MAID.

Air — "The Rambling Sailor."

I.

I LOVED a maid by Geerait's lea,
    And knew by many a token
That love dwelt in her heart for me,
    Though long it lived unspoken;
I loved her well, I loved her true,
But she has crossed the ocean blue;
Yet can the links that fondly grew
    Thus round our hearts be broken?

II.

Ah! many a morn and starry night
    May sink down Time's dark river,
And youth may fade, like all things bright,
    But nought our souls can sever;
For love shall live, the love of yore,
That filled our hearts by Geerait's shore,
Though angry oceans spread and roar
    Between us still forever.

III.

There's many a maid 'neath Daragh's crest
    Whose fond love I might waken,

But never from my lonely breast
  Can thought of her be taken;
I gaze on them, but constantly
Think, think on her beyond the sea;
Thus love and grief have dwelt with me,
  And ne'er my heart forsaken.

THE RIGHTFUL POWER.

I.

"Let every soul be subject
  Unto the higher powers."
We bend our souls to God alone
  In these our darkest hours;
For if the Saxon's burning chain
  Was ever made for us,
Designed it was in Satan's brain,
  And forged in Erebus!

II.

"Let every soul be subject
  Unto the powers that be."
To power designed by Lucifer
  We cannot bend the knee;
But preachers, interested, vain,
  The text interpret thus,
And bid us wear the demon chain
  Was forged in Erebus!

III.

Believe them not, — the prosperous Frank,
  He owns his blood-bought field;
The Teuton gathers as his own
  Whate'er his valleys yield;
His own the peasant counts the plain,
  E'en in the land of Russ;
And is our portion but that chain
  Was forged in Erebus?

IV.

A brehon of our land once said,
 "Let each man have his own."
Another, that "a battle-field
 Was the best brehon known."
We'll follow out their judgments plain,
 Though stern and dangerous;
We'll have our own — we'll break that chain
 Was forged in Erebus!

V.

"Let every soul be subject
 Unto the *rightful* power."
Thus rendered we the holy text
 In many a trying hour:
A trying hour is come again, —
 A mighty hour for us, —
We'll hurl the tyrant and his chain
 Back into Erebus!

JESSY BRIEN.

AIR — "As through the Woods I chanced to rove."

I.

JESSY BRIEN! the livelong day,
 Down by Funcheon's river;
I think of her from June to May,
 Down by Funcheon's river;
I love her not for golden dower,
But O, that she's the fairest flower,
In lowly cot or lordly bower,
 Down by Funcheon's river.

II.

Ne'er were eyes so clear and blue,
 Down by Funcheon's river;
Ne'er was heart so good and true,
 Down by Funcheon's river;

And her long hair is so bright,
That it shines by day and night,
Like a cloud of golden light,
　Down by Funcheon's river.

III.

Within the chapel on the green,
　Down by Funcheon's river,
O, could you see my bosom's queen,
　Down by Funcheon's river,
Kneeling at the Sunday prayer,
She looks so bright and lovely there,
You'd deem she was an angel fair,
　Down by Funcheon's river!

IV.

And I will love my maiden mild,
　Down by Funcheon's river,
While lasts the water's song so wild,
　Down by Funcheon's river;
And sweetly as that fairy song,
While blest with love so true and strong,
Our lives in joy shall glide along,
　Down by Funcheon's river.

THE FORSAKEN.

Air — "The Gaddhe Gráine."

I.

The flowers are blooming by stream and fountain,
　The wild birds sing with a joyous tone,
And gladness gushes o'er vale and mountain,
　But I am left to my grief alone —
To wail alone in love's deep devotion,
　For young Dunlevy of the raven hair
Has left his mountains and crossed the ocean,
　To fight for France and for glory there.

II.

They tell me that his love is burning
  For me as fond as e'er it has been;
But when, ah! when comes his sweet returning
  To Erin's hills and his dark Eileen?
They tell me one sweet, pleasant story, —
  My young Dunlevy's brave pride and joy,
When he had won the bright meed of glory,
  A captain's sabre at Fontenoy!

III.

The foreign maidens could ne'er have bound him
  In love's bright fetters, though fair they be;
Yet ah! he comes not, though fame has found him,
  And well I love him, and he loves me.
Alas! their vengeance is not half taken
  Upon the Saxon for his tyrannie,
And O, how long shall I sit forsaken,
  To wail alone by the murmuring sea?

JOHNNY'S RETURN.

Air — "In comes a Croppy."

I.

As Johnny came full merrily
  By Mona's ancient tower,
He saw his true love drearily
  Sit in the wild ash bower;
He spoke to her full cheerily,
  But aye she made her moan:
    "O, I'm left to weep all drearily
      My misery alone,
    For he whose words fell merrily
      On my poor heart is flown."

II.

"When winter blasts were roaring wild,
  My love left me to weep;
And ere the larks were soaring wild,
  He'd crossed the stormy deep."

Then Johnny spoke full merrily,
  But aye she made her moan:
"O, I'm left to weep all drearily
  My misery alone,
For he whose words fell cheerily
  On my poor heart is flown."

III.

O, dead her young heart's gladness then,
  For two long, weary years,
And wild she wailed her sadness then,
  And fast fell down her tears;
Yet Johnny spoke full merrily,
  But aye she made her moan:
"O, I'm left to weep all drearily
  My misery alone,
For he whose words fell cheerily
  On my poor heart is flown."

IV.

He'd come disguised full drearily
  On his returning day;
With laugh and fond word cheerily,
  He cast it now away;
He ran where Eileen drearily
  Sat making her sad moan:
    And merrily, O, merrily,
      His arms were round her thrown,
    Crying, "Joy is dawning cheerily,
      And sorrow's night is flown!"

SWEET IMOKILLY.

I.

I MET, within the greenwood wild,
  My own true knight, that loved me dearly,
When summer airs blew soft and mild,
  And linnets sang, and waves rolled clearly;
And O, we pledged such loving vows
  In moss-grown glade, all green and rilly,

Where lightly waved the rustling boughs
  Of thy green woods, sweet Imokilly!

II.

I met my love in festive hall,
  'Mid lords, and knights, and warriors fearless,
And there my love among them all
  To my fond heart was ever peerless;
And he was fond, and time could ne'er
  His love for me make cold and chilly;
Ah! then I knew nor grief nor care,
  'Mid thy green woods, sweet Imokilly!

III.

From Rincrew's turrets, high and hoar,
  When autumn floods were wildly sweeping,
I saw my love ride to the shore,
  I saw him in the torrent leaping,
To meet me 'neath the twilight dim,
  In bowery nook, secure and stilly,
But the ruthless waters swallowed him,
  By thy green woods, sweet Imokilly!

SHANE GOW; OR, THE BOYS IN GREEN.

A. D. 1798.

I.

Up comes Shane Gow,*
  With his hammer in his hand:
"Tell me, tell me how is Ireland,
  And how does it now stand?"
"Through and through old Ireland
  There is war now between
The gory Saxon despots
  And the gallant boys in green."
  O, the gallant boys in green —
May the God of battles bless them,
  The gallant boys in green.

* John the Smith.

II.

Then he dashed down his hammer,
  And he took up his gun,
And he swore each jovial tradesman
  Should join us every one;
And he marched in review
  With a brave and manly mien,
And prepared with his comrades
  To join the boys in green.
  O, the gallant boys in green —
May the God of battles bless them,
  The gallant boys in green.

III.

Then up comes a captain,
  With a burly seaman's shape,
Saying, "I have a ship in company,
  With green to her cape;
If you want to cross the ocean,
  Her prow it is keen,
And I'll land you all in Ireland,
  To join the boys in green."
  O, the gallant boys in green —
May the God of battles bless them,
  The gallant boys in green.

IV.

So we sailed and we sailed
  Till we crossed by Cape Clear,
And at sight of old Ireland
  We gave a hearty cheer;
And we landed in a bay,
  By the enemy unseen,
The first immortal shipload
  That joined the boys in green.
  O, the gallant boys in green —
May the God of battles bless them,
  The gallant boys in green.

V.

Now fill me up a tankard,
  And fill it to the brim,
And, brothers of my bosom,
  I'll drink a health to them

Whose green flags are flying,
   And whose pikeheads are keen
In the fight for Ireland's freedom,
   The gallant boys in green.
    O, the gallant boys in green —
May the God of battles bless them,
   The gallant boys in green.

I WISH I SAT BY GRENA'S SIDE.

Air — "I wish I had the yellow Cow."

I.

I wish I sat by Grena's side,
With the friends of boyhood-tide,
With the maids, the brilliant-eyed,
   Playful, wild, and airy,
Who taught me that love could go,
Worship bright eyes to and fro,
But turning with fonder glow
   Back to you, my Mary!

II.

I wish I sat by Grena's stream,
In the ruddy sunset beam,
Where the waves leap, glance, and gleam
   On through dell and wildwood;
Ne'er half so fleet and free,
As the fairy feet of glee
Which danced 'neath the summer tree
   In our dreamy childhood.

III.

I wish I sat by Grena's shore,
With the green boughs waving o'er,
Where the glens and mountains hoar
   Shine, one land of faery;
Then, O, how I'd muse and dream
Long beside that haunted stream,
And all on one golden theme —
   You, my lovely Mary!

IV.

I wish I sat by Grena's wave,
Hopes fulfilled that boyhood gave,
Where the woods clothe gorge and cave,
   Storied hill and plain, love;
You placed beside me there,
Laughing, loving, wildly fair,
Long parted, lost, but ne'er,
   Ne'er to part again, love!

ROVING BRIAN O'CONNELL.

Air — "How do you like her for your Wife?"

I.

"How do you like her for your wife,
   Roving Brian O'Connell?
A loving mate, and true for life,
   Roving Brian O'Connell?"
"She's as fit to be my wife
As my sword is for the strife,"
Said the Rapparee trooper,
   Roving Brian O'Connell!

II.

"Ne'er to Mabel prove untrue,
   Roving Brian O'Connell,
For O, she'd die for love of you,
   Roving Brian O'Connell."
"O, my wild heart never knew
A flame so constant too,"
Said the Rapparee trooper,
   Roving Brian O'Connell!

III.

"Never man my child will take,
   Roving Brian O'Connell,
Save him who'd die for Ireland's sake,
   Roving Brian O'Connell."

"O, I'd die for Ireland's sake,
And her bonds we soon will break,"
Said the Rapparee trooper,
   Roving Brian O'Connell!

IV.

"Her father died as dies the brave,
   Roving Brian O'Connell,
Beneath the blow the Saxon gave,
   Roving Brian O'Connell."
"Next we'll meet the Saxon knave,
He'll get pike, and gun, and glaive,"
Said the Rapparee trooper,
   Roving Brian O'Connell.

V.

"How will you your young bride keep,
   Roving Brian O'Connell?
The foeman's bands are ne'er asleep,
   Roving Brian O'Connell."
"In our hold by Conail's steep,
Who dare make my Mabel weep?"
Said the Rapparee trooper,
   Roving Brian O'Connell.

VI.

"This day in ruined church you stand,
   Roving Brian O'Connell,
To take your young bride's priceless hand,
   Roving Brian O'Connell."
"O, my heart, my arm, and brand,
Are for her and our dear land,"
Said the Rapparee trooper,
   Roving Brian O'Connell.

THE ADVICE.

Air — "The Advice."

I.

Redmond spoke the wise old man, —
  Redmond Clare of Corrin's highland, —
"O, win my maid I never can,
  The proudest heart in Erin's island;
Day by day I've gone to woo,
  And found but pride and black displeasure."
Then said the sage, "If love won't do,
  Go court her all with golden treasure."

II.

Redmond was the comeliest man
  From Brandon hill to Barrow's water,
Yet high howe'er his passion ran,
  She frowned on all the love he brought her;
And Redmond came of gentle kin,
  But ah! he lacked fair Fortune's measure,
And when he failed her heart to win,
  'Twas but for want of golden treasure.

III.

To foreign climes he never ran,
  But wrought within his native island,
Until, at last, the richest man
  In all the glens of Corrin's highland,
He went to woo the maid again,
  And met all smiles and courtly pleasure,
And found, proud woman's heart to win,
  There's nothing like the golden treasure!

THE FLAME THAT BURNED SO BRIGHTLY.

Air.—"Saddle the Pony."

I.

There was a light in the window pane,
    Still burning, brightly burning,
And it gleamed afar over Cleena's main,
    On Donall's bark returning;
And he looked up, the cliffs between,
    Where the hamlet glimmered nightly,
And thought he saw his own Kathleen
    By the flame that burned so brightly.

II.

It was upon All-Hallow's night,
    When the candles bright were burning,
That the beams fell from that constant light,
    On Donall's bark returning;
It lit like a star the darkening scene,
    And made his heart beat lightly,
For he thought he saw his own Kathleen
    By the flame that burned so brightly.

III.

He moored his bark the hamlet near,
    Where the candles bright were burning,
But a mournful wail met his startled ear,
    All-Hallow's night returning;
And he heard a name in that piercing keen,
    And saw a shroud gleam whitely—
'Twas the waking light of his own Kathleen,
    The flame that burned so brightly!

EILEEN'S LAMENT FOR GERALD.

Air —"Slan lath a chur."

I.

By loud Avondhu,
While the sweet flowerets blew,
I've mourned for my Gerald the long summer through,
And autumn falls lone
On Kilmore's mountain zone,
But Cleena, still Cleena ne'er heedeth my moan.

II.

O, sweet fell the hours
By Crom's lordly towers,
When we strayed, ever loving, through Maig's blooming bowers—
From bright June to May
Was one blissful day,
Ere my true love was borne from his Eileen away.

III.

With gems of red gold
Gleamed his mail in the wold,
As he slept where the lone Druid worshipped of old;
But the young Fairy Queen
Passed there in the e'en,
And the flash of his bright mail was never more seen.

IV.

She bore him that night
To her palace of light,
In this rock wild and lone, by the spells of her might,
And she keeps him in thrall,
The bright prince of her hall,
While she heeds not my wailing, and hears not my call.

V.

And thus I must weep
By Cleena's gray steep,
Joy faded, hope clouded, and sorrow more deep;
Yet firmer and true
To the one love I knew,
Till I die in my sorrow by loud Avondhu!

THE HOLLY TREE.

Air — "I met a maid, she asked my trade."

I.

"O, DAUGHTER, lovely daughter,
  Sit by my elbow-chair,
And you shall have for birthday gift
  Yon flax-field shining fair."
"The flax may vie with summer's sky
  In azure and in blue,
But I must have a better gift,
  O mother, dear, from you."
    Sing ho! he! he! the holly tree,
      Its leaves are always green,
    And thus may shine love's flowers divine,
      And ever bright be seen.

II.

"Cheer up, my blooming daughter,
  You'll have a gift instead,
Yon gentle flock of snowy sheep
  Upon the hill-side spread."
"O mother, dear, I'll card the wool,
  And spin the worsted fine,
But you may keep both flax and sheep,
  For better gifts are thine."
    Sing ho! he! he! the holly tree
      Is green through winter's gloom,
    And thus may shine love's flowers divine,
      Forever bright in bloom.

III.

"Now laugh, my merry daughter,
  I'l give thee ten times more —
Yon spotted herd of lowing kine
  That graze beside the shore."
"I'll milk the kine, O mother, dear,
  At morn and evening's fall,
But de'il may take the gifts you make,
  I hate them, one and all."

Sing ho! he! he! the holly tree,
  Its leaves are always green,
And thus may shine love's flowers divine,
  And ever bright be seen.

IV.

"Then sing! You'll get, sweet daughter,
  For husband a young man!"
"Ho! ho! ha! ha! O mother, dear,
  And see how well I can.
For, O, I love a nice young man —
  I cannot tell you how;
But ten times more than fields of flax,
  And more than sheep or cow."
    Sing ho! he! he! the holly tree
      Is green through winter's gloom,
    And thus may shine love's flowers divine,
      Forever bright in bloom.

V.

And she embraced her mother,
  No more to sigh or crave;
Like the cracking of a hazel-nut,
  The hearty kiss she gave:
Then danced, with strapping, twinkling feet
  A reel the kitchen round,
Till pots and pans, and plates and cans,
  Gave back the gladsome sound.
    With ho! he! he! the holly tree,
      Its leaves are always green,
    And thus may shine love's flowers divine,
      And ever bright be seen.

MERRILY, MERRILY PLAYING.

Air — "Gleantaun Araglin ěving."

I.

Merrily, merrily playing,
　Dances the rill away,
Where breezes soft are straying,
　And linnets sing all day;
Sweeter than wood-rill's glee is,
　Sweeter than linnet's tune,
My Helen's voice to me is,
　All in the rose-bright June.

II.

My love than the rose is sweeter
　That blooms in yonder dell,
And far I've come to meet her,
　For, O, she loves me well;
And the stream by the gay beams lighted
　Shall freeze in the summer noon,
Ere we break the vows we've plighted
　All in the rose-bright June.

MY TRUE LOVE.

Air — "The May Morning."

I.

My love has a form of splendor;
　My love has an eye divine;
My love has a heart full tender,
　And I know that heart is mine;
Her swan-like neck and bosom
　Are softly fair and pure
As the snowy wild-rose blossom,
　Or the white flower of the moor.

II.

The summer streamlets playing,
　Flow down in light and song,
So my thoughts to her go straying
　Through night, and all day long,
And to the bliss which crowned me,
　When I kissed her o'er and o'er,
When my true-love's arms were round me,
　By the wild lake's rocky shore.

III.

My love's like a bright May morning,
　So pure, so mild, so bland;
My love's like a rose adorning
　A bower in some fairy land.
How I long for red eve's shining,
　To see my true-love stand,
Her golden tresses twining
　With her snow-white lily hand.

IV.

There's a stream in the wild-wood springing,
　Where the birds chant on each tree:
O, I deem them forever singing,
　My mountain maid, of thee.
And that stream the mountains blue, love,
　A deep sea shall o'erflow,
Ere I forsake my true-love,
　Or my heart one change shall know.

SONG OF SARSFIELD'S TROOPER.

Air — "Here's our brave Lord Lucan."

I.

The night fell dark on Limerick, and all the land was still,
As for the foe in ambush we lay beside the hill;
Like lions bold we waited, to rush upon our prey,
With noble Sarsfield at our head, before the break of day.
From Dublin came the foeman, with guns and warlike store —
To gain the walls of Limerick he'd want full ten times more;
And little was he dreaming, that there to work his doom,
We'd come with gallant Sarsfield, far down from wild Sliav Bluim.

II.

At the lonely hour of midnight each man leapt on his steed,
And 'cross the bridge of Cullen we dashed with lightning speed;
And up the way we thundered to Ballincety's wall,
Where lay our foes securely, with guns, and stores, and all.
When they asked for the password, "Ho! Sarsfield is the man!
And here I am!" our general cried, as down on them we ran;
Then God He cleared the firmament, the moon and stars gave light,
And for the battle of the Boyne we had revenge that night.*

III.

When we'd slain them all, brave Sarsfield he bade us take that store
Of baggage-carts, and powder, and arms and guns galore,
And pile them by the castle, and place the fuse full nigh;
And that we did right speedily, and blew them in the sky!
How pleasant spoke our general as fast we rode away!
And many a health we drank to him in Limerick next day:
Here's another health to Sarsfield, who led us one and all,
And took the foe's artillery by Ballincety's wall!

* These two lines are from an old song on the same subject, the fragments of which remain still among the peasantry.

THE WANDERER.

Air — "Slan Beo."

I.

O, GREEN are the woods that circle my Helen's wild home,
O, sweetest her smiles from Houra to Cleena's bright foam,
And brightest her eyes 'mong the blue eyes of splendor that beam
    'Mid the hills of the South, by wild-wood, and fountain, and stream.

II.

I sat all alone by the wood-screened banks of the Suir,
While the calm sky of eve shone bright in its breast fresh and
    pure;
O, every fair cloud, like a gold-winged angel above,
Left an image below — a glory-robed trace of my love.

III.

And once by the marge of Cleena's waters I lay,
In a sweet dream of love and joy at the opening of day;
The beams of the morn smiled over the blue billows there,
The smiles of my love, the wreaths of her long golden hair.

IV.

By Shannon's green shore my wandering footsteps I stayed
On a wave-worn steep, to dream of my yellow-haired maid;
I thought of her archéd brow and fair neck of snow,
As I saw the fleet wing of the white gull gleaming below.

V.

And thus as I stray by river, and wild-wood, and sea,
All Nature still paints but one lovely image for me;
And, O, for the joy when standing by Ounanar's tide,
In the greenwood again, with my bright-eyed love by my side.

FAIREST AND RAREST.

Air — "The rarest Maid."

I.

Fairest and rarest
  Of all the maids that be,
Sweetest and meetest
  For minstrel's love is she,
She who loved me longest,
  When far, far away; —
With a love the strongest
  I love her to-day.

II.

Keep me and steep me
  In black Sorrow's wave,
Fair dreams and rare dreams
  Of my love could save; —
Save my heart, and borrow
  Light in such dark doom,
Make, 'mid desert sorrow,
  Joy's gay flowers to bloom.

III.

Deeming, sweet dreaming,
  Such a joy to me,
How bright with joy's light
  Must the present be!
When her eyes are shining,
  Void of care and pain,
When her arms are twining
  Round me once again.

COME, ALL YOU MAIDS, WHERE'ER YOU BE.

Air—"Come, all ye Maids."

I.

Come, all you maids, where'er you be,
　That flourish fair and fine, fine,
To young and old I will unfold
　This hapless tale of mine,
　　　　Mine,
This hapless tale of mine!

II.

The sun shall set upon my grief,
　The sun shall rise the same, same,
And ever so shall live my woe,
　Enduring as his flame,
　　　　Flame,
Enduring as his flame.

III.

My home was in the border land,
　Where the flashing streams rush down, down,
From Houra's hill; there with gallant Will
　I met in the autumn brown,
　　　　Brown,
I met in the autumn brown.

IV.

He said, his love so fond and true
　Would never die for me, me,
That my eyes shamed the hue of the violet blue,
　And my lips the red rose tree,
　　　　Tree,
The bloom of the red rose tree.

V.

Alas! I liked and loved him well,
　Though I answered cold as stone, stone,

So he turned his steed to the wars with speed,
  And he left me weeping lone,
           Lone, —
  To sigh and weep alone.

VI.

Grief made my love burn wild and strong,
  So I followed him full fain, fain,
But by Knock'noss Hill, O, my gallant Will
  Lay dying amid the slain,
           Slain,
  Lay dying amid the slain!

VII.

And down I knelt by my true love's side,
  And he bent his eyes on me, me;
One long, long look of love he took,
  And he died on that blood-stained lea,
           Lea,
  He died on that blood-stained lea!

VIII.

The sun shall set upon my grief,
  The sun shall rise the same, same,
And ever so shall live my woe,
  Enduring as his flame,
           Flame,
  Enduring as his flame!

IRELAND OUR QUEEN.

AIR — "Irish Molly, O!"

I.

COME all you Irish maidens, and Irish wives also,
I pray you teach the young men the way that they should go;
A martial lady walks the land, — our long-dethronéd queen, —
Her banner is the Sunburst grand, her color is the Green!

II.

As I went out one morning along the river side,
Down by the tumbling water, this lady fair I spied;
Bright and rosy were her cheeks, and raven-black her hair,
And the robes were all of green and gold this Irish queen did wear.

III.

Her shoes were of the Spanish buff, bound round with silken sheen,
And 'cross her breast a baldrick blazed — a baldrick of the Green;
And from that flashing baldrick bright an Irish blade hung down,
And on its emerald hilt was graved the Harp without the Crown!

IV.

And she that was so sorrowful and sad in days gone by,
The light of hope was on her brow, and war was in her eye.
"O, why are you so glad, bright queen, that wept so long and sore?"
"Because the morning dawns," she cried; "my sons arise once more.

V.

"And not as they were wont to rise, undisciplined and rude,
With creed 'gainst creed, and brothers' swords in brothers' blood imbrued;
But hand in hand throughout the land my faithful sons are seen,
With hopeful words and ready swords to battle for the Green!"

VI.

With cap in hand down knelt I there before my noble queen;
She drew her sword and dubbed me, too, a soldier of the Green;
I kissed its hilt, and vowed unto the God whom I adore,
That I would die a soldier's death or free my native shore!

VII.

Come, all you Irish young men, now list to what I say:
Have weapons bright and powder dry before the coming day —
The morning clears — awake! arise! and rally round your queen,
And show the world that Irishmen still love their native Green!

MARY, THE PRIDE OF THE WEST.

Air — "Nancy, the Pride of the East."

I.

The summer shines bright from the plain
    To the hills where the gray rocks are piled;
The birds sing a clear, joyous strain,
    And the flowers are in bloom o'er the wild;
But a flower all these fair flowers above
    In sweetness, blooms deep in my breast, —
'Tis the lone flower of fondness and love
    For Mary, the Pride of the West.

II.

There's an ash-tree that blooms light and fair,
    Where the linnets in May make their bower;
There's a rose-bush beyond all compare,
    By the walls of the gray mountain tower;
But how lovely soe'er that lone tree,
    And the bush all in white blossoms dressed,
As fair and as lovely is she,
    My Mary, the Pride of the West.

III.

When she goes from the wild hills among
    To the town on the verge of the plain,
Could you see her sweet face 'mid the throng,
    You ne'er would forget it again;
And the gallants who pass, when they see,
    And the crowd, think her brightest and best,
And they ask who such fair maid can be,
    My Mary, the Pride of the West!

IV.

When each night at her father's broad hearth,
    I sit near my love by the fire,
I have all that my heart on this earth
    Can love, and adore, and admire;
Then her eyes, like two clear stars above,
    With their kind looks on me often rest,
Till I'm wild, wild with fondness and love
    For Mary, the Pride of the West.

MY LOVE IS ON THE RIVER.

Air—"Ta mo grad sa ar an abainn."

I.

Sliav Gua's highlands shade meadow and moor,
And guard the green islands of the golden Suir:
The Tar brightly sallies from their cooms, wild and fleet,
And sings through the valleys that bloom at their feet.
More bright to-day than they e'er shone before,
Shine castle gray, and green height, and shore;
O, the splendors that quiver o'er wildwood and lea,
While my love is on the river in his light boat with me.

II.

Swift as foot of the beagle from the hills doth he hie,
Bright as glance of the eagle the glance of his eye;
When the Green Flag's unfurled he is straight as its tree,
Never heart in the world could be fonder of me.
Outlawed and lone lived he many a day
In his cold cave of stone, 'mid the hills far away;
But truth conquers ever, and my love he is free,
On the Suir's golden river, in his light boat with me.

III.

Sweet songs are ringing from the birds of the grove,
But sweeter the singing of my own gallant love;
O, his brave words first found me in sadness and pain,
But they soon strewed around me joy's bright flowers again.
And he never more from my arms shall be torn;
The fair chapel door shall receive us next morn;
And the green woods shall quiver to our bridal bells' glee,
For my love is on the river, in his light boat with me.

GLENARA.

Air — "She is my true Love."

I.

Grand are the mountains that circle Glenara,
See-Fein, wild Corrin, Knockea, and Sliav Dara;
Proudly their summits look down where its sheen flood
Lies coiled in the gorges or sunk in the greenwood.

II.

Sweet are the scenes where that wild flood enlarges,
Peaceful the homes by its flower-scented marges;
Fair are the maidens with eyes brightly glowing,
Who bide by its windings and list to its flowing.

III.

Ever the fairest 'mid Beauty's gay daughters,
Dwells my young love by the sound of its waters;
Roams she at eve through its fairy recesses,
My maid of the blue eyes and long, golden tresses.

IV.

One summer even I sped to the fountain,
Sped to her side from my home o'er the mountain:
There a lone dreamer to sweet bliss awoken,
My fond vows of love to a fond heart were spoken.

V.

Far from my dear mountain home as I wander,
Ever with joy on that evening I ponder,
Thinking and dreaming how fraught with sweet glory
My days by her side, 'mid those hills wild and hoary.

ASTHOREEN MACHREE.

Air—"Astoria Machree."

I.

Summer with gay flowers the hills was adorning,
   Streams through the wildwood sang sweetly and free,
As I 'scaped from my cell at the dawn of the morning,
   My dark tyrant scorning, Asthoreen Machree.

II.

O, in that prison my heart was all sadness;
   O, but the long days fell heavy on me,
Still thinking I never might see thee in gladness,
   Brooding in madness, Asthoreen Machree.

III.

Now I have 'scaped, but such darkness was never;
   How could the brightness arise save from thee?
Woe and despair, they have crossed my endeavor,
   Thou sleeping forever, Asthoreen Machree.

IV.

Out in the forest the branches are shaking;
   There the sad Banshee is wailing for me;
Down from the trees the strong boughs she is taking,
   My bier she is making, Asthoreen Machree.

V.

Soon shall we meet in the grave's silent dwelling;
   O, but 'tis joy thus to slumber with thee;
Soon shall the keeners my hard fate be telling,
   My death-bell loud knelling, Asthoreen Machree.

THE UNDERTAKERS.*

Air—"The Boys of Wexford."

I.

When Ginkell signed his king to bind
   On Limerick's treaty stone,
We thought us free from th' enemie,
   Our good lands all our own.
That felon plot, it freed us not,
   But wrought us woe and shame;
For, gorged with blood, the demon brood
   Of undertakers came;
     And O, they racked the Irishman,
       And ground him fierce and sore,
     Like Israel's clan, 'neath Pharaoh's ban,
       In Egypt's land of yore.

II.

And though our proud, sad hearts we bowed
   In peace beneath their sway,
They broke their troth and plighted oath,
   And robbed us day by day.
Honor and trust, in blood and dust,
   They trampled madly down,
'Cause on their hordes we bared our swords
   For Ireland's old renown.
     And O, they racked the Irishman,
       And ground him fierce and sore,
     And still to-day their children play
       That black game played of yore!

III.

With penal laws they doomed our cause
   To wreck by slow degrees,
But hope still bloomed, howe'er they doomed
   The homeless Rapparees;
With bloodhounds good they tracked each wood,
   Our cavern lairs to find,

---

* The soldiers of King William, to whom the confiscated Irish lands were granted after the siege and treaty of Limerick.

Till you could see on every tree
  Some corpse swing in the wind.
For O, they racked the Irishman,
  And ground him fierce and sore,
And who'll deny that still they ply
  That black trade plied of yore?

IV.

And though we now ply spade and plough,
  Who'll reap the crop he sows?
Ah! plough and sow; but reap and mow
  Are other things, God knows.
The good, strong hand that tills the land
  The agent sweeps away,
Like those lost hearts who bore their parts
  'Neath th' undertakers' sway.
And O, they racked the Irishman,
  And ground him fierce and sore;
But Israel's clan from Pharaoh's ban
  Were freed in days of yore.

MARGREAD BAN.

Air — " The old Astrologer."

I.

My wild heart's love, my woodland dove,
  The tender and the true,
She dwells beside a blue stream's tide
  That bounds through wild Glenroe;
Through every change her love's the same, —
  A long, bright summer dawn,
A gentle flame, — and O, her name
  Is lovely Margréad Bán.
O, joy, that on her paths I came,
  My lovely Margréad Bán!

II.

When winter hoar comes freezing o'er
  The mountains, wild and gray,

Her neck is white as snow-wreaths bright,
  Upon thy crags, Knockea;
Her lips are red as roses sweet
  On Dara's flowery lawn;
Her fairy feet are light and fleet,
  My gentle Margréad Bán;
And O, her steps I love to meet,
  My own dear Margréad Bán!

III.

When silence creeps o'er Houra's steeps,
  As blue eve ends its reign,
Her long locks' fold is like the gold
  That gleams o'er sky and main.
My heart's fond sorrow fled away
  Like night before the dawn,
When one spring day I went astray,
  And met my Margréad Bán,
And felt her blue eyes' sparkling ray,
  My lovely Margréad Bán.

IV.

One summer noon, to hear the tune
  Of wild birds in the wood,
Where murmuring streams flashed back the beams,
  All rapt in bliss I stood;
The birds sang from the fairy moat,
  From greenwood, brake, and lawn;
But never throat could chaunt a note
  So sweet as Margréad Bán,
As through the vales her wild songs float,
  My lovely Margréad Bán.

V.

O, would that we for love might flee
  To some far valley green,
Where never more, by rock or shore,
  Dark Sorrow could be seen.
I know a valley, wildly fair,
  From strife far, far withdrawn;
And ever there the loving air
  Of gentle Margréad Bán
Would keep this fond heart free from care,
  My lovely Margréad Bán.

OVER THE HILLS AND FAR AWAY.

AIR—"Over the Hills."

I.

From night till morn, from morn till night,
My thoughts dwell with a sweet delight,
And all upon a maiden bright,
Who dwells by Houra's rocky height,
  Over the hills and far away,
  Over the hills and far away;
  I think of her both night and day,
  Over the hills and far away.

II.

And is my maid a proper theme?
And is she worthy of my dream?
Go, catch her smile and clear eyes' beam,
By Houra's hill or Grena's stream,
  Over the hills and far away;
  And ne'er was one, you'll think and say,
  So lovely as my maiden gay,
  Over the hills and far away.

III.

And have you seen the violet blow?
Its tints within her fond eyes glow?
Her skin is fair as blooms that grow,
In wild March on the fragrant sloe,
  Over the hills and far away,
  Over the hills and far away,
  I think of her both night and day,
  Over the hills and far away.

IV.

Yet 'tis not for her sweet smile's charm,
And 'tis not for her graceful form,
But for her heart, so true and warm,
My love burns on, through calm and storm.
  Over the hills and far away,
  Whate'er my lot, where'er I stray,
  I'll think of her both night and day,
  Over the hills and far away.

THE GREEN AND THE GOLD.

Air — "Neil McCreaman was a braw Hieland Soldier."

I.

In the soft, blooming vales of our country,
  Two colors shine brightest of all,
O'er mountain, and moorland, and meadow,
  On cottage and old castle wall;
They shine in the gay summer garden,
  And glint in the depths of the wold,
And they gleam on the banner of Ireland,
  Our colors, the green and the gold.
    Then hurrah for the green and the gold!
    By the fresh winds of Freedom out-rolled,
  As they shine on the brave Irish banner,
    Our colors, the green and the gold.

II.

In the days of Fomorian and Fenian,
  These colors flashed bright in the ray;
And their gleam kept the fierce Roman eagles
  In Rome-conquered Britain at bay;
When Conn forgot his hundred red battles,
  And the lightning struck Dathy of old,
As he bore through Helvetia's wild gorges
  Our colors, the green and the gold.
    Then hurrah for the green and the gold!
    May they flourish for ages untold,
  May they blaze in the vanguard of Freedom,
    Our colors, the green and the gold.

III.

Up many a grim breach of glory,
  In many a fierce battle's tide,
Flashing high o'er the red, gleaming surges,
  Our banners swept on in their pride,
From the day when triumphant they fluttered
  O'er the legions of Brian the Bold,

Till with Sarsfield they streamed down the Shannon,
　Our colors, the green and the gold!
　　Then hurrah for the green and the gold!
　In Victory's van, as of old,
　May they flash over new Irish legions,
　　Our colors, the green and the gold!

IV.

In these dark days of doom and disaster,
　Is it dead, the old love for our land?
Are our bosoms less brave than our fathers'?
　Comes the sword-hilt less deft to our hand?
No; we've proved us the wide world over,
　Wherever War's surges have rolled,
And we'll raise once again in old Ireland,
　Our colors, the green and the gold!
　　Then hurrah for the green and the gold,
　　And hurrah for the valiant and bold
　Who will raise them supreme in old Ireland,
　　Our colors, the green and the gold.

MY HANDSOME YOUNG MAN.

Air.—"John the Journeyman."

I.

My handsome young man is no coward or slave;
He's kindly, he's pleasant, he's brilliant and brave;
On the throne of my heart, since our courtship began,
In the warm light of love sits my handsome young man.

II.

His laugh is like music, his words ever gay,
And he smiles like the sun on the morning of May,
And the warblings of birds in the Moat of Dunsan
Are less sweet than the songs of my handsome young man.

III.

His short, curling hair in the sun shines like gold,
And his step's like the step of a chieftain of old;
For the pure Irish blood that through centuries ran,
Throbs warm in the heart of my handsome young man.

IV.

My handsome young man at the muster is seen,
With his jacket of blue and his feather of green.
"May the brave wind of Freedom those green feathers fan
To the land of my birth," says my handsome young man.

V.

"In the land of my birth still the dark tyrants reign,
And they mocked all our efforts to sever their chain;
But the next time they'll find it no flash in the pan,
When we rise in our wrath," says my handsome young man.

VI.

Then all you young maidens, ne'er smile on a slave;
Choose a sweetheart, like me, from the ranks of the brave,
From the soldiers who'll fight against Tyranny's ban,
For the land of their birth, like my handsome young man.

OUR SONG.

AIR — "Cannon Balls and Bombshells."

I.

O, you at home preparing,
  And you who in the fray,
Beneath each foreign banner,
  Fought well to win the day,
Come join, no more to sunder,
Old Ireland's banner under,
For now her shouts of Freedom
  Along her mountains thunder!
    Hurrah! hurrah! hurrah!
    United, heart and hand,
  We'll die like gallant soldiers,
    Or free our native land!

II.

"Who makes the bravest sweetheart?"
  I asked my Irish maid;
She said, "A jovial soldier,
  Who wears the green cockade!"

I took it as a token,
So fond her words were spoken,
That me my maid will marry,
When Ireland's bonds are broken!
Hurrah! hurrah! &c.

III.

The night that wrapped old Ireland
In centuries of gloom.
The dazzling beams of Freedom
Its fading skirts illume;
Nor long shall tyrants wound her,
Nor slavery confound her,
For soon in bright battalions
Her children shall surround her!
Hurrah! hurrah! &c.

IV.

O, you who wear the Orange,
Our ancient, sturdy foe,
With you, for sake of Ireland,
Our contests we forego;
One kindly mother bore us,
One tyrant ever tore us;
Then let us join together
In Freedom's thundering chorus!
Hurrah, hurrah! &c.

V.

O, gayly shines our banner,
With white, and gold, and green,
With a sunburst like the morning,
And shamrock's gleaming sheen;
Our blood shall stain her splendor,
Ere dark defeat attend her,
With our war-cry, "Fag-an-Bealach!"
Our watchword, "No surrender!"
Hurrah! hurrah! &c.

VI.

Then, comrades, gallant comrades,
Now join this prayer with me:
Confusion to the tyrants
Who cause our slavery;

May traitors rot and moulder,
May Ireland's sons behold her
On Freedom's field triumphant,
Stout shoulder unto shoulder!
Hurrah! hurrah! hurrah!
United, heart and hand,
We'll die like gallant soldiers,
Or free our native land!

THE WITHERED ROSE.

Air — "The Orange Rose."

I.

Fair blooms array the summer bowers
  Along the woodlands airy,
But fairer still this flower of flowers
  I got from my dear Mary.
The purple heath-bell paints the steep,
  Wild rock and glen illuming;
More dear this withered flower I keep,
  Than all the wild flowers blooming.
    O, fair the blooms that deck the bowers,
      And paint the mountains airy;
    O, fairer still this flower of flowers,
      I got from my dear Mary!

II.

O, sweet the days of long ago,
  When love with joy was weaven,
When in the fairy dells below
  We met each summer even;
When Mary sat in beauty nigh,
  And sang the songs I taught her,
And spoke the love that ne'er shall die,
  By Grena's sunny water.
    O, fair the blooms that deck the bowers,
      And paint the mountains airy;
    O, fairer still this flower of flowers
      I got from my dear Mary.

III.

It was upon a Saint John's night
  She gave me that red blossom;
'Twas blooming in its freshness bright,
  Upon her loving bosom;
And since, through changing joys and tears,
  Though Fate her smiles denied me,
O, ever since, for five long years,
  I've kept that flower beside me.
    O, sweet the blooms that deck the bowers,
      And paint the mountains airy!
    O, sweeter still this flower of flowers
      I got from my dear Mary!

IV.

And when once more I meet her gaze,
  By Grena's crystal water,
How sweet to talk of those young days
  When by the wave I sought her;
When care is fled, and woe is dead,
  And joy alone is shining,
When meeting them in that wild glen,
  Her arms are round me twining,
    O, then beside our native bowers,
      Amid the woodlands airy,
    This long-kept, priceless flower of flowers
      I'll show to my dear Mary.

LAMENT OF MARION CREAGH.

Air—" Margaret Roche."

I.

The woods of Drumlory
  Are greenest and fairest,
And flowers in gay glory
  Bloom there of the rarest:
They'll deck without number
  A grave red and narrow,
Where he'll sleep his last slumber,
  Young Hugh of Glenurra.

II.

The canavaun's blooming
  Like snow on the marish,
The autumn is coming,
  The summer flowers perish;
And though Love smiles all gladness,
  He's left me in sorrow,
To mourn in my madness
  Young Hugh of Glenurra!

III.

Sweet love filled forever
  His kind words and glances;
Light foot there was never
  Like his in the dances,
By forest or fountain,
  In goal on the curragh,
Or chase on the mountain,
  Young Hugh of Glenurra!

IV.

When cannons did rattle,
  And trumpets brayed loudly,
In the grim van of battle
  His long plume waved proudly;
As the bolts from the bowmen,
  Or share through the furrow,
He tore through the foemen,
  Young Hugh of Glenurra!

V.

Alas! when we parted
  That morn in the hollow,
Why staid I faint-hearted,
  Why ne'er did I follow,
To fight by his side there
  The red battle thorough,
Or die when he died there,
  Young Hugh of Glenurra?

VI.

Ah! woe is me, woe is me,
  Love cannot wake him;
Woe is me, woe is me,
  Grief cannot make him

Quit to embrace me;
 This red couch of sorrow,
Where soon they shall place me
 By Hugh of Glenurra!

THE GREEN FLAG.

I.

Prepare, prepare, with silent care,
 And trust to words no longer,
We've had enough of such false stuff,
 And we are nought the stronger;
Those mountebanks who fill their ranks
 By lying all in chorus,
Of them beware, and still prepare
 For the Green Flag flying o'er us.

II.

In days of yore, when talkers bore
 A sword, like men of valor,
From every fight they led the flight
 With base and coward pallor;
Such worthless men, by voice and pen,
 With faction cursed and tore us;
We'll strike them dumb, with fife and drum,
 And the Green Flag flying o'er us.

III.

Prepare, prepare, in joy or care,
 To fill the gap of danger,
And silent force will run its course
 To swamp the subtle stranger;
Within that gap our chains we'll snap,
 And conquer all before us,
If we prepare to do and dare,
 With the Green Flag flying o'er us.

IV.

In other days, the peasants' gaze
 Drooped slavish down to no man;

Unskilled and rude, they sank in blood
  Before their serried foeman.
Shall we like those confront our foes,
  Their blood-red tale before us?
No; we'll prepare, then do and dare,
  With the Green Flag flying o'er us.

V.

And when the time of deeds sublime
  Shall light the way before us,
With patriot wrath we'll clear our path,
  And free the land that bore us;
The nations round shall hear the sound
  Of our triumphant chorus
Of drum and fife, in Freedom's strife,
  With the Green Flag flying o'er us.

THE JOY-BELLS.

AIR—"The Bells of Barna."

I.

BLITHESOME is our marriage morn,
  Blithesome are our hearts and gay,
Though in no high carriage borne,
  Though we've neither pomp nor sway;
And the joy-bells' constant ringing
  Floats upon the mountain wind,
Ringing, ringing, sweetly bringing
  Many a glad thought to my mind.
    O, the joy-bells! O, the joy-bells!
      Ringing, ringing sweet and clear,
    In the May-time of our loving,
      And the May-tide of the year.

II.

This small chapel by the mountain
  For our bridal's fittest place,
With its fairy thorn and fountain,
  And its old familiar face;

With the gray priest vested meetly,
  Like a saint from Heaven above;
With our parents smiling sweetly
  On our fond and deathless love.
    O, the joy-bells! O, the joy-bells!
      Ringing, ringing sweet and clear,
    In the May-time of our loving,
      And the May-tide of the year.

III.

Once the golden *Mi na Meala**
  With its sunny hours is o'er,
Grief may come, but joy must follow
  When I pass my husband's door,
For my Donall loves me kindly,
  And though love the judgment dim,
'Twas but slow, and 'tis not blindly
  That I gave my heart to him.
    O, the joy-bells! O, the joy-bells!
      Ringing, ringing sweet and clear,
    In the May-time of our loving,
      And the May-tide of the year.

JOHNNY DUNLEA.

Air — "Johnny Dunlea."

I.

There's a tree in the greenwood I love best of all, —
It stands by the side of Easmore's haunted fall;
For there while the sunset shone bright far away,
Last I met 'neath its branches my Johnny Dunlea.

II.

O, to see his fine form as he rode down the hill,
While the red sunset glowed on his helmet of steel,
With his broadsword and charger so gallant and gay,
On that evening of woe for my Johnny Dunlea.

* The Honeymoon.

III.

He stood by my side, and the love-smile he wore
Still brightens my heart, though 'twill beam nevermore;
'Twas to have but one farewell, then speed to the fray;
'Twas a farewell forever, my Johnny Dunlea.

IV.

For the red Saxon soldiers lay hid in the dell,
And burst on our meeting with wild, savage yell;
But their leader's black life-blood I saw that sad day,
And it stained the good sword of my Johnny Dunlea!

V.

My curse on the traitors, my curse on the ball
That stretched my true love by Easmore's haunted fall;
O, the blood of his brave heart ebbed quickly away,
And he died in my arms there, my Johnny Dunlea!

THE JOLLY COMPANIE.

AIR — "The Jolly Companie."

I.

O, WE are jolly soldiers,
  Of courage stout and true,
Some in strife grown hoary,
  And some to battle new;
We're going to the wars
  Beyond the Irish sea,
Our green flag o'er us waving,
  A jolly companie!
  A jolly companie!
  A jolly companie!
In bivouac, or wild attack,
  A jolly companie!

II.

When we sailed from the harbor,
  Our hearts were sad and sore
For the girls we left behind us
  Upon the Irish shore:

Though the girls in France are fair,
  To our own still true we'll be,
As we fight our way to glory,
  A jolly companie!
  A jolly companie!
  A jolly companie!
Around the can, or man to man,
  A jolly companie!

III.

Here's a health to good King Louis,
  Our friend forevermore,
And a health to poor Righ Shamus, —
  May his troubles soon be o'er.
Where'er the pike we trail,
  We'll smite his enemie
To the tune of "Fág an bealach,"*
  A jolly companie!
  A jolly companie!
  A jolly companie!
In peace or fight, by day or night,
  A jolly companie!

IV.

When we look upon our flag-staff,
  Of the hardy Irish oak,
'Twill remind us of our country,
  'Mid the battle's dust and smoke;
In Danger's stormy gap
  Our gory bed may be,
But we'll die like sons of Ireland,
  A jolly companie!
  A jolly companie!
  A jolly companie!
In bivouac or wild attack,
  A jolly companie!

* "Fág an bealach," Clear the way.

THE FIRST NIGHT I WAS MARRIED.*

AIR — "The first Night I was married."

I.

The first night I was married, and made a happy bride,
The captain of the cavalry he came to my bedside, —
"Arise, arise, new married man! arise, and come with me,
To the lowlands of Holland, to face your enemie!

II.

"Holland is a pretty place, the fairest I have seen,
With the waysides glittering all in flowers, the fields so bright
    and green;
The sunshine lights the clustering grapes, the vines hang from
    each tree;"
And I scarce had time to look about when my love was gone
    from me.

III.

O, weeping, weeping sorely, I waste each day and night,
Thinking of the hours I spent with my own heart's delight:
My curse upon the cruel wars that drove him o'er the sea,
To the lowlands of Holland, far, far away from me.

IV.

I built my love a gallant ship to bear him o'er the main,
With four-and-twenty sailors bold, all for a fitting train;
The storm came down upon the sea, and the waves began to
    roar,
And dashed my love and his gallant ship upon the Holland
    shore!

V.

Says the mother to the daughter, "What makes you so lament?
Is there no man in Ireland to please your discontent?"
"There are men enough in Ireland, but none at all for me,
For I never loved but one young man, now far beyond the sea."

---

* From the fragments of an old ballad, about the time of the "Wild
Geese," or recruits for the Irish brigade.

VI.

"I'll build my love another ship, and give its sails the wind,
And search among the bold brigade my gallant love to find;
I'll search among the bold brigade, with heart full fond and fain,
And I'll bring back my true-love from the wild, wild wars again."

THE NIGHT BEFORE FONTENOY; OR, THE GIRLS WE LEFT BEHIND US.

I.

The watch-fire's light falls gayly bright,
  Upon our harness gleaming,
And long we've eyed its flame to-night,
  O'er mournful memories dreaming.
Now fill each glass, and raise each hand,
  And pledge the loves that bind us, —
A health unto our native land,
  And the girls we left behind us!

II.

We've left the sickle and the spade
  At home beyond the water,
We've come to learn the soldier's trade
  In many a field of slaughter;
And soldiers of the best once more
  The Saxon foe shall find us, —
Then a health unto our native shore,
  And the girls we left behind us!

III.

We've drawn the sword for France's land,
  Our knowledge dearly buying,
But we've one heart and we've one hand,
  And we have faith undying,
That with that sword we'll break the rod
  Of foes at home that grind us, —
Then a health unto our native sod,
  And the girls we left behind us!

IV.

Ah, many a girl our hearts adore, —
   Bright Alice, Kate, or Mary, —
From Antrim's cliffs and Kerry's shore
   To glens of green Tipperary, —
Fair maids that with one witching smile
   Could round their fingers wind us, —
Then a health unto our native isle,
   And the girls we left behind us.

V.

Fill high, and drink their health to-night
   In bumpers brimming over;
Some glorious day in fond delight
   May each one clasp her lover,
When side by side, with sword in hand,
   At home again they'll find us, —
Then a health unto our native land,
   And the girls we left behind us!

VI.

Fill high the glass, — the watch-fire light
   Will soon be dimly burning,
And some of us, so hale to-night,
   May lie full low at morning;
May those at home forevermore
   In memory fondly mind us,
When Freedom gladdens Ireland's shore,
   And the girls we left behind us!

FANNY.

AIR — "Green Leaves, so green, O!"

I.

WHERE Anner flows by fairy wrath,
   And tower, and gray rocks many,
One Sunday noon, in woodland path,
   I met my blithesome Fanny.

Her hair was like the yellow blooms
  That deck the meadows early;
Her eyes like heaven, when spring illumes,
  They shone so kind clearly.

II.

We sat to hear the river's tune
  'Neath trees all mossed and olden,
And talked and laughed that autumn noon,
  With thoughts full sweet and golden; —
I built a palace in my brain,
  As fond I gazed upon her,
And in its bright hall she did reign,
  My queen of love and honor.

III.

The palace towers may all depart,
  And cruel Fate may sever,
But in my brain and in my heart
  Her form shall live forever; —
At Beauty's shrine the worshippers
  Judge fond, and rash, and blindly;
Yet ne'er was form more fair than hers,
  And ne'er beat heart more kindly.

THE BRIGADE'S HURLING MATCH.*

Air — "The Game played in Erinn go Bragh."

I.

In the South's blooming valleys they sing and they play
By their vine-shaded cots at the close of the day:
But a game like our own the Brigade never saw —
The wild, sweeping hurlings of Erinn go Bragh.

II.

Our tents they were pitched upon Lombardy's plain;
Ten days nigh the foeman our army had lain;
But ne'er through his towers made we passage or flaw,
Till we showed them the game played in Erinn go Bragh.

* This story is told among the people of Cork and Limerick.

III.

Our sabres were sharp, and a forest was nigh;
There our hurleys we fashioned ere morning rose high;
With the goal-ball young Mahon had brought from Dunlawe,
We showed them the game played in Erinn go Bragh.

IV.

Our captain stood out with the ball in his hand;
Our colonel he gave us the word of command;
Then we dashed it and chased it o'er esker and scragh,
While we showed them the game played in Erinn go Bragh.

V.

The enemy stood on their walls high and strong,
While we raced it, and chased it, and dashed it along;
And they opened their gates as we nearer did draw,
To see the wild game played in Erinn go Bragh.

VI.

We left the round ball in its roaring career;
We turned on the foe with a wild, ringing cheer;
Ah! they ne'er through our bright, dauntless stratagem saw,
While we showed them the game played in Erinn go Bragh!

VII.

Their swords clashed around us, their balls raked us sore,
But with hurleys we paid them in hard knocks galore;
For their bullets and sabres we cared ne'er a straw,
While we showed them the game played in Erinn go Bragh.

VIII.

The fortress is taken! our wild shouts arise;
For our land and King Louis they swell to the skies.
Ah! he laughed as he told us a game he ne'er saw,
Like the wild, sweeping hurlings of Erinn go Bragh!

ADIEU, LOVELY MARY.

AIR — "Adieu, lovely Mary."

I.

"Adieu, lovely Mary; I'm going to leave you,
   And to the West Indies my sad course to steer;
I know very well my long absence will grieve you,
   But I will be back in the spring of the year."

II.

The May-fires were burning, and ships were returning,
   But word never came to allay her sad fear,
And sorely and sadly young Mary sat mourning
   The loss of her love in the spring of the year.

III.

And summer thus found her, and wooers came round her,
   Yet deep in her bosom one form she held dear;
She answered them, weeping, "My love I am keeping
   For one who'll be back in the spring of the year."

IV.

The old man with treasure, the young man with pleasure,
   Still courted till autumn was yellow and sear;
No fond vows were broken, the same words were spoken,
   "My love will be back in the spring of the year."

V.

Next spring flowers were shining, and Mary sat twining
   A wreath of their blooms, and her heart was not drear;
For O, with love glowing, when soft winds were blowing,
   Her true love came back in the spring of the year!

I'M FOURTEEN YEARS OLD UPON SUNDAY.*

AIR — "As I went a walking."

I.

Adown by the Suir, in a May morning's shine,
I saw a young maiden a milking her kine;
And she sang, "O, my bosom no more shall repine,
 For I'm fourteen years old upon Sunday,
 And I shall be married on Sunday!"

II.

"O, love is the fondest the day it is new,
And the heart is a rover, and often untrue;
And will he be fonder, the bridegroom of you,
 But fourteen years old upon Sunday,
 And after your wedding on Sunday?"

III.

"I know him too truly, my brave Conor Lee!
His mind from all thoughts of a rover is free,
And I'm sure in my heart he'll be fonder of me,
 But fourteen years old upon Sunday,
 And after our wedding on Sunday.

IV.

"On Saturday night I'll be void of all care,
With my new bridal dress, and the flowers in my hair,
With three pretty maidens to wait on me there,
 And to dance at my wedding on Sunday,
 For I shall be married on Sunday."

* From fragments of an old song.

THE LINNET.

I.

I've found a comrade, fond and gay,
  A linnet of the wildwood tree;
We hold sweet converse, day by day,
  My heart, my rambling soul, and he.
He sits upon the blossomed spray,
  Within the hollow, haunted dell,
And every song-note seems to say
  That wild bird knows and loves me well.
    Sweet linnet, sing all merrily
      Beside the glittering streamlet's shore,
    For love-bright dreams thou bring'st to me
      Of Rosaleen forevermore.

II.

As I lie in my waking dreams,
  And dreamy thoughts successive rise,
Down from the blooming bough he seems
  To look on me with human eyes;
And then he sings, — ah, such a song
  Will ne'er be heard while seasons roll,
Save thy dear voice, that all day long
  In memory charms my heart and soul.
    Sweet linnet, still sing merrily
      Beside the haunted streamlet's shore,
    For many a dream thou bring'st to me
      Of Rosaleen forevermore.

III.

If souls e'er visit earth again,
  With one my little friend's possessed;
Each dulcet, wild, Elysian strain
  Springs so divinely from his breast.
Those fairy songs, that earnest look,
  Some minstrel's sprite it sure must be, —
Anacreon's soul, or hers who took
  The love-leap by the Grecian sea!
    Sweet linnet, still sing merrily
      Beside the murmuring streamlet's shore,
    For happy dreams thou bring'st to me
      Of Rosaleen, forevermore.

THE SUMMER IS COME.

Air — "The Summer is come."

I.

The summer is come, and the grass is green,
The gay flowers spring where the snows have been,
The ships are sailing upon the sea,
And I'll soon get tidings of Gra Machree.

II.

O, weary, weary, the long, dull night;
I think and think of my heart's delight,
And in my dreamings constantly see
The stately form of my Gra Machree.

III.

The birds are singing from brake and bough,
And sweetly, sweetly remind me now
The day we danced by the village tree,
When I won the heart of my Gra Machree.

IV.

I'm sure, I'm sure, while the sunbeams glow,
While flowers are springing, and soft winds blow,
The white ships sailing upon the sea
Will soon bring tidings of Gra Machree.

OVER THE MORNING DEW.

Air—"As truagh gan peata vier agum."

I.

It is the sweetest hour for love:
The sun is o'er the eastern grove,
And nought is heard but coo of dove,
    And wild streams in the greenwood.
Over the morning dew,
Over the morning dew,
Come with me, young Gra Machree,
    Unto the leafy greenwood.

II.

With flowers that bloom so sweetly there
I'll deck thy dress and golden hair,
And thou hast never looked so fair
    As then in that wild greenwood.
Over the morning dew,
Over the morning dew,
Come with me, young Gra Machree,
    Unto the leafy greenwood.

III.

There rears the Rath its lonely height,
Where fairies dance at noon of night,
And there my faith I'll fondly plight
    To thee in that wild greenwood.
Over the morning dew,
Over the morning dew,
Come with me, young Gra Machree,
    Unto the leafy greenwood.

IV.

O, fear not here to stray with me;
You know me from your infancy:
I'll ask but look of love from thee,
    And fond kiss in the greenwood.
Over the morning dew,
Over the morning dew,
Then come with me, young Gra Machree,
    Unto the leafy greenwood.

THE KNIGHT'S LAY.

I.

As I stray on my gallant steed from thee,
    By river and mountain hoar,
O, thou dost rise before mine eyes,
    In thy loveliness evermore;
And evermore as I speed to thee
    From tourney, tilt, or fight,
My guerdon sweet in thy smiles I meet,
    And thy love, O, my lady bright.

II.

O, lovely is the eventide,
    And the sunset's purple shine,
But as I gaze through its glorious blaze,
    I see but thine eyes divine;
And all through the morning heaven wide,
    Whatever shines brightly there,
But fills my breast with its sweetest guest,
    Thy form, O, my lady fair.

III.

As we camp at night by the mountain wood,
    I and my charger free,
The night bird's strain but brings again
    Thy words of love to me;
And the flowers I see by the fountain flood
    In the spring-time of the year,
In their sheen of gold I ever behold
    Thy bright locks, my lady dear.

IV.

The scarf thou gavest me long ago
    Sees many a gory field,
But it giveth light to my heart at night,
    As I rest on my dinted shield.
This heart must be leal and strong, I trow,
    That so well hath toiled and strove;
'Twas hope in you made it toil so true,
    So long, O, my lady love.

THE BOYS OF WEXFORD.*

Air — " The Boys of Wexford."

I.

In comes the captain's daughter, the captain of the Yeos,
Saying, " Brave United man, we'll ne'er again be foes.
A thousand pounds I'll give you, and fly from home with thee,
And dress myself in man's attire, and fight for libertie."
    We are the boys of Wexford, who fought with heart and hand
      To burst in twain the galling chain, and free our native land.

II.

And when we left our cabins, boys, we left with right good will,
To see our friends and neighbors that were at Vinegar Hill;
A young man from our ranks a cannon he let go;
He slapped it into Lord Mountjoy — a tyrant he laid low.
    We are the boys of Wexford, who fought with heart and hand
      To burst in twain the galling chain, and free our native land.

III.

We bravely fought and conquered at Ross and Wexford town,
And if we failed to keep them, 'twas drink that brought us down.
We had no drink beside us on Tubber'neering's day,
Depending on the long, bright pike, and well it worked its way.
    We are the boys of Wexford, who fought with heart and hand
      To burst in twain the galling chain, and free our native land.

IV.

They came into the country, our blood to waste and spill,
But let them weep for Wexford, and think of Oulart Hill.
'Twas drink that still betrayed us, — of them we had no fear,
For every man could do his part, like Forth and Shelmalier.

* Two verses of an old song are incorporated in this.

We are the boys of Wexford, who fought with heart and hand
To burst in twain the galling chain, and free our native land.

v.

My curse upon all drinking, — it made our hearts full sore, —
For bravery won each battle, but drink lost evermore;
And if for want of leaders we lost at Vinegar Hill,
We're ready for another fight, and love our country still.
    We are the boys of Wexford, who fought with heart and hand
To burst in twain the galling chain, and free our native land.

SWEET GLENGARIFF'S WATER.

Air — "As I was riding out one Day."

I.

Where wild fowl swim upon the lake
  At morning's early shining,
I'm sure, I'm sure my heart will break
  With sadness and repining.
As I went out one morning sweet,
  I met a farmer's daughter,
With gown of blue, and milk-white feet,
  By sweet Glengariff's water.

II.

Her jet black locks, with wavy shine,
  Fell sweetly on her shoulder,
And, ah! they make my heart repine
  Till I again behold her.
She smiled, and passed me strangely by,
  Though fondly I besought her,
And long I'll rue her laughing eye
  By sweet Glengariff's water.

III.

Where wild fowl swim upon the lake
  At morning's early splendor,
Each day my lonely path I'll take,
  With thoughts full sad and tender;
I'll meet my love, and sure she'll stay
  To hear the tale I've brought her,
To marry me this merry May
  By sweet Glengariff's water.

THE FAITHFUL LOVERS.

Air — "Along with my Love I'll go."

I.

"O'er wildwood, hill, and valley
  Sound the piercing pipe and drum;
On the shore our kinsmen rally,
  And our parting hour is come."
"O, love, we'll ne'er be parted, —
  Side by side against the foe
You and I will stand true-hearted,
  And along with my love I'll go."

II.

"The steel-cap will dim the brightness
  Of your golden, curling hair;
The sword-hilt will spoil the whiteness
  Of your hand so small and fair."
"I mind not these long locks twining,
  I heed not this white hand's snow,
And where'er our flag is shining,
  Along with my love I'll go."

III.

"The roads they are rough and dreary;
  They will scar your milk-white feet;
If you go on our marches weary,
  You must lie in the open street."
"No danger can confound me;
  Through sunshine or wintry snow,

With my horseman's cloak around me,
  Along with my love I'll go."

IV.

" On your sleep the battle's warning
  Shall the pipes and trumpets bray;
Woman's fear and pity scorning,
  You must rush to the gory fray."
" By your side no coward pallor
  This dauntless brow shall know;
Through the fray, with a soldier's valor,
  Along with my love I'll go."

V.

" In the fight, the foe prevailing,
  May strike us ruthless down;
Can you look on death unquailing,
  On red field and blazing town?"
" In the fight, when death has found me,
  Fear nor pain my heart shall know;
To the grave, with your arms around me,
  Along with my love I'll go."

VI.

The battle trumpet sounded
  By Shannon's gory strand;
They fell, by foes surrounded,
  Side by side, for their native land.
In her eyes shone love immortal,
  As his blood stained her breast of snow,
And she cried, " Through Death's dark portal
  Along with my love I'll go."

VII.

And there in death together
  They sleep since that battle-day;
O'er their grave blooms the purple heather,
  With many a floweret gay;
O, fair maids, when 'gainst the stranger
  For Ireland we strike the blow,
May you cry, " Through death and danger
  Along with my love I'll go." *

---

* The incident of this little ballad is **historical**. The lovers fell, as related, at the battle of Ballintubber. See Annals of the Four Masters, about the year 1650.

AMONG THE FRAGRANT HAY.

Air.—" Young Roger was a Ploughboy."

I.

Young Johnnie, in the autumn,
 To Limerick he came,
And none could tell what brought him,
 And none could tell his name;
  But he sat by Bessie Gray,
  That sunny autumn day,
And he told her sweet romances 'mid the new-mown hay.
   Then O, for fields lighted
    By sweet autumn's ray,
   When loving vows are plighted
    Among the fragrant hay.

II.

When, ere the next sweet morning,
 Young Johnnie had fled,
With envy filled and scorning,
 The village maidens said.—
  O, they spoke of Bessie Gray,
  And they said she'd rue the day
When she heard the sweet romances 'mid the new-mown hay.
   Then O, for fields lighted
    By sweet autumn's ray,
   When loving vows are plighted
    Among the fragrant hay.

III.

Young Johnnie's happy dwelling
 Lay fast by the Lee,
And in manly parts excelling,
 But few like him you'd see;
  And so thought Bessie Gray
  Since that lovely autumn day
When she heard the sweet romances 'mid the new-mown hay.
   Then O, for fields lighted
    By sweet autumn's ray,
   When loving vows are plighted
    Among the fragrant hay.

IV.

Young Johnnie could remember
His vows and his flame;
He came in dark December,
And told his kin and name;
And there was a wedding gay,
And the bride was Bessie Gray,
And all from these romances 'mid the new-mown hay.
Then O, for fields lighted
By sweet autumn's ray,
When loving vows are plighted
Among the fragrant hay.

THE SADDEST BREEZE.

Air — "Johnnie, lovely Johnnie."

I.

The saddest breeze in all the land,
It blew across the sea:
It drove a brave ship from the strand,
And bore my Hugh from me;
And long I sat beside the rill
To weep my fate alone,
Till leaf and flower from wood and hill
With summer beams were flown.

II.

The gladdest breeze e'er swept the vales
To-day blew from the sea;
It swelled a good ship's snowy sails,
And brought him back to me;
And now 'tis rushing wildly past,
With wintry sleet and rain,
Yet e'en I love the cold, cold blast
That brought my Hugh again.

ALMANSA; OR, O'MAHONY'S DRAGOONS.

Air.—"The Bold Dragoon."

I.

Brave comrades of the sword,
  Sing with me Almansa's day,
How fought our bold dragoons
  Through that fierce and fiery **fray**,
And how they won to deathless **fame**,
  Old Ireland's chivalry,
Our dashing, bold dragoons, with their long **swords flashing**,
  And their bridles flowing free.

II.

When the sunset light fell red
  On that battle's trampled ground,
On our front the flam of drums,
  Mingled with the trumpet's sound;
And thither rolled the English line,
  Horse, foot, artillery,
To surround us bold dragoons with our long swords flashing,
  And our bridles flowing free.

III.

As nearer and more near
  The threatening foemen came,
Their flanks all rolling smoke,
  Their front all fire and flame,
Loud spoke our colonel's trumpet,
  "Boot to boot and knee to knee!
Forward! Charge! my bold dragoons, with your long swords
    flashing,
  And your bridles flowing free!"

IV.

Then each charger shook his mane,
  From the scabbard flew each brand,
And our country's name and fame
  Nerved each gallant rider's hand,
And like the deafening thunder clap
  That roars down Barnagee,

Sped we forward, bold dragoons, with our long swords flashing,
    And our bridles flowing free.

v.

Through the fire and through the smoke,
    Through the bayonets and spears,
Through their serried ranks of foot,
    And their pluméd cavaliers,
As a boar-hunt through a meadow,
    One wild hurricane went we,
Brave O'Mahony's dragoons, with our long swords flashing,
    And our bridles flowing free.

vi.

Then we wheeled unto the right,
    And fell thundering on their flank,
Till we reached the crimsoned sward,
    Where our gallant major sank,*
And we heard his voice of valor
    As he died in victory,
"Well done, my bold dragoons, with your long swords flashing,
    And your bridles flowing free!"

vii.

When the trumpet's loud recall
    To our ears its cadence bore,
Sword and saddle, rein and plume,
    Horse and man, were wet with gore;
Yet we mourned full many a comrade,
    Many an empty saddle-tree,
We, O'Mahony's dragoons, with our long swords flashing,
    And our bridles flowing free.

viii.

Come all ye soldiers true,
    Who bear the belt and brand,
Here's to those, the Brave who died,
    Here's the memory of our land.
A field of fame like this some day
    In Ireland may we see,
To charge like bold dragoons, with our long swords flashing,
    And our bridles flowing free.

---

* The gallant Philip O'Dwyer, aid-major of the regiment, a cousin of O'Dwyer, the banished earl of Kilnemanagh, in Tipperary.

MY LOVE IS AT MY SIDE.

Air — "I once loved a Boy."

I.

The lone hill's dells are blue with heather bells,
  The wild flowers bloom along the moor,
The soft winds glide, and my love is at my side,
  On the banks of the calm, golden Suir,
            Bright and pure,
  On the banks of the calm, golden Suir.

II.

By upland springs a lonely linnet sings
  All of love from his leafy wildwood tree,
Of smiles and sweet sighs, and the loving, star-bright eyes
  That are gazing so fond now on me,
            Trustingly,
  That are gazing so fond now on me.

III.

The soft airs blow, and wildly wandering go
  To tell where the woodlark builds its nest,
Of bliss that knows no care, and the maiden young and fair,
  That I'm clasping so fond to my breast,
            Dearly pressed,
  That I'm clasping so fond to my breast,

IV.

O, bright flow the rills, and this river by the hills,
  Telling, telling as they go to mount and moor,
That my love's at my side, that she'll be my own dear bride,
  On the banks of the calm, golden Suir,
            Bright and pure,
  On the banks of the calm, golden Suir.

WHERE ARE YOU GOING, MY PRETTY MAID?

Air—"Tha na la."

I.

"Where are you going, my pretty maid,
 While heather bells the mountains cover?"
"I'm going to Dallan Green," she said,
 "To dance a reel, and meet my lover.
  Hi, ho ho! while sunbeams glow,
   We'll banish care and worship pleasure;
  Hi, ho, ho! with heel and toe,
   On Dallan Green we'll dance a measure."

II.

"And who is he has made you feel
 Within your heart a love undying?"
"A soldier in his jack of steel,
 With jangling spurs, and green plume flying.
  Hi, ho, ho! while sunbeams glow,
   And gild the flower, and brown the berry,
  Hi, ho, ho! with heel and toe
   We'll foot it round in laughter merry."

III.

"And does he fight for English sway,
 Or for the brave old land that bore him?"
"My pride, my love rides through the fray
 With Ireland's green flag floating o'er him.
  Hi, ho, ho! while sunbeams glow,
   His maid returns the love he brought her;
  Hi, ho, ho! with heel and toe
   We'll foot it round by Dallan Water."

IV.

"And why do you love him, gentle maid,
 For love and war bring woe and danger?"
"For he loves me, and for the blade
 He draws against the Saxon stranger;
  Hi, ho, ho! while sunbeams glow,
   We'll taste the joy, though Love's the giver;

Hi, ho, ho! with heel and toe
 We'll foot it round by Dallan river."

V.

"Good men, fair maid, have lived and died,
 Although the foreign laws have bound them."
"They're slaves, not men," she proud replied,
 "Who wear the Saxon chains around them!
Hi, ho, ho! while sunbeams glow,
 I care not for such slaves a feather.
Hi, ho, ho! with heel and toe
 We'll foot it round and round together."

VI.

"And when, fair maid, in wedlock's band
 Will he and you hear joy-bells ringing?"
She tossed her head, she kissed her hand,
 And vanished down the woodland, singing:
"Hi, ho, ho! while sunbeams glow,
 We'll banish care, and worship pleasure;
Hi, ho, ho! with heel and toe
 On Dallan Green we'll dance a measure."

SONG OF GALLOPING O'HOGAN.

Air — "He thought of the Charmer."

I.

Hurrah, boys, hurrah! for the sword by my side,
The spur and the gallop o'er bogs deep and wide;
Hurrah for the helmet and shining steel jack,
The sight of the spoil, and good men at my back!
 And we'll sack and burn for king and sireland,
 And chase the black foe from ould Ireland.

II.

At the wave of my sword start a thousand good men,
And we ride like the blast over moorland and glen;
Like dead leaves of winter, in ruin and wrath
We sweep the red Saxons away from our path,

And we'll sack and burn for king and sireland,
And chase the black foe from ould Ireland.

III.

The herds of the foe graze at noon by the rills:
We have them at night in our camp 'mid the hills:
His towns lie in peace at the eve of the night,
But they're sacked and in flames ere the next morning light;
  And we'll sack and burn for king and sireland,
  And chase the black foe from ould Ireland.

IV.

And so we go riding by night and by day,
And fight for our country and all the rich prey;
The roar of the battle sweet music we feel,
And the light of our hearts is the flashin' of steel.
  And we'll sack and burn for king and sireland,
  And chase the black foe from ould Ireland.

THE LABORER.

Air — "Granua weal."

I.

I LABOR and sweat for the poor shilling fee
Through the days of my manhood, but what's that to me?
When age steals upon me, I'm left in the lurch,
Fallen, wretched, and poor as a mouse in a church;
Then the laws must be rotten — the de'il in the sham
Of state-craft that leaves me to-day what I am.

II.

If I make of the desert a fair, smiling land
By the sweat of my brow and the strength of my hand,
Then the rent it is raised, or my cabin and all
That I've built, and I've planned, by the crowbar must fall.
For the laws they are rotten — the de'il in the sham
Of state-craft that leaves me to-day what I am.

III.

The rich they are made of the fine porcelain clay,
And I of the turf-mould, plebeian, they say;
But the tall, graceful frame, and the clear, flashing eye
Of the poor Irish toiler will fling back the lie.
'Tis the laws that are rotten — the de'il in the sham
Of state-craft that leaves me to-day what I am.

IV.

A little bird sang in my ear one fine morn,
"Poor toiler, arise from thy bondage forlorn;
You're the tree whose rich fruit makes the wealth of the
 great, —
You're the strong, sturdy pillar that props up the state."
So the laws must be rotten — the de'il in the sham
Of state-craft that leaves me to-day what I am.

V.

Then I'll look to myself for the remedy true,
And over old Ireland, strong brothers, to you;
For while cursed by dissension, in bondage we groan,
But when banded together, the state is our own.
Yes, I'll look to myself, for the de'il's in the sham
Of state-craft that leaves me to-day what I am.

PATRICK'S DAY.

I.

We cannot be glad: lonely exiles, we borrow
 From pomp and parade but the semblance of glee;
We cannot be glad while in serfdom and sorrow
 Our brothers are pining beyond the sea:
  Though gallant and proud,
  Our heads shall be bowed,
 When we think, mother Ireland, of them and of thee.
  Though flaunting on high,
  Our banners may fly,
Though the trumpets may blare, and the drums roll and
 rattle,
And rifles and bayonets flash bright in the ray,

They make us but sigh for one good hour of battle
On green Irish ground upon Patrick's Day.

II.

We cannot be glad, though the pageant's shrill clangor
From street unto street fill the blue heaven's dome;
We cannot be glad, but the sounds of our anger
Shall be heard far away o'er the wild sea's foam;
  Shall be heard far away
  By the tyrants whose sway
Is the curse of our race, and our green island home!
  Be heard rising clear
  By the despots whose fear
Will make them imagine our rifles and cannon
Are over the water beginning the fray,
That the people have risen, from Bann to the Shannon,
To try their new strength upon Patrick's Day.

III.

We cannot be glad, but the brave hope we cherish
Of raising the green flag afar o'er the main;
That the power of the tyrant before us shall perish,
Assuages our sorrow and soothes our pain.
  So our trumpets shall sound
  All the wide world round,
With the bold voice of Freedom inwrought in the strain,
  And our banners shall gleam
  In each foreign sun's beam,
Till, sons of one mother, we're banded together,
With weapons all glittering in warlike array,
Till we fight the good fight on our own native heather,
And win back our freedom on Patrick's Day.

THERE IS A STREAM.

Air — "As I was riding out one Day."

I.

There is a stream 'mid Houra's dells
　That dances downward fleetly,
That mirrors rocks and heather-bells,
　And sings by wild woods sweetly,
With drooping birch and drinan dhun *
　Its vernal banks adorning,
And there my love with sweet smiles won
　My fond heart in the morning.

II.

God bless the May that brought to me
　The love that nought can sunder;
God bless the odorous drinan tree
　That we sat fondly under.
The skies were blue, the clouds were bright,
　The valleys shade and splendor,
And Annie's eyes were filled with light
　Of love, all true and tender.

III.

And oft within that valley lone
　We met on May-days after,
While aye the stream went murmuring on
　With sounds like fairy laughter;
'Tis there a rill, but far below
　It winds, a calm, bright river;
And thus may our love forward go,
　Increasing on forever.

* The blackthorn or sloe tree.

SAINT STEPHEN'S NIGHT.

I.

WITHOUT, the wild winds keenly blow
O'er weary wastes of wintry snow;
Within, the red fire sheds its glow,
Where round and round the dancers go!
    Merrily, merrily round and round,
    Airily, airily round and round,
    To the sweetest music in Ireland's ground,
    The heart's glad laugh and the bagpipe's sound.

II.

What befits Saint Stephen's Night
But loving words and glances bright, —
But young and old, with main and might,
To dance around in wild delight?
    Merrily, merrily round and round,
    Airily, airily round and round,
    To the sweetest music in Ireland's ground,
    The heart's glad laugh and the bagpipe's sound!

III.

The wren was hunted all the day
By the striplings tall and the children gay;
Now he's dressed in state on the holly spray,
And his noisy captors, where are they?
    Dancing, dancing round and round,
    Airily, airily round and round,
    To the sweetest music in Ireland's ground,
    The heart's glad laugh and the bagpipe's sound!

IV.

Maid and matron, son and sire,
With bounding spirits that cannot tire,
Around the bright Saint Stephen's fire
Joke and dance to their heart's desire,
    Merrily, merrily round and round,
    Airily, airily round and round,
    To the sweetest music in Ireland's ground,
    The heart's glad laugh and the bagpipe's sound!

v.

Round and round so merrilie,
Yet merrier yet that dance would be
If our scattered brothers beyond the sea
Were home returned and Ireland free!
  O, merrily then we'd dance it round,
  Saint Stephen's night, around and **round**,
  To the sweetest music in Ireland's **ground**,
  The heart's glad laugh and the **bagpipe's sound**!

LIFE IS BRIGHT.

DUET.

AIR — "Her Shoes were black, her Stockings white."

I.

(*He.*) With heart full light, in summer bright,
  Or winter's stormy weather,
With rein in hand, with belt and brand,
  And trooper's jack and feather,
A soldier gay, I ride away,
  Across my native heather,
    Singing:
(*Both.*) Life is bright when hearts unite,
  And marriage bells are ringing!

II.

(*She.*) When morning's beam is on the stream,
  And the perfumed zephyrs blowing,
And sheep-bells ring and milkmaids sing
  In the dells where kine are lowing,
I sit anear the streamlet clear,
  My thoughts on you, love, flowing,
    Singing:
(*Both.*) Life is bright when hearts unite,
  And marriage bells are ringing!

III.

(*He.*) In hall and bower, where ladies' power
  Cleaves the soldier's heart asunder,

　　　　　　Or where beams glance from sword and lance,
　　　　　　　　And the cannons roar like thunder,
　　　　　　This jack of steel, a heart full leal
　　　　　　　　To thee, fair maid, beats under,
　　　　　　　　　　　　Singing:
(*Both.*)　Life is bright when hearts unite,
　　　　　　　　And marriage bells are ringing!

　　　　　　　　　　　IV.

(*She.*)　When, far from me, you wander free,
　　　　　　　　I ever think of you, love;
　　　　　　Your smile so warm, your gallant form
　　　　　　　　In constant dreams I view, love;
　　　　　　Where'er you go, in weal or woe,
　　　　　　　　You are my only true-love!
　　　　　　　　　　　　Singing:
(*Both.*)　Life is bright when hearts unite,
　　　　　　　　And marriage bells are ringing!

　　　　　　　　　　　V.

(*Both.*)　When hearts entwine, like yours and mine,
　　　　　　　　No power their bonds can sever;
　　　　　　Through joy's gay light, misfortune's blight,
　　　　　　　　Or envy's false endeavor,
　　　　　　Our love's bright flame shall burn the same,
　　　　　　　　Calm, warm, and true forever!
　　　　　　　　　　　　Singing:
　　　　　　Life is bright when hearts unite,
　　　　　　　　And marriage bells are ringing!

O, BLEST BE THE BOWER.

Air — "The Shandhina."

I.

O, BLEST be the bower where we sat all alone, love,
Where the stream murmured down with a wild, fairy tone, love;
Where I looked in your eyes, that so tenderly shone, love,
And kissed you so fondly, and called you my own, love!
How white shone that bower with the hawthorn blossom,
Like the sheen of your brow and the snow of your bosom, —
How sweet sang the wild-birds from brake and from tree, love,
But the fond tale you told me was sweeter to me, love!

II.

On harebells at morning the dewdrops shine clearly,
And fair is the blush of the wood-roses early, —
Like dew on those harebells your sunny eyes shine, love,
And your cheek's like the blush of the roses divine, love;
Your form is as fair as the ash by the mountain,
Your heart is as pure as the waves of the fountain,
And light as the breezes that sunny hills range, love,
Yet true as the pole-star that never can change, love.

III.

I wake in the morning from fair dreams of you, love,
I walk in the noontide, and think of you too, love;
I sit in the evening by mountain or river,
And my soul with your form is illumined forever!
I look on each beauty the summer has brought us,
I gaze on each glory that nature has wrought us;
But the splendor of earth or the heaven's sunny hue, love,
Was dreary, and cheerless, and dark without you, love!

  Then blest be the bower where we sat all alone, love,
  Where the stream murmured down with a wild, fairy
   tone, love,
  When I looked in your eyes that so witchingly shone,
   love,
  And kissed you so fondly, and called you my own, love.

BY THE SHORE.

AIR—"Mo Wokir trè Volla gau gouglum."

I.

FULL oft in the morn I look sunward,
   An exile's sad look o'er the brine,
With the hopes of my heart trooping onward
   To thy mountains, O, dear land of mine;
And a vision I see brightly gleaming,
   In glory the blue billows o'er,
Thy green flag of splendor outstreaming,
   And thy war-harness glittering once more.

II.

I list to thy drum-roll defiant,
   As its thunder sounds loud through the hills,
From the rock-pillared Pass of the Giant
   To the farthest of Desmond's wild hills;
And I see the white camps of thy valor
   Shine bravely by mountain and plain,
And the tyrant crouch down in his pallor
   'Neath the sword of thine anger again!

III.

On thy great day of need and commotion,
   When thy broad flag of battle out-waves,
At the sword-point we'll prove our devotion,
   Fair land of our forefathers' graves!
On that day may all false traitors shun us,
   As we sweep o'er the red field of gore,
May the great God of battle smile on us,
   And we'll crown thee with freedom once more.

TO MARY.

I.

O, WHAT were my student life but gloom,
   While the moon shines in through my window pane,
If I could not dream in my lonely room,
   And call up Fancy's aerial train?

II.

The moon is up o'er the eastern rocks,
   And shineth bright through my window pane;
The small clouds float by her face, like flocks
   Of gorgeous birds on an orient plain.

III.

And aye as the sweet moon smiles on me
   With a holy smile through my window pane,
O, many a dear, dear dream of thee
   Enlivens my bosom and fills my brain.

IV.

O, many a mile in thought I rove,
   While the moon shines in through my window pane,
Till I clasp in my arms my own dear love,
   And thy lips of coral I kiss again.

V.

Then a paradise gleams around me clear,
   While the moon shines in through my window pane;
And I hear thy voice, and I see thee near,
   And I drink thy murmurs of love again.

VI.

Then what were my student life but gloom,
   While the moon shines in through my window pane,
If I could not dream in my lonely room,
   And call up Fancy's aerial train?

OLD LAND.

AIR — "My Father built a Baby House."

I.

Old Land of English **knavery**,
Misrule, misfortune, **slavery**, —
Old Land of Irish bravery,
    With **you** we'll fall or stand;
And though we're exiled far away,
For you we work, for you we pray,
And raise our good swords high, and say,
    "A health to you, Old Land!"
    Sing hey! sing ho! the Irish Green!
    Sing hey! sing ho! our weapons keen
    Shall plant it where the Red has been
      On all thy shores, Old Land!

II.

Old Land, a lesson sad we've got;
Amongst ourselves we raged and fought,
And your destruction nearly wrought,
    Each fratricidal band;
But we will make our promise good,
We'll join in faithful brotherhood,
And on the red field spill our blood,
    Or free you yet, Old Land!
    Sing hey! sing ho! &c.

III.

Old Land, if 'mid thy teeming race
There grew some traitors, bad and base,
Yet sure even murderous Cain's **disgrace**
    Our primal Mother banned;
And those fell traitors you have nursed,
Of foes the deadliest and the worst,
Earth holds their villain names accursed
    Forevermore, Old Land!
    Sing hey! sing ho! &c.

IV.

Old Land! May God inspire our souls
To safely steer o'er Faction's shoals,
And sure as yonder sun outrolls
    At morn his banners grand,
Our breast will make a shield for you;
We'll die on War's red field for you,
And win, but never yield for you
    One inch of ground, Old Land!
    Sing hey! sing ho! the Irish Green,
    Sing hey! sing ho! our weapons keen
    Shall plant it where the Red has been
      On all thy shores, Old Land!

EILEEN OF THE GOLDEN HAIR.

Air—"Eileen Bàn."

I.

Come with me to Mora's bowers,
    Far in wild Glenara's dell,
Where the sunny sward with flowers
    Glitters round the fairy well;
Where the green leaves quiver o'er us
    To the jocund summer air,
All things bright, and life before us,
    Eileen of the golden hair.

II.

Darkness reigned within my bosom,
    By our early sorrows cast;
Thou hast set a blooming blossom
    In that desert land at last;
Thou hast taught my soul to borrow
    Sun-bright hope from black despair;
That there comes a gladsome morrow,
    Eileen of the golden hair.

III.

Then away to Mora's bowers,
  Deep in wild Glenara's dell;
There we'll spend the summer hours,
  'Neath the green leaves, loving well.
Not a cloud shall linger o'er us,
  Cloud of woe or blighting care, —
All things bright, and life before us,
  Eileen of the golden hair.

www.ingramcontent.com/pod-product-compliance
Lightning Source LLC
Chambersburg PA
CBHW051732300426
44115CB00007B/522